Writing in Motion

Writing in Motion

BODY—LANGUAGE—TECHNOLOGY

Kenneth King

*With a Foreword
by Deborah Jowitt*

**Wesleyan University Press
Middletown, Connecticut**

Published by Wesleyan University Press, Middletown, CT 06459

© 1992, 1993, 1994, 1996, 1999, 2003 by Kenneth King

Printed in the United States of America

5 4 3 2 1

Library of Congress Cataloging-in-Publication Data

King, Kenneth, 1948–
Writing in motion : body—language—technology / Kenneth King ; with a
foreword by Deborah Jowitt.
p. cm.
ISBN 0-8195-6613-6 (cloth : alk. paper)—ISBN 0–8195–6614–4
(paperback : alk. paper)
1. Dance criticism. 2. Dance—Philosophy. 3. King, Kenneth, 1948–
I. Title.
GV1600.K56 2003
792.8'09—dc22
2003015186

FOR MARJORIE GAMSO,
WITH APPRECIATION

Dancing in all its forms
cannot be excluded from
the curriculum of all noble
education; dancing with
the feet, with ideas, with
words, and, need I add
that one must also be able
to dance with the pen?

Friedrich Nietzsche,
Twilight of the Idols

Since the 1960s I have been creating a range of texts that move between and across categories and disciplines; many were originally prerecorded and used to accompany dances or were spoken and acted. During the last two decades I've turned to the essay, a form that I consider the most formidable and challenging. The reciprocity between dancing and writing engages a double motion and involves a synergy, even symbiosis, that animates not only the body but also words, ideas and ambient, too. The dancing body fields impulses, signals and signs that can be transmitted, deciphered, amplified and translated—to court the kinetic cogito. Dancing outdoes any teleprompter—words, sentences and ideas pop into one's field or inner screen, materialize in the air, brain, or somewhere in between. There's information in movement, even a text, and more!

Dance is the most ephemeral of arts. It evaporates as soon as it is performed. Writing endures. Once words are arranged and fixed on the page, they remain and can be reexperienced. There's a kinesis to syntax too; I've aspired to a motion grammar that links word and gesture, envisages dancemaking as writing in space, and I sometimes feel writing in motion might actually be a better mimetic transmitter than video. It's a little bigamous, too; the writer is always trying to steal time to read and the dancer rebels, insisting it's time to work out and rehearse! In 1973 when I performed at the Autumn Festival in Paris, a booking agent told me I could dance anywhere in Europe if I'd only give up my texts and use music instead. HA! There's an alternative future.

The reader should feel free to move around in this collection and read the texts and essays in any order. Even when writing for a dance, the challenge was always that the texts were meant to stand separately as independent literary works. (A dance too is a text.) As with dancing, I enjoy pushing the limits, making syntax overreach itself, stretching language further than it can go, jumping contexts, sometimes by coining words to bridge conceptual differentials and dissimilar discourses—to make it know more than it can. Like a cryptologist, I scout out words within words and have even mistaken a semicolon for a semiconductor, hoping to squeeze as much conceptual leverage into a sentence as possible. Even before the Internet, I sensed that the information age, trumpeted during the 1960s by Marshall McLuhan, would challenge reading in a new way, increase the mindfield and payload of syntax, and enable it to bundle together and encode more diversity and interdisciplinary freight. For the generations of readers after the Internet, and for the connoisseurs of poststructural and postmodernist logophilia, here's toasting you!

First, *express* thanks go to Jill Johnston for originally contacting Suzanna Tamminen, Editor in Chief at Wesleyan University Press, or this wouldn't have happened. Since the 1960s Jill's virtuosic, live-wire writing and liberating media performances have had the most impact on me of all the practitioners of the Judson Church vanguard, and I salute her! Suzanna Tamminen was patient, supportive and persevering through the long editorial review and production process and thanks too are due to the press's Director, Tom Radko, Assistant Editor, Leonora Gibson, Wesleyan University Press's entire staff, Nils Nadeau for his extraordinarily perceptive and cogent copyediting, Darwin Campa at Barbara William & Associates for the dynamic cover design, Lisa Sacks, Production Editor at University Press of New England, for her careful organizational oversight, helpful advice and generous guidance, Amber Frid-Jimenez, Designer and Charles Coates, Typesetter, for their expertise in bringing this long project to completion. Special appreciations go to Deborah Jowitt for gracing this volume with her eloquent introduction and for her enthusiastic and generous critical commentary over the years. One of the earliest and staunchest literary supporters has been Richard Kostelanetz, a prolific historian, critic and artist who ranges over many disciplines; since 1967 I have been indebted to him for getting many of my texts and writings into print.

The book is dedicated to my good friend Marjorie Gamso, dancer-choreographer, writer and autodidact, for the stimulating camaraderie of regular, often weekly, marathon conversations over the better part of three decades that consistently have helped stimulate, catalyze and probe emerging impressions and ideas, as well as for guiding me to important and often unfamiliar sources. I thank Frances Alenikoff, our celebrated dancing octogenarian, writer and multimedia artist, with whom I've collaborated, for sustaining me with much stimulation, knowledge and support, assuring me this book would happen. Without attorneys to thank—Linda Lovett, Esq., Holly Schepisi, Esq., and especially Jeffry Hoffman, Esq.—this might not have been possible; additional thanks too to Grant King, Arnold Horton, Gina Bonati and Elena Alexander.

Finally I salute the late Susanne K. Langer, philosopher extraordinaire, proficient in many disciplines spanning the arts and sciences with an unmatchable literary genius, for her conversations and inspiration. And these souls, teachers, free spirits and liberators across the great divide: Roberta Dauernheim, Anna Loessen, Karin Martello, Keith McGary and my brother, Joseph D.

February 2002
K. K.
New York City

Reading—in some cases, revisiting—these essays by Kenneth King, I feel my brain start to whirl, to become hyper-aware of its own circuitry, to shy away from discursive thinking. It's a familiar sensation. Almost forty years of watching-hearing-reading the works of King, perhaps our only dancing philosopher, have attuned me to his unique voice and vision. Through him, I learned to sense dance as language—not in the sense of bearing a narrative, but as a language with formal correlations to spoken and written word structures, a language whose significance flashes out from the patterns it traces on the floor, from the alterations in the air as one body passes another. Dancing, to him, is "writing in space." Like early ritual dances that mapped visions of stellar order, King's choreography, for the watcher as for the doer, flared along the nerves and muscles, hinting at cosmic correspondences you couldn't explain yet somehow comprehended. The experience went beyond watching, say, one of George Balanchine's storyless ballets and attributing human feelings to patterned interactions; it made you sense a system operating at full steam— or the design of a system. Long before postmodern theorists from a variety of disciplines discovered "the body," and science promoted the notion of cellular intelligence, King had wreaked havoc with the old mind-body split.

For him, dancing may have triggered the impulse to create the texts that often accompanied his performances. When I interviewed him in 1976 for the *Village Voice*, he remarked that "Language is bound up with how we see in ways we're not even aware of. And often when I do a movement, words come to mind—not because the movement *means* them, but because the gestures, the act of dancing, become a reflective device."

This was when he was finishing *Battery: A Tribute to Susanne K. Langer*. (Langer, a philosopher he deeply admires, wrote in her three-volume *Mind* about the role of primal choric dance and rhythmic chant in stimulating the frontal lobes of the brain to invent symbolic thought.)

Whether dancing, talking, dancing-while-talking, or writing, King's linguistic processes are exhilarating, not to say occasionally hilarious. Dense with movement and/or words, they explode and reconfigure the familiar, crack syntax open, invent startling words. Always extraordinarily well-read, he gained new brain fodder from French literary theory but gave his intricate and witty theoretical musings the rhythms and dynamics of a dance:

> Let's face it, the French have turned thinking into a glamour industry; they furnish the latest *trompe de textes* or *topos logos du jour*. And more specifically, marketing *difficult*, abstruse thinking freighted in sparkling, complex rhetoric that stymies in the effort to liberate itself from *ontometaphysics*, it ends up being even *more* para-cryptic. They've refined, defined and redefined the exigencies and border turfs of modern philosophy, poststructuralist exegesis, cryptoanalysis, and non-narrative narrativity. They resurrect and exergeticize Descartes daily, jousting with a Cartesian cottage industry on the scale of the Taj Mahal! ("Writing Over History and Time: Maurice Blanchot & Jackie O")

His mind absorbs what he reads, and he's off—as if literature were fodder for a veritable Preakness of intellectual acrobatics. In his fascinating essay "Dreams and Collage," he begins by referring to Aristotle's *On Dreams*, moves to bring in Langer, Michio Kaku's explication of string theory, Freud, and Simone de Beauvoir *on* Freud, before launching into a discussion of collage and dreams as saboteurs of linear continuity. Wilhelm Reich also figures in this piece of writing, as do Mircea Eliade, the Lascaux caves, and MTV: "Collage objectifies the mimesis of oneiric configurations and unlocks the keys to dimensionalizing how many strata of brain, mind, being and world resonate simultaneously, thus moving representation beyond representation, and thereby telescoping cognitive and systemic transferences." (How typical of King's mindplay—that "unlocks the keys.") And the references are no scholarly showing off; they're another sort of collage, in which sharp minds, brought into proximity, clang satisfyingly off one another.

When Kenneth King began to show dances in New York in 1964, he was still a student at Antioch. The college's work-study plan enabled him to spend several months a year in the city. He couldn't have arrived at a better time. The vanguard bunch of dancer-choreographers, musicians, and visual artists grouped under the rubric of Judson Dance Theater had, a couple of years earlier, radically redefined what constituted a dance and being a dancer. The field was wide open for a bright iconoclast to romp in. In those days, King, Meredith Monk, and Phoebe Neville formed a trio of young Turks, in tune with the times but more interested in theatricality than their immediate elders, who were largely concerned with the everyday. The Judsonites' investigation of "objective" performing, however, did influence them. The title of a 1964 dance-theater piece of King's, *cup/saucer/two dancers/radio*, made it clear that the objects and the objectlike humans were to be considered equals. In it the choreographer, dressed in underwear and a tie, and Neville, wearing a bra, girdle, and hair-curlers, stood side by side for a long time staring straight ahead. I think the radio played. They each held a cup and saucer below their chins. Gradually their hands began to tremble, making the cups chatter against the saucers with increasing volatility. Finally the pair tilted the cups as if to drink, but, since the cups were well below their mouths and their focus never deviated, they instead poured streams of colored liquid down their white garments. Spectators, shocked by the act, with its connotations of unacceptable behavior or extreme disassociation, could also think about what was absent—the identities of these two, their histories, their feelings.

I discern in King's work an ongoing interest in what is absent or hidden. He devotes an essay to "Sight and Cipher." His thoughts in "Appeal to the Unknown; Prayer to the Great Void (Mappings for a Metatheology)"—presented as part of a collaborative performance event in

1972—riff brilliantly on nothingness, which "by being revealed . . . is only further concealed." Concealment is the theme of his piece on the influential and reclusive French philosopher Maurice Blanchot and the enigmatic, limelight-evading Jacqueline Onassis. He is drawn to the art of Joseph Cornell, whose fastidious arrangements of objects in boxes intimate that everything is there: the box is open, the small world complete in itself. Yet Cornell's works also provoke questions about what *isn't* seen (the imagined scenario that expands beyond the confined space and the moment of viewing): "*Aviary* houses a parrot perched within a recessed compartment surrounded on three sides by racks of miniature drawers, with a curiously placed coil beside its mouth, as if echoing or conversing with its invisible *other*, intimating further, its own tacit or silent voice, or the collusive symbiotic contour of such a potency" ("A Pipe of Fancy [Vision's Plenitude]: Joseph Cornell, An Appreciation").

Some of King's politically conscious dances of the 1970s referred in dazzling accompanying wordplay to codes, hidden agendas, and espionage. In the 1972 *Metagexis* (part of whose text is included in this collection), he danced—some of the time as Joseph K. Devadesa of the "Inner Seercret Service"—during a disquisition on the double negative ("He ought to be being being naught so not not to be caught"). During *Word Raid* (1979)—text also included here—he and a partner convulsed the audience with tongue twisters in which "meaning" took a header down the rabbit hole:

A SPIFFLY CLIPPED HIP AND STRICTLY TIGHT-LIPPED CRYPTIC SCRIPT IS SIMPLY SIFTED AND SIPPED THEN ON A TIMELY TIP SLIPPED ON A SECRET SHIP ADRIFT A THRIFTY TRADE TRIP THEN SWIFTLY STRIPPED AFTER A STIFF SHIFTY RIFT BY TWO TONGUE-TIED TIFFED AND MIFFED TWIN KNIT-T'WITS! (TO: WIT) . . .

An interest in Jungian archetypes and altered states generated a variety of personae who frequently concealed King in performance, especially during the later sixties and seventies. There was "Pablo," who wore a lab coat and a black hood, whom King has described as "an oracular figure that resides in the consciousness, that announces or directs like a guardian or a guide." There was "Sergei Alexandrovitch," a Russian dancer, "Mater Harry," an androgynous blonde spy who talked in a stentorian whisper from behind a fan, "Tallulah Bankhead," and "Pontease Tyak," the grey-bearded curator of the Trans-Himalyan Society, mysterious beneath dark glasses, hat, overcoat, and thick Slavic accent.

When, in the late sixties, King moved away from theater pieces with pop art imagery in which he moved very little, it was clear he was a dancing marvel. His style showed a kinship to that of Merce Cunningham, with whom he studied and whom he greatly admires. They're both essentially tall, lean, long-necked, and naturally erect; in different idiosyncratic ways, their arms and legs twist, whirl, and probe the air from an elongated but flexible spine. Cunningham has written that if a fine dancer simply invests himself or herself in the movement, allowing feelings or qualities to emerge unplanned, he makes "of himself such a kind of nature puppet that he is as if dancing on a string which is like an umbilical cord:—mother nature and father spirit moving his limbs, without thought." King dancing has seemed a medium, fielding messages from the unknown (it is interesting to learn that he loved puppets as a boy). An admirer of Marshall McLuhan, he has remarked that "the media (re)circuit and act as extensions of the central nervous system"; *his* central nervous system often has seemed besieged by mysterious information. Stillness was never a feature of his style, as it is of Cunningham's. And spectators noticed right away his extraordinary buoyancy—how he was often on tiptoe, or skimming the floor with seemingly unpunctuated chains of small, light hops, skips, and leaps. (Perhaps I should recast that last sentence; in "Transmedia," he writes that his dancing "is more like high-interface action verbs than nouns or subjects.")

The eighties were perhaps the heyday of King's group choreography. He had splendid dancers and collaborated with videographers as well as composers. Some pieces involved text; some did not. Some had you laughing at the wit of his words and how they collided with the moving figures; others were just plain beautiful. I should say, though, that beauty and wit did not rule each other out. In the 1984 *Moose on the Loose*, skeins of complex, out-of-kilter dancing by five individuals beguiled us while Pam Tait, as a kind of anthropologist-journalist, gabbled moose-talk. At one point, King pranced up to her and asked accusingly, "Who do you think you are, Jacques Derrida?"

Pieces such as *Moose,* the 1983 *Lucy Alliteration (A conceptual oratorio), Critical Path* (1985, dedicated to Buckminster Fuller), *How to Write (Digital Picnic)* (1987), *If Iphigenia* (1988), *Correlations* and *The Si(g)ns of the Wor(l)d* (both 1989), and *Galvanic Mix* (1990) were what King called "process-generated" dances. That is, they involved a high degree of improvisation around a known structure. He appreciates the connections between improvisation and ritual, the responses that seem programmed into our genes, the not-so-buried treasures of the collective unconscious. For the dancer, improvisation can blur boundaries between the known and the unknown, affirm habits or knock them askew. King likes to use the word "programming" to describe his process: ". . . constantly breaking down and repeating movement with an eye to the various matrices of possibilities, recombining in any number of ways steps, changes, rhythms, textures, etc., as well as their density of relay and delay so that any and all elements, components and permutable options can be retrieved, (re)assembled or juxtaposed at any moment by, or between, any dancing body" ("Transmedia").

The process involved the performers learning many movement possibilities that would constitute a common warehouse. Learning not just the steps but the ways in which these could be transformed by altering sequence, dynamics, path, etc. Trained in wiliness as well as physical agility, he and his dancers then made instant-by-instant choices in performance. Even if you didn't know they were improvising, you would have been struck by their air of intense concentration and the excitement that crackled in the patterns they mapped. The choreography presented the audience with an image of decision-making and with a web of dancing that emerged over and beyond anyone's single activity and any individual's plans. The orbits, the sudden slash of a diagonal path, the near collisions, the moments of congruence that inevitably slid apart were fascinating, exhilarating, sometimes maddening, incendiary.

Like the work of all truly innovative theater artists, King's choreography was not the sort to appeal to a mass audience. His company didn't make its living touring; the spaces it performed in were usually not proscenium stages but black-box theaters or luminous New York houses like St. Mark's Church and the Merce Cunningham studio. At one time, when the weather was warm, he and his dancers rehearsed in Battery Park because it was free (this was captured in *Making Dances*, an important 1980 documentary on experimental choreographers—King was one of seven on whom the film focused).

He no longer has a company, although he occasionally performs himself, and has devoted himself more intently to writing essays—the business of creating dancing wor(l)ds on paper. There is little I can say about what Kenneth King does that he couldn't say better. On the other hand, he never had the pleasure of sitting in a theater as I did, feeling his creations fire up the brain and the surrounding air.

[I]

One can know self and world, b e i n g and mind, simply by moving the body. Moving the body—dancing—can be synonymous with seeing, thinking, doing—with *action*! There's more to dance than companies, careers, foundations and corporations. That's all temporary. There's a bigger connection.

Believe it or not, it's possible to move through all of space (it's a paradox), out of the linear into the relativistic and synchronistic. It's also possible to stop or step out of t-i-m-e, just by . . . dancing! Dancing is a *t r e m e n d o u s* motion—movement connects everything across spacetime. Kant was right—space and time are (only) the *conditions* of our experience . . .

I can't wait for the day when the computer is a domesticated appliance we can have in the home, when dance can have its own *channel*, poetry, theater, and the other arts their own channels too. Can you imagine how computer, cable and satellites will alter and transform the perception (of perception) and the operations of spacetime? Not to mention institutions, cities, governments and nationalisms as well. Probably it's because of Watergate that we don't have it already. I'd also like to be in a research center (while you're asking) where I could work with my company, space, video and computer. We need new ways to see and *be* totally. The crisis seems to be about specialization.

You ask about . . . labels and categories. I'm not sure w h a t kind of choreographer I am. Actually, I may be a dancemaker instead—I generate movement possibilities from processes, schemes and puzzles rather than manipulate bodies in a predetermined form. But—I might be a superrealist too, and, after all, on Fridays a futurist!

Seriously, though, I prefer the word *transmedia* because it's movement that connects and extends whatever we see or know, in our heads, on the page or stage, across a room, or on a screen: even across disciplines. I also like the word *k i n e t r i c s* as the movement of bodies, ideas, images, lines, words, letters, concepts, tracks, designs, structures, *systems*, etc., through and across one another. The many texts I've written for my dances can stand and have been published separately. I also incorporate projections, films and video in my dances. *Space City*, a film collaboration with Robyn Brentano and Andrew Horn, was premiered in June 1981 at Lincoln Center's International Dance Film Video Conference. Channels, circuits and media interfacings let spaces, resources, concepts and perspectives become interpenetrating and interexchangeable. Movement—following Marshall McLuhan's startlingly insightful lead—extends the signs and signals as well as the ambient of the central nervous system, connecting all perceptual processes. There may be only five senses but a virtually unexplored and unlimited number of sense "ratios." (Kinaesthesia and extrasensory perception, for example, may be amalgams and combines of these ratios.)

Ever since I began making dances in the early 1960s, I've *programmed* movement—I like that word—meaning constantly breaking down and repeating movement with an eye to the variations matrices of possibilities, recombining in any number of ways steps, changes, rhythms, textures, etc., as well as their density of relay and delay, so that any and all elements, components and permutable options can be retrieved, (re)assembled or juxtaposed at any moment by, or between, any dancing body.

As a dancemaker I program structural and organizational options rather than just set, specifically repeatable phrases, so the generation of (im)pulses, and the tracing and tracking of "circuits" in space, activate the firing and fielding of signs and signals that synchronistically become part of the formal performance process. It's asking a lot from dancers, but there's an organization to the dancing body transversing s p a c e that is quicker than the structural logic that the brain can decide, know or predetermine. It's a kind of *digital*-kinetic semiotic . . .

Just how there are pulses, images and imageries in the movement stream, sometimes just below the visible surface or dynamic, appearing automatically in the density of high-frequency field formations, or through the warping and deporting of line, time and contour, intrigues me enormously. Sometimes the imagery only *seems* to be emitted, setting up semblances and (co)correspondences; sometimes it's actual, visceral, mimetic, tacit or disembodied. Dancing brings us to, through and across— sometimes beyond—the thresholds of the visible and invisible, the seen and unseen, the contained and uncontained . . .

And one wonders too just what *is* the connection between TV and the kinet(r)ics of perception *and* the dance (and media) explosion. The *programming* of parts, elements, units, modules, and matrices (including texts, voice, music, projections, transparencies, film and/or video) can stimulate if not create a synchron(icit)y of pulses, pictures and information relays; behind and through the moving body are other *orders* of projectable imageries. With the computer age there will be dancing words, kinetic grammars, information channels, conceptual continua, data process services, synchromimetic teletexts and electric dance mosaics, as there now are concerts and performances.

After six or seven generations, modern dance is still in its initial "volcanic" stage, and necessarily so! I have this expression about the dance explosion—"the f-i-e-l-d is bigger than the form"—meaning that the combined, concatenating activities of all those working in dance today have extended the parameters and boundaries of the idiom in a kind of joint exchange enterprise—there's now a pool of extended possibilities, structural and conceptual, rather than fixed or enforced styles, genres and schools. Postmodernism might be paradoxically an open-ended systemic pluralism . . .

I feel that the art of choreography has reached an intriguing "pass." John Cage has reportedly said he doesn't think there will be composers in the year 2000—complex aural resonances and synchronistically engineered sound environments will preclude their relevance. (There will be sound engineers and musicmakers.) I've long suspected the same about dance. A dance *can* make itself, even, w i t h o u t a choreographer!

I'm interested in ballet, modern (and postmodern) dance and "natural" movement coming together and f - u - s - i - n - g. One could consider classical alignment and turnout as a kind of technology for locomotion through space, but the tilting, multiple contractions, streamlining of line, pulse, spiral, and the twisting and skewering of line and form by the rotation of the torso—what Merce Cunningham ingeniously discovered—have expanded and changed all priorities. Sometimes I like to try shifting back and forth between "movement" and "dance"—they really can't be separated! I like the idea of a technic rather than a technique, because there are larger, organic, holistic connections in the moving body, and another *energy resource*. I mean, with whom or where can one train to move synergetically?

I started out as an aspiring actor while in high school and early college and did three years of summer stock, the first in 1959 as an apprentice at Adelphi College, where I was fortunate to witness a lecture by Ruth St. Denis. Much of my early work from 1964 to 1975 was theatrical and had dancing and talking characters, and props. Maybe the drama of the moving body was my first connection.

I went to Antioch College, which has a work-study program, so every three or six months I'd trek from Ohio to New York City for my jobs. My first was as a hospital orderly at New York University's Rusk Institute of Physical Medicine and Rehabilitation (1961). Evenings I decided to study dance. I don't know how or why, but I found Syvilla Fort's name in the phone book! She was *fabulous*—a passionate and inspiring teacher who had danced with Katherine Dunham, later teaching and collaborating with many many people, including John Cage (for whom he composed the first piece for prepared piano). She taught primitive, modern and basic ballet. And she encouraged me!

In the early 1960s I went to a variety of studios like New Dance Group and Ballet Arts and then found Paul Sanasardo, who had the patience and dedication to teach carefully and explain alignment, placement, phrasing, combining ballet and modern, even at the barre. Paul also incorporated what I'd call a kind of adapted dramatic "method" or

Stanislavskian approach to dance projection, performance, motivation
and focus.

I also went, of course, to the Martha Graham School. It was by then a high drama dance factory with lots of conflicting currents and intrigues. Right after college I took ballet with Mia Slavenska (1965). She didn't talk about electromagnetic currents or archetypes, but about the *skeleton*. She was both outrageous and endearing, when she wasn't poking or insulting you. She told me I had arms like sausages and was hopeless; it was v e r y inspiring!

In an early existentialism course at Antioch we read Nietzsche's *Thus Spake Zarathustra* and that started everything. Isadora Duncan has written that besides the Bible she kept *Zarathustra* on her bedstand throughout her entire life. In 1974 I presented a Nietzsche portrait-play entitled *High Noon*, assembled after carefully researching his writings. Nietzsche has a master key to the dance.

While at Antioch, my most important experience was our much revered "guru" philosophy professor, Keith McGary. He really made things happen! To this day he's really been the biggest influence, meaning one who l i b e r a t e s. In his aesthetics class (a turning point) we read Susanne K. Langer. It was a breakthrough. Her writings have been of enormous importance, especially the later *Mind: An Essay on Human Feeling*. During 1975–76 I presented a Bicentennial dance tribute to her called *Battery*, with ten dancers at the Cathedral of St. John the Divine. I've met her several times and had the opportunity to visit and talk with her in her home in Old Lyme, Connecticut.

In the summer of 1966 I got a scholarship and studied briefly with Merce Cunningham and Carolyn Brown. Merce is the Einstein of modern dance. For more than fifteen years I've watched all his work with great excitement and appreciation. He and John Cage are major artistic influences—they're a new juncture point and whole new axis in the experience of movement and sound in spacetime. I consider Merce Cunningham to be our first s p a c e dancer.

There have been many other influences—Balanchine, the Judson Dance Theater, and oh, I'd better mention Charlie Chaplin too—a favorite—he was certainly an early modern dancer, no?—while we're bantering terms.

More recently (1978) Maria Theresa Duncan—the last of the "Isadorables" (at the heroic age of eighty-four)—provided a profound experience in restaging and performing three separate concerts of the heritage of Isadora. It was so important I had to write a long appreciation entitled *Vision Dancing*.

Maybe you're wondering how I've kept my head together . . . New York *is* mania and madness. Ha! OK—I'll confess—only by reading and exploring Krishnamurti, for the past decade. He shows you how to see the *whole* mind—instantly. He's an expressway.

Reading and research are a tremendous and important influence. Here are some thinkers and authors I could not have done without: Nietzsche, Edmund Husserl, Ernst Cassirer, Sigmund Freud, Carl Jung, Wilhelm Reich, Norman O. Brown, Marshall McLuhan, Jacques Ellul, Ludwig Wittgenstein, Gurdjieff-Ouspensky-Nicoll, E. E. Cummings, Walt Whitman, John Cage, Marcel Duchamp, Arthur Koestler, Jean-Paul Sartre, Simone de Beauvoir, John Cunningham Lily, Alice Bailey, Nikola Tesla, Virginia Woolf, Gertrude Stein, Susanne Langer and Simone Weil.

I always encourage students to bring something else or o t h e r—an interest, avocation, a study, system, even another art—to the dance, to discover a larger organic understanding of the moving body. And in the classroom I insist on being a student too and sharing in the collective kinetic investigation and exchange.

I want dancers to be able to move and generate a dance using their own inner rhythms and body clocks (reaffirming both Isadora and Stanislavski) and to be able to patternate and problem-solve with an eye to compositional development, design, modulation, exchange—not just present a preset, mechanically manipulated piece. I WANT TO SEE A DANCER'S AWARENESS, INTELLIGENCE AND SPONTANEITY *ALLOWED* TO FUNCTION ON STAGE.

There are so many formidable challenges to making dances. First and foremost it's the action of dancing that completes my own sense of being. It is a way to bridge the mind-body schizsplits that have fragmented our whole Western field of experience. Dancing is the means to recover the whole being, the primal man—archetypally the way perhaps the shaman is a unitive being before history's specializations divide him into poet, oracle, priest, medicine man, mystic, medium, magician, etc.

In *The Making of Americans*, certainly the one work that crowns Ger-

trude Stein a philosopher, there's a big humorous clue in her exclamation
at the outset that she wants to have in her all the b e i n g of *all* those
who have ever lived, are living or will be living. Finally the reason for
dancing: ontological lust!

The challenge of training is discovering one's body—all the ways it
can move and the reflexive underlying principles that connect the diversity of its processes and resources. Also, finding new energy thresholds,
other senses and sense ratios by changing the total body *frequency* and
engaging multiaxial electromagnetic body field alignments. Dancing into
the space age, into and through s p a c e . . . finding a bridge between technics and technique, art and science, investigation and discovery, the abstract and the concrete, programs, entertainment, and i n f o r m a t i o n.

Because of the concatenation of diverse styles, techniques and systems
during the last two decades, I sometimes think the only way to cross the
new threshold is to work with "open form" and process choreography.
Dance is about constant transformation. Even formal choreography can
include elements of improvisation, which can, I think, be a kind of metascience—rigorous, formal, systemic, complex and spontaneously revealing of how movement *itself* generates and derives energy, structure,
grammar. The most rewarding response to my work by both critics and
audiences alike is wondering, and wanting to know, what's set and what's
not set—it becomes a puzzle for them watching, just as it can be for us
d o i n g ! Dance can be larger than a choreographer's brain and the sum-
mation of its linear organizational structures. I always feel that dancers,
given the chance, can bring as much new information to a work in pro-
gress as any of the choreographer's (pre)suppositions. Movement has its
o w n *intentionality*; dance doesn't need a psyche or psychology to motivate it, it has its own "MOTORvation" . . .

What's challenging is constantly pushing against one's limits, conceptions and possibilities. One can never rehearse enough. What's challenging about performing is the o t h e r (larger) projection threshold and the
surplus of energy the audience supplies. Marcel Duchamp clarified the
modernist intention—the audience provides the energy and attention to
complete the action of the work. Meaning and stories are now long beside
the point, because movement as a paranarrative phenomenon automatically expresses and reveals so *many* things. Performing is a tremendously
exciting, transforming experience, almost like turning yourself inside out

or having a double. Dancing can bring forth the mythic temperament, and I seem to have a large dose of that too. Dancing is always apocalyptic, i.e., revelatory.

The environment is in such DANGER—nukes, chemspills, military, commercial (not to mention political) overkill—we need to rediscover another radiant energy within our bodies. Intelligence doesn't have to be contained by a body or institution but can inhabit a field or ensemble of dancers. And gesture itself is a secret art—it can reveal, conceal, inform, heal and transmute conflict and tension, then embrace and celebrate mystery. Einstein: "The most beautiful thing we can experience is the mysterious. It is the source of all true art and science" (*What I Believe*, 1930).

Since the mid-1970s my work has changed in that it involves more and more dance, music and transmedia exploration, less characters and overt polemics. The information is in the dance; the *doing* is the finding and knowing. Right from the outset in 1964 my dance developed from working with language, the voice and various kinds of texts to explore a larger sense of deep structure. In the information age there emerges a complex digital action to all the parameters of the wor(l)d—all its rhythmic, intrasyntactical and *coded* coefficients. Left brain/right brain research has shown that duality *is* physiological, but there are means and programs that can recoordinate polarity and holistically recircuit the brain's separate processes. I've found ways to "synapsulate" both body and rhythm, phrase, sequence and voice with my "t-e-l-e-g-r-a-p-h-i-c s-o-n-g-s," puns, word games and tongue twisters that atomize, particalize and reduce to essential rhythmic bits the modules and matrices of steps, patterns, phonemes, gestures and vocables and activate their complex, *primal* mix.

Another challenge: that the body when heated, toned, and prepared can r e l e a s e itself from (the force of) gravity. Even if only temporarily, for a few moments it's an incredible, even revelatory experience.

I'm a tall, lean, slim person and I like that feeling, the body being light and unimpeded. I like to move full out, very expansively and rapidly. I've devised a lot of arm and spine movements that are all my own, so the body coils, twists, bounds, spins, spirals, gyrates, dips, bounces and curves . . . The arms scallop spatially and gesturally, revolving around a constantly rotating body axis, revealing intersecting zones and interstices. I turn and counter torque, whirl, glide, skim, travel, and dive the vectors. Dancing is more like high-interface action verbs than nouns and subjects. I'm very interested in the *electric* threshold: dance can be like live voltage, or crossing realms. Sometimes the body is flooded and energized by an excess of impulses, spasms, jerks, shakes, tremors, and responds with quirks and undulations. Sometimes the channel or energy stream makes cresting gestures: the body tracks, paces, swings, pivots, gallops, darts, slashes, skewers, scoops, scampers, vaults, jousts, rotates, balances and springs into the air. I don't like to jump mechanically but be *lifted* into the air. Dancing is immensity.

I've worked a lot with speed, fluidity and compression of phrase, step, gesture, rhythm and activating a rapid-fire pulse. But the most important thing is to find out how one dances for one's self. I can't quite teach what I do entirely yet. I try to and like working best by "osmosis" with dancers. The eye is mimetic and dancers should be able to "read" and transfer movement connections instantly. In my company work I try to draw on dissimilarities and differences to find or allow another sense of continuity and unity. I'm not trying to have dancers be homogenized doing "my" style; I want them to "translate" and problem-solve by isolating and formally recombining the ingredients. I teach specific steps, matrices and units specifying how to use them in various ways, but let them find and make the connections. My role is generator, conductor, catalyst.

First I give the dancers "space maps"—i.e., grid structures with specific locomotor instructions. During the last few years, starting with my dance *Wor(l)d (T)raid* (1978), it's been three grids: horizontal/vertical, diagonal, tilted, rotated, circuited, diamond-shaped and circular. It's about how very simple basics can visually and rhythmically quickly generate a complex field and fold, and numerous, simultaneously interlocking structures. One can use any battery of movements, though I prefer mixing the basic principles of both modern and ballet. Steps can include tendus and tracking laterally with the legs at 90-degree angles, pivoting the sense of line and structure, then adding lunges, walks, porte de bras, contractions, tilts, attitudes, triplets, turns, battements, etc. The steps per se are really about "geometry" (i.e., how axis, center, weight, etc. move the body through and across space) and "geography" (or topography, mosaic-style), revealing how a discontinuous field of multioptional possibilities

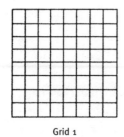

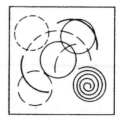

Grid 1   Grid 2   Arcs/circles/spirals
                                                    rotors (moving arcs)
                                                    Grid 3

and interlocking, intertwining structures break through to, or simulate, a kind of kinetic motor or holotropic calculus.

Look at this. Would you believe it's all of geometry and geography in only three grids!

In the random action of assembling parts and steps, dancers develop "radar"—in fact, all technological projection systems have their source in our central nervous system. And this is not just "my" choreography or "a" dance but also the means anyone could use to explore generative structures, process composition, kinetic geometry, etc. It's what I often teach and work with in workshops and residencies.

To develop and coordinate the rhythmic folding and the overall dynamic, I'll give images—for example, for the first grid I'll suggest moving as if traveling, scurrying, darting through a labyrinth, or demarcating precise sets of interlocking puzzles, like Chinese boxes, because space can reveal its intersecting layers, integers, rhythms. The circular grids, arcs and "rotors" (rotating arcs), as well as interpenetrating circles, generate contours, vortexes of energy, and punctuate line with surprising changes of direction, making for relays, delays, recoils, dynamic change and curvilinear detail. As the dancers learn to ply the changes automatically, they find that dancing can happen faster than it seems one *can* think, arrange, plan, predict, coordinate or predetermine. That's the idea! There *is* a tremendous action and motion within what we call spontaneity and synchronicity that is mysterious because it carries us beyond the known limits and parameters of the ways we *think* it possible to move. Isn't that postmodern?!

To develop and coordinate the rhythmic folding and the overall dynamic I'll suggest typography clues—for example, *Currency* (1980) grew
out of the tight formal gridwork of *Wor(l)d (T)raid* but spun through
space with a looser, freer-wielding abandon punctuated by sudden clusters of configurations that continually arose like bubbles or eddies, and it
was one of the most open-form works I've generated. Conceptually, the
collective motorizing action of the ensemble makes for rotating axial
"spools," coiled and sprung vectors, vortexual pools and a constantly
shifting center requiring multiple foci as the eye "reads" the rapidly assembling and disappearing formations and patterns. (We generated the
dance outdoors in the summer in Battery Park in Lower Manhattan, using video to develop it.)

Because *Currency* was generated with five dancers (Carter Frank, Shari
Cavin, Bryan Hayes, Bill Shepard and myself, and videographer Tim Pur-
tell), a kind of rapid-fire digital shifting from symmetrical to asymmetrical clustering of configurations made phrasing break through to a kind of
interlaced kinetic circuitry, threading bodies, lines and patterns through
one another, constantly realigning and recycling itself through space, permuting torque play, direction, shifts of perspective, and energetically
switching the focus between foreground and background and thus
throwing depth of field and dimensionality into relief. I also cited Duchamp's *Nude Descending a Staircase*—the first time we see the fragmented rotation of a post-cubist spine in space; also the suprapositional
overlays of M. C. Escher and Joseph Cornell's enchanting poetic collages
were inspirational too.

A CAPS grant (thanks again) enabled me to purchase a color video
VHS system to regularly tape and playback rehearsals both in the studio
and outdoors in Battery Park. Memory is not just in the brain but in the
visceral and muscular reflexes entrained by visual and kinetic relays connecting axis, spine, and the scan of the gaze. The spine functions like a
revolving antenna. The firing of (im)pulses and signals sets up intertwining, sprocketing patterns, ribbons, waves and threads so that parts, modules and steps can be vigorously (re)assembled, plied, transformed, per-
muted, even fragmented from day to day, performance to performance.
The video soundtrack amplified the invasive cacophony of the urban
soundscape, simulating a William-John Tudor score, a composer with

whom I've collaborated since 1976. Later he watched the video to plot the time changes, then adapted and composed an electronic score for the dance.

As Marshall McLuhan explained, television is about constantly reassembling clusters and configurations of image, word, picture, information, etc. The dizzying juxtapositions, rapid jump cuts, zero-degree zooms and staggered panning shots seem to throw the viewer out of his body, or one's eyes out of perspective! Rather than paper and money, the "pulse" may now be the real basic unit of currency and exchange in the digital transformations of our overloaded modern world.

For me, a very active, dense field and stage fabric can be very satisfying because of the bounty and networks of signs and signal circuits elicited. Besides, computers are going to make for whole new orders and registers of program possibility where word, image, pulse, design, configurations, and data transparencies with high-density ratios and motor mimetic transactions will take precedence in redefining our perceptual-kinetic and visual-mimetic currencies. One sees its intimation in the intense, spellbound fascination youngsters have riveted to electronic pinball and public computer games, or in business transactions at banks, airlines and corporations that are beginning to confront the high-process assemblage and digital transformation of high-frequency clustered configurations, feeding and engaging the total scanspan of our mindfields.

Instead of steps and structures, the layering of post-choreographic space is really negotiated by *codes*—complex ways we assimilate and process the raw data of steps, phrases, signals, directions, lines, vectors, matrices, trajectories, changes, etc. Merce Cunningham made and coined the language and vocabulary and the Judson Church experimentation furthered the transformational rules, i.e., performative grammars.

New dance has entered another whole realm, or order of coordination, organization, structuring, energy and intelligence that can function when bodies move. Inner space and o u t e r space—*why* separate them! The body *is* contained, but—dancing is *uncontained* . . . We can move to know ourselves and dance to s e e the wor(l)d . . . It's the riddle of being— and goodness! n-o-t-h-i-n-g-n-e-s-s and the mystery of holy universe that keeps dancers making dances, and—dancers! E-U-R-E-K-A!

February 19, 1981

The human body is poised to undergo unprecedented digital transformations that will create another frontier of corporeal extensions comparable
to the technological advances that have changed the entire physical landscape during the last century, as laser meets psychomimesis and biotech-
nology releases the capacities of cell and gene, confounding the credulity
of science fiction. After multimedia on stage, technology *in* and *as* the
body. The regeneration and simulation of body parts—synthetic skin,
lightweight joints, transplanted organs, cyber prostheses, bionic implants
and genetically altered programming will be taken for granted. Virtual
memory and cybermnemonic technology—*neurothetics*—will be pioneered by glasses with two-way neurotransference and micro cellphone
earpiece adaptors to extend the interactive capacity of the Internet, surpassing screen and monitors to spacialize displays like a combo fusion of
freeform 3-D and teleprompting. Imagine dancers channeling choreography *during* performance.

All technology externalizes and exemplifies principles already residing
within the body. Marshall McLuhan clued us in to how the media are
externalizations of the senses and nervous system, as the Net is of the
brain. Technology began with the alphabet, media are different languages,
and information is processed with peripheral vision, as dancers can read-

ily testify. The body is the wor(l)d and the planet made flesh is the dance of digitality. No wonder French logotechnicians have extolled the death of the author and the disappearance of the subject! There's just the coextensivity of the *textendable*, the Web's unimpeded circulation and distribution of signs, data, sites, images, texts and information links that make mind *Mind*—a (co)coextensive epic hyperphenomenon, a supraterrestrial neurosphere.

Merce Cunningham pioneered digital dance long before the PC. His system dances, such as *Canfield* (1969), *Landrover* (1972) and *Torse* (1976), made long before his use of Life Forms computer software, transected the realms of discontinuous spacialization and hyperdimensional vectorization—the first time the kinetic spectra of the bioenergetic field in *motion* was seen on stage. *Canfield* was dedicated to Nikola Tesla, who pioneered AC-DC current, radio and laser, but also foresaw wireless planetary power—a futuristic possibility. (The CIA reportedly confiscated his papers right after he died, so the full scope of his secret inventions hasn't been released.) Tesla, Wilhelm Reich and R. Buckminster Fuller have made biosyncretic advances that choreographers have only begun to tap.

Electricity changed everything. It shifted the transference boundaries between inner and outer, continuous and discontinuous, choreography and improvisation, turning the wor(l)d into a hypertrophic field continuum. Electronics repositions and erases temporal boundaries, virtualizes history and shifts registers between self and other as it catalyzes dimensional exchanges and overrides categories. Microscope, camera and movie projector magnified vision, opened it to other orders of reality and perception, and zeroed in on the hyperdimensionality of information hidden in the interstices between ultimate units—atoms, genes, cells, codes, frames, bytes, and ciphers. Phonograph and radio extended the frequency range of aural and audial ambients; dancers who improvise know how to *listen* to movement. Lightbulb and locomotive catalyzed the topology of the nation's landscape and spawned the growth of cities and technology. Cars privatized and reconfigured space and property, opened the radial vectors of highways and, coupled with drive-in movies, liberated sexuality. The airplane converted the motivity of the railroad, expanding rail lines into flight vectors whose interprecessionary meridians criss-cross the globe like matrices of planetary dendrites. Multimedia mapped interface capacities between technologies, reembodied by the Internet. Dance, the *exstasis* and reflexion of being (being) in motion, continues to confound itself with the desire for antigravitational (ups)urges. (-Cellular activation, magnetization of lymphatic fluids and electromimetic frequency acceleration are means to suspend gravity.) Hark the body digital.

Information is tactile, kinetic and autonomic. Its currency is the sign. A sign can be kinetically activated by an impulse, flexion or isomorph and stand proxy for a constellation of interconnectivities—even a shoulder shrug, finger snap or body tic can generate a kinetic matrix. Dance, being a continuum of coordinated patterns, aligns processes that link different orders of signals and signs that are converted into codes, virtual correlatives and symbiotic analogues transmitting sensibility, information and cognition. Merce Cunningham used chance to expand the permutability index of movement—collaged fragments and compossible structures synergized parts into several greater wholes. He actualized holistically kinetic choreographic circuitries that displayed the architectonics of anarchistic logic(s) before chaos theory (other modes of order and design revealed in what appears to be disorder). The *synapse* is a secret agent: the spaces and integers between bodies, limbs, isomorphs, patterns and scalar ratios reveal the mysteries of the invisible—and its readability. The release of cellular energy mirrors the orgonomic discoveries of Wilhelm Reich, the father of body work. Buckminster Fuller worked out the synergetic architectonics of frequency engineering, the first requirement for scripting the biosystemics of the digital body, akin to dancing the Pentium chip.

Dancing is an information system. Dance technique too is a virtual technology—turn-out, contraction, ballon, etc. move and lift the body, eideticizing space and perception. Philosopher Susanne K. Langer was the first to write about art as virtual form (*Feeling and Form*, 1958) with reference to the projections, semblances and esthetics of representation that can embody different modalities, including the real, unreal, irreal, surreal and hyperreal. The virtual extends physical parameters too and is more than surrogate or substitute—future body links have to be more than disembodied hologramic homunculi or video spectres hovering on the Net. Langer also wrote about physiognomic seeing—compositive, configurative scanning of detail and pattern recognition that collages how perception visualizes phenomena, after cubism and gestalt theory (*Mind: An*

Essay on Human Feeling, 1965). Windows greatly amplify the potential physiognomic capacities of cyberocularity—seeing the wor(l)d through the readability of its extensions. Vectors, meridians and circuits link computer, body and language. Technology amplifies the kinet(r)ics and culture of corporeality.

The transistor miniaturized circuitry, made equipment transportable and turned space inside out before the microchip compressed energy and provided analogs for virtuality and digital memory (which resides in brains and *cells*). Gestures anchor spacial vectors and act as connective agents for the transmissivity of movement codes. Gestures can activate genetic potential, too. The father of digital transmissivity, Alan Turing, a British mathematician and cryptanalyst, helped pioneer the Collasus deciphering machine during World War II that cracked the Germans' infamously permutable, nearly indecipherable Enigma code. Turing discovered how to transform an algorithm into an electronic circuit so the computer could perform many more functions than highspeed calculation. Turing paved the way for the idea(s) of programming, digital memory and pulse frequency modulation.

There needn't be a separation between movement and the information it carries or transmits (a signal can bypass becoming a sign and the sign likewise its symbol or signifier), instantly opening windows and kinelexically linking views, mimetic perspectives and hyperdimensions. How do we read the codes and ciphers of the dancing body? *Semionostics*— technics for seeing and cognizing a field of motion sign(al)s—extrapolates references, patterns, associations, and correlatives and frees dance from literal and symbolic meaning, symbiotizing doer and viewer. Around 1920 German phenomenologist Ernst Cassirer, assimilating the discoveries of neurology and brain surgery, realized *all* perceptual and esthetic processes engage language elementally, and psychoanalyst Jacques Lacan has written that the unconscious is structured like a language. Undoubtedly the digitizing of its elements will continue our preoccupation with integrating its communicative ratios and bundling its code matrices to speed the transmission of thought, information, conception and movement. Movement links primordiality and futurity as it rides the divide and plays out dialectical resolutions between history and prehistory; kinemorphic *transcription* engages multiple and simultaneously extended

scapes, images and meanings. Dance partners the invisible. Meaning is
polyvalent and multisemic.

Dance companies have become late-twentieth-century hyperconsu-
merist *institutions* whose intractability can limit the art's growth potential. Dance is *more* than choreography; art always exceeds its form(s).
Mercea Eliade's book *Shamanism* offers a sobering reminder that there
have been legions of anonymous dancing healers, prophets and poets
throughout all history in all parts of the world whose names have not
been recorded and whose great accomplishments never terminated in
packaged choreography and history-obsessed career trips. After all, making and selling dance is a capitalistic enterprise. The French post-
Hegelians were right to celebrate the end of history, which is not *not* the
same as the ending of time. Virtuality again.

One of the biggest millennial frontiers will be ageing and longevity;
there's little or no literature on it for dancers, but already more are challenging the stereotype. Maria-Theresa Duncan commanded the stage at
eighty-three with indelible presence; Maya Plitsysteskia astonished a couple of seasons ago at seventy. With uncanny vitality, Frances Alenikoff,
approaching eighty, fondly recollects being enthralled by the great Spanish dancer Escudero when he was an octogenarian. Less than a decade
ago there were between 30,000 and 40,000 people who lived beyond one
hundred; now it's surpassed 400,000. Vigorous exercise is the first best
redemption, but ever-expanding herbal, homeopathic and nutritional
supplements have made incredible advances, and biochemical breakthroughs cannot be far away. For joints: glucosamine/chrondroitin sul-
fate, joint factors (Twin Labs or Solgar), parsley, horsetail/chapparel
combo, marshmallow, slippery elm and mucilaginous foods such as oat-
meal. For tissues, cells and ligaments: MSM (methylsulfonylmethane)
and N-A-C (n-acetyl-L-cysteine). Anti-ageing: gingko biloba, DHEA-25
(dehydroeplandrosterone with bioperine); PS-100 (phosphatidylserine),
gotu kola, acetyl-L-carnitine and lecithin all help maintain brain and cognitive function; alfalfa, coenzyme Q10, siberian ginseng, spirulina, and
liquid chlorophyll boost energy; hawthorn supports the heart; fresh aloe,
Q10 and any number of conditioners fortify the skin. (NAC and Q10 are
also powerful antioxidants. I owe most of this to Frances Alenikoff and
Gina Bonati.) Check out Gary Null's website, <www.garynull.com>; he's

the pioneering health guru and nutrition expert who understood well in advance of medical practitioners how to galvanize the immune system to combat AIDS, cancer and environmental illnesses such as multitoxic and Epstein-Barr syndromes.

The formidable technological challenge for dance education in the twenty-first century will be joining mind and body. Since the 1930s college and university curricula have generated a new grade of practitioners (even though dance departments often operate under the limited auspices of phys. ed. rather than fine arts). But the field remains isolated and politically naive though the body is a super matrix and movement an international currency. Journalists don't have the space to do it justice; dance writing needs wider parameters. The merger of TV, cable, film and video on the Net will give the arts a big shot in the arm: broader, more diversified bases and support linked to increased centers of outreach and development, programmatic options, literary outlets, and hopefully more hip, daring, outspoken practitioners like crackerjack culture critic Camille Paglia (<www.salon.com>). Virtuality accelerates the reciprocities of bodies and wor(l)ds, the circulation of signs and isomorphs, the exhilaration of linked motion; luckily the planet too has dreams and orgasms . . .

(1999)

Walt Whitman's celebrated, still incantatory words from *Leaves of Grass*, magical and evocative, timeless and modern, pry open one of the perennial mysteries about the voice—or multiplicities of voices surging through one's throat like a sonic river (reading him aloud), refocusing all the conceptions and preconceptions about identity. One body, one voice—hardly. Singularity's song spins a tumultuous plurality of voices and poetic constellations of concatenative signs: "Through me many long dumb voices . . . Through me forbidden voices . . ." The phenomena of the transformations of vocal registers, whether that of a transcendental poet like Whitman, hip-hop rappers whose speeding, popping fusillades of hyperflexed, steady stream phonemic collisions and rhythmic elisions reach thresholds of genuine digital transmissivity, popular comics like Randy Credico, Lily Tomlin, Rich Little or Dana Carvey, direct voice mediums such as Leslie Flint and John Sloan, evangelical legends like Aimee Semple McPherson speaking in tongues, or the indefatigable Tallulah Bankhead with her overproduced, dramatically deep, drop-dead diction—voices of otherness hold one rapt like the embrace of supernatural paradox.

We all enjoy playing with voices, the child humorously lampooning adults by mimicking them and adults endearingly and ridiculously adopting simpering voices when pampering and playing with children, animals and pets. William James has written about some of these primal impulses of mimicry in his *Principles of Psychology*; Joseph Cornell's parrot habitat series, visually silent but poetically resonant, connotatively evokes an implicitly arresting double mimicry, an absurdist entendre bonanza. James: "Vocalization . . . the child imitates every word he hears uttered and repeats it again and again with the most evident pleasure at his new power . . . The child's first words are in part vocables of his own invention . . . man is essentially *the* imitative animal . . . For a few months in one of my children's third year, he literally hardly ever appeared in his own person."[1]

Just by compressing, foreshortening or elongating one's trachea, (epi)glottis, mouth muscles, or angle of delivery, voices slide through a host of mercurial registers to surprise by their sudden othernesses; the comedic causes one to "double" up—the euphemism for laughter is metaphysically sacrosanct. The ability to take on an authentic, other vocal signature and imitate the factorial specificities of a foreign voice always proves a delightful surprise.[2] The euphonic voices *in* the voice hovering over and through it, permeating it, alter and lead one through the passes of compossibility—an entrancing audiophilia.

The voice, any voice, inherits language, whose awesome pregiveness and anteriority transform it into its double, then supply the figure it inhabits with a shadow (the *mark* of existence) through innuendo, contiguity, reflexion and resonance. Maurice Merleau-Ponty: "Language is the double of being . . ."[3] Jacques Derrida: "There is a double effect of the medium, a double relation between logos and sense . . ."[4] The voice's power rides the disembodied edge and ontic margins of phenomenality and provides a reciprocal guarantor *for* language as its producer and praxeologer. How curious that seeing and hearing *and* hearing and seeing language and language *voiced* reverse, transpose, transfigure and *tropize* orders, priorities, contexts, codes and logics. It is vocal production, motoric and mimetically embodied in its virtual, acoustic spectra, and retroactively mnemonic, that makes language exceed itself, scrambles its rules, contexts and proprioceptive proprieties. Every voice embodies a malleable spectrum of potentially permutable and paramimetic modes that has the potential to hyperflex the entire psyche. A voice even slightly altered takes on the eidetic signature and numinous profile of a character and is thus both more and less than a given identity (that is consequently tacitly traced by the iteration of figuration). Even in solitary confinement, the voice creates the Other; language, too, elides *its* identity. In *Speech and Phenomena* Jacques Derrida, tracing the fissures and analytics of voice and speech, delves into the lubricous manifolds of ciphers that embed and entrain identity and perception, the psychomimetrics of the dance of signs: "Hearing oneself speak is not the inwardness of an inside that is closed in upon itself; it is the irreducible openness in the inside; it is the eye and the world within speech."[5] Words become eyes, and signs become their sensors and antennae.

Through listening (an art unto itself) the potential is aroused for a reflexive aurality in the production of the vocal stream; the motoric (im)pulses, flexions and vocopathic isomorphisms in turn create virtualized hearing (semiotropic, physiognomic, neuroacoustic) *through* the vocalically charged act of speaking. Mimics and impersonators must be gifted with this ability as a natural talent. Language thus becomes phonemically particalized—constantly sundered and reconstructed to reappropriate the transposition capacities of its registers in moment to moment sonic assemblage; thus the kinetics of vocal production (and its autotranslation into syntactical and symbolically projected mimetic delivery) continually reeideticizes, reconsecrates and reconcentrates all of its elements. *Vocothetics* could be a coinage to signify the homological reflexivities of audioflexions and thereby their intrareferential (co)correspondences underlying the semio-and sonocryptnostics of concatenating sound manifolds that create the neurotropic mazes of likeness, (re)semblance, (re)cognition and wonder.

It is the production of the voice's entire phonological continuum that makes language, and itself, doubly mimetic; this is implicit in, and realized by, the physical projection of making the letter exceed itself. The mimetic disembodies, (re)embodies and catalyzes while it suspends—i.e., foregrounds and backgrounds simultaneously—the concentrated release of mnemonic residues, audiotropic potencies, elements, traces, inferences and characterological substrates that in turn emit energy, affect, connections, messages and meanings and thus configure being. Mimesis is much more inclusive and comprehensive a phenomenon than Aristotle's categorical sense of the imitative. It evokes and activates all the ways the tacit factors of motion, articulation, inscription, energy, psyche, likeness, meaning, sentiency, identity and intelligence inform the animation of words, forms, bodies, personas, gestalts, images, beings and events; and how signs transpire and are made manifest. Since the inauguration of digitality all presentational form(at)s have an immediate and intermediated hyperdimensional capacity to release the palpable impact of their mimicity; through vocalization the animation of the entire phonolexical continuum amplifies and synergizes the signal chains of vocables that congeal into signs, sign manifolds, messages, codes and encrypted transferences. Words entrained as speech and syntax bestow passage, reference, import and communication; obviously voice and language are inextricably interdependent and catalyze one another in incalculably enigmatic ways.

In dance, kinetic and kinaesthetic mimesis arises from the activation and projection of physically activated signals and impulses as well as muscular flexions and sprung gestures that engage the kinelexic play and spectra of corporealized signs in passage. Movement flow, (e)motional tensities and the plastic semblances emitted by locomotion create dialectical contrasts and a kinetic *scripting* that cathect and inscribe, in turn, transferences of shape, contour, isomorphic contiguity and the interpenetrating mosaics of spacialized patterns. If gesture supplied the wor(l)d's first cipher, mimesis provided its first si(g)n—the projected spectacle (ritual) with its concomitant cathexis of desire. Mimesis also summons up a motion currency that evokes reciprocal transparencies between beholder and signifier through the interprecession of sign manifolds, interactive registers, semiotic orders and differential scales that link the spectra of phenomena and the trails and traceries of association that interconnect and overlay forms and media. The mimetic is thus a parasympathetic mediator that delivers up the sensually multisensory interplay of pictures and autonomous images emitted by words and movement, bodies, signals, signs, substrates and ambients in high interface, initiating a dialexis (or double reading) of multiple orders of logical relation whose exchange ratios engage enciphered transferences within and between the virtual continua linking subject and world, as well as their cyberthetic reflexion. Mimesis provides and provokes passage from the known to the not-known and unknown (not *not* the same)—to what is beyond self, body, sight, hearing and the parameters of presentation and appearance into realms bordering the invisible—dreams, secrets, the un-

Kenneth King as three
characters from *Dancing
Wor(l)ds* (1990):

As Mr. Pontease Tyak
the philosopher
vaudevillian in "Who's
Kidding Whom?"
© Johan Elbers.

As Mr. Snail in "Ask Mr.
Snail" © Johan Elbers.

As Tallulah Bankhead
in "The Tallulah
Deconstruction"
© Johan Elbers.

derworld (and undertext), as well as the subaltern domains of the taboo and forbidden.

The lure of forbidden voices—the andryogenic, hermaphrodictic, apocrophantic and phantomimic—broker psychosthetic secrets and engage ontolexic ciphers that exceed containment and move identity beyond and through the sonic contours of orality and over the ocularmetric thresholds of the retinal blink—mimesis is now *prestidigitalization*!

(*1993*)

Have you been noticing the newscasters? They've been messing up, stuttering in suspicious and revealing ways. Like the newscasters, I've been finding myself getting more and more tongue-tied, so I decided to put it to work! Have you ever tried to *write* a tongue twister? At first it seems really impossible. (Tongue twisters are concentrated alliterative chain clusters of easily garbled, usually nonsensical structures whimsically mindboggling to the point of suggesting a kind of twilight zone where riddle, pun, aphorism and anagram meet and trade their secret mirrored i-n-t-e-g-e-r-s . . .)

THE CHEAP SHEIKH AND THE CHIC SHAH SEEK TO SPEAK AT A SECRET SPA ((THE CHEAP SHEIKH AND THE CHIC SHAH SEEK TO SPEAK *CHEEK TO CHEEK* AT A S-E-C-R-E-T SPA . . .))   *(heavy Slavic/Hungarian shadow voice, like a spy)*

THE SHEIKH'S SLEASY SNEAK SWEEP IN SLUSH AND SLEET OF THE SHINY SLEEK SLEEPING SHEEP IS THE SPICY SPEAK OF *SHEEEEEEET* STREET . . .   *(same)*

THE SHADY SHODDY SUPER SURE SHOTS AND SHALLOW SNIDE SNEAKING SNOTS SCHEMING WITH SLIPPERY SNOOPING SCHLOCKS SELLING AND SHELLING STOLEN SLOT STOCKS FROM THE SHAH'S QUEASY SWEAT SHOPS SWOOP AND SWAP SLEEPY SWABS STAKING SHAPELESS SLOBS SCOUTING SURE AND SAVVY SECRET S-A-B-O-T-A-G-E . . .   *(same)*

A FLAKY FLEET OF FAT FRATTY FLAT-FOOTED FRUMPY FUNKY FREAKY FLUNKIES FRAZZLES A FRANKLY BEDAZZLED FRANTIC FRONT LINE RANK OF REGULARLY WRANGLED RANKLED YANKS FRAYED AND FLAYED BY THE FLASHY FLESH AND FLEECY FLANKS OF FORTUNE . . .

THE WORLD'S A DRAMA LIKE A TEENY TOT'S CAREENING TEETER TOTTER UNTETHERING A SCREAMING GLOBAL TROT AND A ZESTY BUT TESTY TEETHING TRAUMA . . . *(high British)*

A SPIFFLY CLIPPED HIP AND STRICTLY TIGHT-LIPPED CRYPTIC SCRIPT IS SIMPLY SIFTED AND SIPPED THEN ON A TIMELY TIP SLIPPED ON A SECRET SHIP ADRIFT A THRIFTY TRADE TRIP THEN SWIFTLY STRIPPED AFTER A STIFF SHIFTY RIFT BY TWO TONGUE-TIED TIFFED AND MIFFED TWIN KNIT-T'WITS! (TO: WIT) . . .

XERXES ZERO-DEGREE XEROX ZIPS ZIG-ZAGS AND Z-O-O-M-S ZEALOUSLY THROUGH ZENOBIA WHILE ZENO'S ZESTY JESTING ZAFTIG ZEBRA AND XY-LOPHONE ARE Z-A-P-P-I-N-G ZEN'OPHOBIA . . .

SHIVA'S SHINY SHUNTED SHEAVES ACHIEVE THE DARING DAIRY DEED OF CLEAVING TO THE CHEESY SHREDDED CHEATING SEEDY SLEEVES OF SLEAZY SEETHING SLEEPING THIEVES FROM THEBES . . .

GIVE HER A GRIMMER GRAMMAR RATHER THAN A SLIMMER GLIMMER OF GLAMOUR ((GIVE HER A GRIMMER G-L-I-B-B-E-R GRAMMAR RATHER THAN A SLIMMER GLIMMER OF GLAMOUR)) . . .

NEFERTITI'S NEAT NEW ESOTERIC EDEN EATERY ETCHED IN KITSCHY KINKY GRAPHIC GRAFFITI EAST OF THE GREAT GREEK CONCRETE CRETE CREEK IN TROPICAL TAHITI BY THE GLEAMING GREEN TEA SEA WITH SCREAMING SLEEK SCENERY GREETS THE BLEARY WEAK AND WEARY WITH A WAFER AND A TREATY . . . *(British)*

SELECTIVELY KEPT S-U-S-P-E-C-T AND *ANTIC*SEPTICALLY SWEPT WITH SHINY SEARING SALTY SWEAT WHILE SECRETLY CRAVING CRUETS AND CREPES **SARA AND CLARA** SLEPT IN THE SAHARA THEN ADEPTLY CREPT SKEPTICALLY SCHLEPPING SHEP'S SCHWEPPS UP STEEP STEELY STONY STEPPES . . .

THE CLIQUEY CHIC BLEAKLY STREAKED FREAK BOUTIQUE SELLING PETE'S STEEP SLEEK HOMEMADE PETITE PEAK PEKOE PEE TEA TEAK REAL CHEAP IN CHEEKY MOZAMBIQUE SPEAKS TO THE WEAK TWEAKED BEAK OF A SNEAKY SNEEZING SQUEAKING SHEIKH AND (CREAKING) SCREECHING S-T-R-E-A-K-I-N-G GREEK'S MEEKLY REEKING (BLEEPED) OBLIQUE COMIQUE . . . *(Trinidadian)*

THE KOO-KOO CUCKOO'S SLEW OF CHEWED STEWED SKY BLUE SKEWERED HIGH CLUES ON THE RUDE OVERDUE RUE RUE RUE RUE *RUSE* OF "WHY I DO HAIKU ON TOP OF A CHOO-CHOO" INSTEAD OF IN (AN) IGLOO HYPES (THE) HIDE IN I DO INTO WRY WIRED EYE GLUE . . .   *(high-pitched Chinese)*

NIMBLY NIBBLING AND NUMBLINGLY NODDING THEN SNOBBISHLY PLOD-DING HOPPING COPPING HOBBLING AND SLOBBERINGLY HOBNOBBING WITH EGG NOG AND A SOGGY WATER-LOGGED CORN COB **THE SLIP-SHOD CLOD** CODDLED CLOBBERED AND CLOGGED THE CON OR COD IN GARBO'S CARGO'S COCKLED COBBLED GARDEN'S GARBLED CARPETED CARBON COG JOB FLOGGING A BOTTLED GLOB OR BOGGLED HARD-BOILED GARGOYLED BLOB IN BROWN BOONDOGGLED JOGGING GOGGLED GARB . . .
(Cockney/British)

A TORMENTED MENTOR MADLY TORN BETWEEN THE RENT THE SCENT THE RENTED SCENT THE SCENTED RENT THE C-E-N-T-E-R THE SENDER AND THE ASCENDED CENTAUR WHO SENT HER SAYS "IT *S T I L L* MAKES A DENT IN DO OR DIE" . . .

ASIDE FROM THE ((*S-I-G-H*)) SIGN *C Y A N I D E* IN THE NIGHT SIDE OF THE SHY SIREN'S SLY SNIDE STRIDE SIRING AND SQUIRING HER IRE ASTRIDE THE WILD IDLING SIDLED SLIDE DOWN THE WIDE WIRE IRISH TIDE OF UNTYING THE UNTRIED (TITLED) IDOL SIDE OF THE PSYCHE'S IRON ICON IDE (E-Y-E-D) . . .   *(whispery but emphatic dream voice)*

A SPECTRAL SPARTAN SPATE OF LATE NITE EIGHTY-EIGHTS SCREAM AND CAREEN DOWN SLIGHT SIGHTED SLIDING STREET SCENES SHOWING THE SHEER SHINING STREAMING STEAMY STEAMS OF LIQUID LIGHT-LINED D-R-E-A-M-S . . .   *(British/Irish overlay)*

A SEXY SUPPLE SWINGING COUPLE'S SLINKY SINGING STRUT SHOVE STUFF AND SHUFFLE CAPPED THEIR NAUGHTY BUT SUBTLE GROOVY GRIND OF SMUTTY NUTTY SNUFF AND UPPERS BUMPTIOUSLY SUMPTUOUS NUP-TIAL SUPPER . . .   *(clipped hipsterese a la Mae West)*

THE BRUTELY BRASH SPLASHY BRANDY BASH BACK BY THE BLOOMING BRUSH OF THE BLACK BLUSHING BERRY BUSH BRUISED THEN SOOTHES THE BURNT BUNS AND BOOT SOOT ON THE (TRUTH: FORSOOTH!) SMOOTH SUPER SLEUTH'S BAD BARED BLUE SUIT . . .   *(gravelly southern twang)*

A GRUESOME TWOSOME WITH SPRUCED BUT TATTERED BOOTS AND A TACKY TROUPE FROM HOUSTON TREKKED THEIR TRAMPY TROUSSEAU SHOW TO TUCSON TO TRY THEIR TRADE OR TRUCE ON . . .   *(Irish brogue)*

SUSIE'S CHI CHI SHOE-IN SUSHI (SO WHO'S *S H E ?*) IS SO SO SO *SO* S-L-E-E-K AND SHE SPEAKS AND SWEEPS REAL CHIC AND HER SUIT SEAT SQUEAKS (SO TO SPEAK) SO SHOULD SHE SOUS SOUS SLOW SHOW SHOP CHEAP STREAK SLEEK OR SNEAK SLEEP OFF PEAK?? ((SNEAK SLEEP OFF PEAK)) . . .

THEY SCOURED THE ROUTE OR RUSE OF **THE SCREWY SOUP** FOR THE CHOP SUEY SLEUTH AND THE ROOSTED RUINED ROOT FOR THE SCOOP OF THE CRUDE ROTTEN TRUTH BEHIND THE RUDE FOOT-LOOSE ROOSTER AND HIS LUCKY LONG LOST LOOT OR LOOP TO SCORE OR SPRUCE UP THE TROUBLED TRUCE BEFORE THE SNEAKY SNOOPING TROOPS STOOPED TO SHOOT OR SCATTER-SLOOP THEIR STREWN SKEWERED COOPS . . .
(deep Irish brogue)

A GAGGED AND BADGERED RAGGED BLACKGUARD BAGGED AND DAGGERED A BRAZEN BRAGGART SWOONED SAGGED AND STAGGERED JAGGEDLY THEN SWAGGERED HAGGARDLY NAGGING A LAZY STRAGGLED LAGGARD . . .
(old, gravelly, deep Irish brogue)

THE SEQUESTERED QUEST FOR THE MAD MOD MARRED MOBBED M-A-U-V-E MARKED KEY AND THE QUEASY MARQUIS' QUIRKY QUEER KIWI QUICKLY QUICKENED QUILTED QUIPS AND QUESTIONS QUELLING QUERU-LOUSNESS QUITE Q-U-A-R-A-N-T-I-N-E . . .   *(a dandy)*

LOLITA'S LECHEROUS LITTLE PEEPING PECKER PEEKERS PIQUED AND POOPED WITH PUNK POP AND PUNS POKES THE POST OR PAST PASSED THE PORK OF POOR PORT PEORIA'S ORAL ARIA . . .   *(a lecher)*

IN VERSAILLES AT A WILD AND WICKED TRYST A THICK-WRISTED TWISTED SISTER ADDICTED TO GLITZ AND GLITTER WITH WISPY SWISHY WHISKERS WEARING WACKY NAPPY WICKED LIQUEURED WICKERED KNICKERS IS THROWN INTO A TAWDRY TIZZY OF TITTERS BY A TOUGH THORNY TONGUE TWISTER AS SHE WHISPERS TO A SICK SITTER A STICKY SLICK PSYCHO

SIZZLER WITH A SLYLY WRY SPRITELY WITTY TWITTER IN HER SLIGHT
SIGHT (*IN V E R S A I L L E S*) . . .   *(deep shadowy British spy)*

A TITAN? A TITAN IS NOT A T-R-I-T-O-N^2 BUT A TYPE OF WRITIN' WITH
TIGHT T-W-A-N-G-Y LIGHTNIN'!   *(light Irish)*

(*1978–1979*)

Alan Turing had not
invented a *thing*, but
had brought together a
powerful collection
of *ideas* . . . the ideas
condensed into exactly
what became "the
computer" . . .

Andrew Hodges,
Alan Turing: The Enigma[1]

Though I've been working on a computer for over a decade, I only recently purchased a Gateway and gained access to the Internet, an event
that occurred coincidentally with plans for an essay to explore how sights
and signs, impressions, ideas and inventions move in sundry tangential
ways from outside the range of conception into the field of vision. How
do certain nascent possibilities and emerging ideas presage the development of new inventions, technology or art forms, and how do they move
from vague possibility, then synergize or piggyback in unexpected ways,
accrue momentum, break through and inaugurate entirely new circuits of
perception and larger cultural constellations? Tracing the idea of the Internet back through the history of the computer is a circuitously complex
puzzle; Alan Turing and Marshall McLuhan might seem to be unusually
paired prongs on history's virtual tuning fork, whose frequencies vibrate
the Web's mystery.

Though Pascal (1623–1662) was the first to consider the possibility of
building a numerical calculating machine, the official trail actually began
with Charles Babbage two centuries later, when he conceived an Analytical (or Differential) Engine in 1837 for mechanically computing mathematical operations long before there was even the possibility of building
one.[2] A century later, Alan Turing, a prodigal mathematician who

worked as a cryptanalyst for British intelligence during World War II, pioneered theoretical breakthroughs that made it possible to develop far more than a high-speed calculating machine. He actually conceived of how to program a digital computer. While I was reading Andrew Hodges's definitive biography *Alan Turing: The Enigma*, another book on Turing was published, *Turing and the Computer—The Big Idea*, by Paul Strathern.[3] Turing's seminal contribution was neglected after his untimely death at the age of forty-two in 1953. Strathern's book, condensed and concise, highlights a prescient overview of just how prophetic Turing was for the development and evolution of the whole digital revolution.

New scientific and technological discoveries, inventions and the evolution of media also move in incalculable ways from the wings of history onto its main stage, their processes masked by upsurges and events that quickly and elusively outflank their tracks while their seismic transformations, similar only in principle, reconfigure the collective cultural apparatus. The train and automobile changed entire landscapes of countries as airplanes did the virtual connectivities and power bases of nations; the lightbulb, movie projector and television completely reconfigured the life world and interior ambient of virtually everyone. The transistor instituted power portability; the microchip further condensed spacetime, energy and memory capacity. How new inventions are first conceptualized, then realized, poses intriguing historical questions that are not always rectified by retrospective analysis. Scientists and engineers, like artists, also have to improvise solutions with often inadequate, makeshift materials. Strathern sketches the prehistory of computers, first citing the abacus, which dates back to approximately 4000 B.C., then William Schickard's "calculating clock" in 1623, William Oughtred's invention of the slide rule during the 1630s, and Pascal's calculating machine in 1642, which Leibniz improved upon and simplified in 1673 so that square roots could be calculated. Finally, in the early nineteenth century, Joseph Marie Jacquard, a technician and weaver, invented cards to control weaving patterns—the first intimation of the concept of mechanical programming. But it is still a giant leap to Alan Turing envisioning the transformation of an algorithm into an electronic circuit to execute a chain of mathematically applied sequences as instructions for *programming* a computer, as well as the idea of a machine making intelligent choices and decisions, thus preparing the world for the digital revolution and artifi-

cial intelligence. Turing's pioneering theoretical and applied work with
cryptanalysis while working as part of a team for British intelligence, and
the inordinately complex capacities of electrically rotorized deciphering
machines like the Colossus in the late 1930s and early 1940s, helped the
Allied Powers win World War II by cracking Germany's infamous, constantly permutating Enigma codes, which were used to deploy their military forces. This provided Turing with the technical leverage that in turn
became the concrete precursor of digital electronics, which would not
gain widespread global momentum for another forty years. In Turing's
case, mathematical logic and cryptanalysis—the flow of secret information through the transformation of codes and ciphers—set the stage for
the electronic revolution.

Early computing machines, large and unwieldy, used punched paper
to encode instructions electrically routed through valves, vacuum tubes
and cables rigged like old-fashioned telephone switchboards, which had
to be laboriously replugged to change each automated function and
served as cumbersome, predigital circuits. Alan Turing stands out as the
unique prophet of digital transmissivity because he conceived a universal
machine, one that could simultaneously perform an unlimited number of
diverse operations utilizing a pulse technology at a time when machine
calculation was still tediously developmental, mechanical and compara-
tively archaic by today's standards. He conceived the idea of generating
what would become software from binary 1:0 code combinations whose
signal chains would be able to execute complex logical operations, hence
instructions, thus preparing electronic circuitry for switching and expanding the options for machine memory, inaugurating the idea of artificial intelligence.

The codes that comprise the ways information can be schematized,
encrypted and routed have extendable analogues and ciphers, whether
this involves strategizing the deployment of aircraft or battleships during
war, calculating a corporation's finances, computing complex demo-
graphic analyses, the distribution of international resources, or the decisions of a chess game. A machine that makes intelligent decisions needs
to be able to adjudicate the duel of dualities that are coextensive with
genuine cognitive potential and that needn't be conceived as competing
with the human brain but rather as supporting a supplemental, parallel
capacity. Turing, who had studied briefly at Cambridge with Wittgen-

stein, later realized that electronic currency could be transacted in pulses and wanted to be able to dialogue with machines. He became preoccupied with the transformation of the analogue, i.e., working out the mathematics of the logistics of instructions to enable a machine to execute a diversity of complex tasks. Long before hypertexting, the analogue extended the cognitive amplitudes of the code and thus the encipherment of intelligence. Turing was convinced the computer could and would have a mind of its own and wanted to build an electronic brain: "he did not mean that the components of his machine should resemble the components of a brain, or that their connections should imitate the manner in which the regions of the brain were connected. That the brain stored words, pictures, skills in *some* definite way, connected with input signals from the senses and output signals to the muscles, was almost all he needed . . ."[4] Information, the strategic organization of signals and signs, is both more *and* less than knowledge; inverse ratios maximize the synergy of their cognitive reciprocity.

An uncanny clue about cognitive analogues could be traced back to Immanuel Kant's concept of the manifold in his *Critique of Pure Reason*, which might now be translated as a matrix that coordinates any given whole: "Every representation contains something manifold . . ."[5]—"every phenomenon contains a manifold . . ." [6]—"But as everything real, which occupies a space, contains a manifold . . ."[7] Kant was a philosopher, not a lawyer; he didn't nail down his terms other than through the accruing shift of contexts, but "manifold" refers to all the compossible vectors and branchings of meaning and reference, the loci of consciousness's matrices of denotation and connotation that are routed through, or rebound from, a sign or signifier and the inextricably compossible dendrites of association that tacitly intersect with, and radiate from, the perceptual nimbuses of phenomena. Understanding presumes meaning as intelligence does consciousness. Webology, on the other hand, involves split-second (re)alignments of often dense constellations of virtual manifolds whose codes and analogues interconnect with and through vast computer banks that relay information systems and data sources accessing intricate (com)possibilities for instant retrieval, enhancing the exchange of symbiotic thresholds. The dualistic limitations of human intelligence as a brain-driven entity can be recircuited by a much larger digitally replicating multiuser electronic network! The Web catalyzes simultaneously plurivalent interprecessionary transactions and thereby extends intelligence as it collectively (re)wires a unified enterprise of digital consciousness that interpenetrates and synergizes the minds of its diverse infoforagers. That artificial intelligence should cybernostically replicate human perceptual and cognitive functions may be to narrow unfairly the scope of its conception and expectation. The digital continuum of the Web's interconnectivities supports a global intelligence that surpasses the definitions of machine and brain; the Net is a gigantic pulsating manifold, a throbbing superterrestial network for synergizing the human resources of intelligence. Turing believed the computer would become a self-contained, independently intelligent entity.

Marshall McLuhan tweaked the other prong of Turing's virtual tuning fork and at the other end of the information spectrum. As the celebrated visionary communications seer and media guru of the 1960s, he presaged the cultural impact of the emerging electronic information age two decades *before* the personal computer would realize it. His keen structural eye and presciently beguiling hypertrophic prognostications traced a host of inscrutable connections that, at the time, exploded the cultural mythology of TV with unusually novel, fancifully bewildering, far-fetched insights imaginatively culled from the history of literature that, in retrospect, were cogently on target and are now taken for granted. His uncannily prophetic analysis of the development of the history of communications in *Understanding Media* transposed systems metaphors, interdisciplinary matrices of facts, fantasy and emerging trends with sly historical acumen harnessed to a razor-sharp wit whose meteor tail of dazzling one-line zingers taught us to look *at looking*, to think about *thinking*, to see *seeing*; and to apprehend the diversely discontinuous ways that modes of perception work to galvanize the central projects and preoccupations of popular culture. McLuhan saw the globe teleholistically and prepared his readers for modes of virtual reality. In retrospect, his Global Village *has* become the World Wide Web, *transploding* space and time, that is, imploding space as distance while simultaneously exploding and transforming the multidirectional vectors and omniradiant trajectories of information flow. That both Turing and McLuhan did more to prepare the world for the Internet encourages scrutinizing and reconsidering their discoveries.

The Web acts as a virtual transformer for the agencies of intelligence and being. McLuhan died in 1980, well before the Internet became operative and reached its presently prodigious proportions. Several years ago *Wired* magazine published the text of an anonymous McLuhan afficionado who claimed to be channeling him with great effect over the Internet. His uncanny trademarks and stylistic panache were so evident that the boundaries between the virtual, incarnate and disincarnate disappeared. McLuhan originally deemed TV a cool medium, and its constantly metamorphosing hypervisual configurations accelerated by the kinetically hypnotic techniques of advertising began a cultural process of intensifying the relay of information ratios whose compression densities, data leverages and digitating matrixes shifted perception and conception significantly, and more so too during the intervening years since multiprogrammatic windows applications have accelerated the capacities of personal computers. Most profoundly, the Internet has changed the *tropisms* of information generation and distribution. The ratios and registers of its operating paradigms have become discontinuously multiconfigurational, disembodied, interprecessionary and hypercontextual.

The Web has become an incredulous supernetwork of virtually proliferating dendrites and exemplifies the extension(s) of mind as an autonomous, disembodied entity. No wonder French logotechnicians have been extolling the death of the author and the disappearance of the subject! There's just the coextensive *textendable* Web, the unimpeded circulation and distribution of signs, data, images, texts and information links that make mind *Mind*—a (co)coextensive epic hyperphenomenon, a superterrestrial neurosphere. (No one owns consciousness; individuation just realizes, tunes and reembodies it.) The composite actions that comprise the intraextendable vectors of cyberocularity involve more than saccadic flexions and exceed even the parameters of visuality and virtuality; the autoscanning mechanisms and automatic interface capacities of both human and biocybernostic vision enable both to break through reciprocally to reflexively amplified relays coursing through hyperdimensional domains with telecognitive f(r)isson. McLuhan's uncanny insights into how the interconnected processes of perception *synthenexeosize* media interfacings have reaped a volumetric escalation of hypervirtualized sightlines, especially with regard to relaying and relating the configurations of signs and schema(ta)s that compose informational matrices, and they have parallels with many other thinkers and artists. Linguist Noam Chomsky,

for example, probed the problematics of the deep structure of language
in an effort to resolve the mysterious puzzle of how young children learn
to understand language, whose grammatical choices transcend many of
its regulatory rules and thus enable them to compose utterances beyond
their grasp; this applies as well to each generation's incremental advance
of knowledge.

For McLuhan, the media were also autonomous languages; multimedia created the basis and protocols of translation and synergy between
(art) forms. He developed a charismatically oracular riff, a hybrid amalgam of hip verbal tripping and dazzling scholastic showmanship that
made purposely preposterous conceptual leaps with unusual flair and
daring. His novel ideas abounded with astonishingly adept metaphoric
relays and prognostophobic links that fissionated surprising insights reconfiguring the contexting of facts, such as that the media (re)circuit and
act as extensions of the central nervous system; the phonetic alphabet
was the source of all technology; newspapers changed the retinal habits
and patterns of reading and favor a discontinuous mosaic assemblage of
news and information fielded by peripheral vision that rapidly scans the
parameters of layout, rather than sequential perception—(TV and now
computer and Internet increase the telemimetic gradients of mosaic scanning); TV immobilizes the eye muscles that usually move while reading,
thus short-circuiting motor response; the retina perceives black and white
on its periphery and color only in its central cone; the power of an ad is
entirely subconscious and should *not* be noticed; computers would eventually be portable; and artists perceive the invisible environment, the one
about to emerge as new technologies evolve.

The forty-year span from television to the personal computer (late
1940s–mid-1980s) witnessed the development of interactive media
(1960s), which began to appear first amongst avantgarde artists testing
boundaries and creating hybrid forms. These transformations provoked a
change from being a passive TV or movie viewer to a more active involvement and also prepared the semiotropically engaged eye to assimilate concomitant shifts of signs, contexts, models, technical vocabularies,
data and information. McLuhan's preoccupation with media grammatology preceded Jacques Derrida's actual systemic coinage of the term.
McLuhan drew attention to a new paradigm that probed how the circuitous circulation of *grammars* of different media impact synergetically on

psyche and culture well before poststructuralism became an international commodity and hot intellectual cottage industry. (Wittgenstein's *Philosophical Grammar* long preceded both as the preeminently seminal metatheoretical text for assaying the (pr)axes of grammatolexical contexts, including the conceptual underpinnings of its metaphorical extensions.) All due credit to Jacques Derrida, grammatology provided a deconstructive (pr)axis for the methodological exchanges of supplemental analytic techniques across disciplines. His writings, such as *Margins*, extended the postmodern praxis of the topoi of the text (about a text) being catalyzed by and at the edges and margins of lexicality, lexicality now also being synonymous with the superspatiality of multiwindowed cyberocularity and the concomitantly intraprogrammatic systemicities of perception. Even when a medium extends one sense, such as the microscope, radar, x-ray, and film did for the proprioceptive eye, gramophone and radio the audiophilic ear, or the computer the processing of high-density digital information ratios, the other senses and their interpressionary ratios are also extended and challenged subliminally, just as the kinetic and motivic action of television links movement, kinelexia, semiotics with the cognitive dance of signs and ciphers.

McLuhan was as much a new breed vanguard philosopher as oracular prognosticator, heralding the synergistic potential of the Global Village which uncannily anticipated the digitally emerging, combinatory structural registers of ideas and telecognitive exchange options that the then separate media were reconfigurating as a new age after the Gutenberg galaxy was blown out by the televisual diaspora—books and print merging and electrically exceeding the boundaries and margins of their topologies. Critics who bemoaned the disparity with, and atrophy of, reading, due to TV, must now be chuckling; the Internet not only demands an acutely intensive semiolexical navigation but multiplies modes and technics of discursive registers and arrays types of intrapenetrating informathics while amplifying the thresholds of icons, images, pictures and virtual dimensions as passage through alternative screens and simultaneously programmatic, intracompositive schemas. It's also supertactilic, another favorite McLuhan theme, as if the keyboard were wired to a kinaesthetic launcher and space probe, the mouse needing only to be clicked to select, reposition, execute, jump, zoom, zip and locate. Clicking of course is *telegrammat(h)ic*. Typing and the tactile transmissability of fingers are imperative to move cyber and cipher capacities with pre- and posthensile dexterity.

Marshall McLuhan did more than other thinkers and practitioners to prepare the public imagination for the emergence of the personal computer and digitized multimedia; his trailblazing impact sensitized the collective consciousness to the possibilities of living and interacting with highly saturated media symbioses. The Internet similarly reifies densely discontinuous, albeit synthetic interfaces between multistructural modalities composited by combinations of sensory inputs. Webology fuses McLuhan's conceptions of cool/hot participation thresholds with high/low information definitions because users are constantly selecting from a maze of options with myriad interface density capacities that synthesize while navigating media and communications exchanges.

Because TV imagery is subliminally hypnotic, socially conditioned and psychically overwhelming, one tends to think of information as being at a lower threshold, having less visceral impact and a cooler objectivity, but the Internet provides options for reconfiguring the matrices and schematas of whatever constitutes (the principles of) configuration itself, and it thereby maintains high visual interface capacity while simultaneously complementing the interconnectivity of intricate, mosaically arrayed, discontinuously discursive registers—doing precisely what TV hasn't managed to do, or has shunned doing. The Net assures symbiotic grammatologies of interactive reading, the teletransference of iconographic gradients, the conversion of simultaneous registers of information gathering, and the processing of random continua via hypertextual conduits. It furnishes a moment to moment methodology to decode the pluralizing (pr)axes of kinelexically morphizing conceptual typologies and ideologies, telecognitive parameters and relays of transposable typographies between and among topologies of events, disciplines, data, discourses and issues when only partial clues are given or available. In turn, the Internet's superfluity of search options, key words, hypertext links, engines and super-scanning protocols develop instantly as one surfs through overload connectivity.

Many times while writing about a number of different subjects, I have found myself repeatedly returning to McLuhan's seminal insight that our perceptual system fields new information—often elusively, inchoately or intuitively—at the margins of perception, via peripheral vision. Choreographers and dancers can readily confirm this; when improvising options in the course of composing dances they depend upon peripheral vision to scan and navigate tangentially through and amongst rapidly moving kinetic continua of interactive signals, signs, and spatial vectors in order to steer their course through incalculably indeterminate, helter-skelter pathways of each others' constantly accelerating bodies. It may not be that artists are so much ahead of their time as that the culture blindsides itself to what is happening peripherally on its margins.

One supplementary clue regarding the apperceptive action of peripheral vision comes from Susanne Langer's cogent commentary about physiognomic seeing developed in *Mind: An Essay on Human Feeling*[8] and her earlier use of the word "virtual" and virtual illusion in *Feeling and Form* (1953) to qualify the aesthetic sense(s) of semblance, artistic projection and perception; these continue to bear in intriguing ways on expanding cognitive thresholds and digital horizons. Like Nietzsche, who postulated a realm beyond good and evil, the virtual combines both while superseding the modalities and techniques that span and realize the real, actual, unreal, irreal, surreal, and hyperreal. Langer used the term "virtual" in part to explicate and extend the discoveries of gestalt theory with a comprehensive philosophical theory of symbolic function that inventoried how artistic form configures the plays of virtual illusions that can involve both a simulation and simulacrum of perception while generating a precognitive reflexion of how an art form can be transparent to its underlying principles, structures, ideas, and feelings. Gestalt psychology analyzed the schematic (ap)perception of forms, structurality, pattern recognition and configuration. The virtuality of digital technology now makes those modalities, models and methods *transposable*. The virtual thus reflects and reflexes interactive registers between and across discursive and nondiscursive realms linking the esthetic and cognitive. It also exercises connectivities between the semantic and visual, semiotic and symbolic, sign and cipher.

Physiognomic seeing, which arrays spectra and patterns in puzzle-like configurations, also has systematic implications for, and is transformed by, intermedia ratios, especially those that mosaicize composites of perceptual functions, which in turn provoke knowledge—the axis and dialexis of prehension and apprehension, recognition and cognition. Physiognomic seeing processes the interconnectivities between correspondences, gestalten, (re)semblances, correlatives and essences; it synergizes the configurations linking similitude and analogue as it collages discontinuous overlays of signs, sights and ciphers. Every search selection ferrets out a given batch of finds, opens up or narrows research parameters, selects leads, indexes and sites that provoke other simultaneous network references from any number of worldwide computer, library and data bank sources that may or may not supply the requested information. Even first time Internet users quickly realize how digital compossibilities arise from the momentum of what continually remains just tantalizingly outside the field of vision. Cyberocularity serves as a virtual prosthesis for compensating the limits of the human field of vision. Overlays and composites simulate overviews; the antidote to concealment is relayed by hypertext links that create complex mazes and contextual (re)placements that make the gaze shift rapidly between screens, menus, selections, topologies, typologies and textual sites to scan options and clues and assemble linkages as the eye processes pictures, images, photographs, icons and texts that create nets of instantaneously branching telecognitive circuits. Search engines can simultaneously narrow the beam of focus while opening up further investigative vectors that nonetheless create compossible sites to be worked over, by and at their intrapressionating margins.

There are now over 300 search engines and 600 data bases (which engage multiple combines at once) such as <www.dogpile.com,> <www.northernlights.com,> <www.allsearchengines.com.> Another favorite is <www.askjeeves.com,> a veritable infotherapist of search engines because it solicits questions that are then broken down and analyzed into possible components and sub-questions whose conceptual parameters refer the user to any number of topological schematas that autogenerate far-reaching crossreferential indexing services of incalculable magnitudes. The densities of Internet links conjoin and contrapose topologies *of* typologies and topographies of topologies, i.e., different interactive mosaics whose transferences of teleconfigurative alignments create instant new paradigms. Instead of hierarchiality, discontinuous, multischematic manifolds generate and disseminate vast data sweeps (this in contradistinction to the Gutenberg era of the book, where the only links were footnotes).

Physiognomostics references the hypersystemicities of eye and vision. It compounds and synergizes all (ap)perceptual processes and thus probes the mosaicizing flexions that occur just before and beyond sight, screen, menu, selection, reference, conception and event. This is what artists do as they follow intuitive leads while conceiving possibilities for a work or as their imaginations scavenge a hunch, work over a set of clues that lie just outside their field of vision, or that initially elude conception. Physiognomostics delineates and qualifies what can be visualized (ideas, topics, topoi, structures, schemas, etc.) and thus amplifies the types, levels and gradients of assemblage and the intercompositivenesses of signs, images and ranges of textual materials that link pictures and screens for probing and combinating data and conception. Physiognomostics also intraconfigures secondary factors, elements, qualities, attributes, gestalts, essences, eideogrammatic coordinates and logothetic components that become intricately condensed and rekeyed (encyphered and encrypted) by eye and mind in the processes of assimilating modalities that act as relays to cathect the mimetics of the interval—the spaces between perceptual units and saccadic flexions that process the apperception of bytes and afterimages. Vision involves more than eye and brain (why Marcel Duchamp challenged the piety and priority of the retinal image); seeing involves one's entire field, brain and being becoming telepermeable. The idea constantly refocuses itself and reocularizes vision.

A similar process occurs moment to moment while navigating the Internet, as hypertextual links create unexpected, virtually omnitropic trajectories and out-of-range connections that amplify synergetic, strategic alternatives. Every new link reconfigures all available conduits whose typographemic relays digitally (re)array the spectra of searchability and knowability. Thus constantly expanding, decomposable typographies (and typographies of typologies) suprapose and surpass the recombinant codes of every new alignment or interface, catalyzing trails of tacit ciphers embedded in the subliminal play of hyperlinked schemas that enable the user to grab and isolate, zoom in on and magnify details, amplify registers, and isolate the overlays and overplays of bytes, ideosigns and ideomorphs. The juxtaposition of icons and toolbars reconfigures the underlying schematic mosaics of cybertopologies to maximize search functions. The constellation of search engines that intraconnect mega computer banks and digital storage capacitors have now exteriorized a globally extended membrane that is a virtual planetary collective of superreferentiating, telecognitive intelligence. Meta- and megasearchers such as

<express.infoseek.com,> <www.theultimates.com,> <www.albany.net/
allinone> engage multiple search engines simultaneously to magnify the
power, outreach and sweep of hyperconfigurative networks.

Media and media awareness have changed the concept of art and artistic techniques. Pop Art was about painting *as media* and provoked the
irony of the retinal image as it blew up and blew *out* the surface of the
canvas by overinflating the iconography and image values of Hollywood
glamour and commercial advertising (Oldenberg, Dine, Warhol, Lichten-
stein, etc.). While it exaggerated the largesse and magnitude of the representational image, it created a barbed undertow and hypertrophic black-
flow of cultural effluvia (comic books, advertisements, Hollywood stars,
etc.) and thereby became a tacit agent of deadpan social commentary.
Beginning at the turn of the twentieth century, the mosaicized extensions
of collage from Kurt Schwitters to MTV have trained the eye to see and
move through dizzying displays of hyperpixilated juxtapositions that
reached a predigital crescendo with abstract expressionism. Jackson Pol-
lock's drip and splatter technique reconfigured a highly kineticized play
of abstractive subaltern gestalten that presaged a randomly hypermimetic
visual combine and exploited the eidetic synchronicities of vision by suspending recognizable figuration per se, training the eye to mosaicize negative space, the virtual, invisible, "non" space(s) between things, contents, shapes, lines, figures and the interstitial matrices of relational
definition. Art as techne and art as media were prime 1960s preoccupations; mixed-means preceded mixed-media that performance art and
technology transmuted into multimedia, generated by artists' hybrid
crossover experiments long before the cyberthetic fusion thresholds of
CD-ROMs.

Looking back, I sensed some of these seeds of awareness in an early
evening-length mixed-means dance theater work of mine, *m-o-o-n-*
b-r-a-i-nwithSuperLecture (1966), which combined an abundance of props,
oversized objects, recorded text and film to mirror the constant bombardment of information. The accompanying prerecorded text was written
in part as a farflung McLuhanesque parody *of* a parody satirically exploit-
ing the irony of overextended and overproduced metaphoric tropes by
making connections between wildly dissimilar phenomena.[9] (McLuhan's
hypertrophy made implausibility plausible and impossibility *com*possi-

ble.) Another dance, *Inadmissleable Evidentdance (The CIA Scandal)* (1971), was digital before there was such a thing. It deployed rapid, high-energy, hyperspatially locomoted dance that combined an open balletic style with a fractured, discontinuous overlay of modern dance—contractions and torqueing of the spine, spinning and semiphoric arm articulations punctuated by vibratory impulses that jabbed, stretched and fragmented the planes and lines in space by "synapsulating" all the kinetic registers of the moving body. The dance was performed to a recorded futurist text that must have seemed like science fiction—a high-tech polemic that foretold the profound cultural, programmatic and political changes that *would* occur once the computer became as widespread an appliance as the TV, detailing how it would amalgamate the separate media, institutions and communications functions and thus eventually absorb post offices, telephone companies, libraries, governments, etc.[10] Electronic communications were already causing seditious internal havoc by undermining the hierarchical security checks and balances among intelligence agencies—the real, but unperceived, scandal behind Watergate that would eventually force the first president from office. This dance started my involvement with *digital dance*, exploring the high energy terrain of movement as a motion *currency* and *carrier* of information, not only for reading and organizing the hyperkinetic density of signals and signs that compose cognitive valences, but as a semiotic reflector and conduit, like a fiberoptic channel made possible by changing the *frequency* of the moving body as it teleprojects its own and transects others' electomagnetic fields. In the 1960s emerging postmodern dance had just managed to free itself from literary interpretation and heavy-handed psychological symbolism, so colleagues would listen with incredulous chagrin when I tried to explain *how* there was *information* in the moving body!

The rapid transmissability of movement made possible by emerging communications technology was part of a cultural transformation that informed how dance (and media) could change the frequency of the body in response to the media changing the modalities of perception. The bioenergetic field, composed of a geodicity of magnetically arrayed, constantly intersecting meridians, energizes, and is energized by, the wor(l)d's hyperextended vectors, which enable it to process and transmit extremely rapid impressions, impulses, signals, information, feelings and ideas. As a dancemaker, I recognized the limitations of choreography as mechanically repeatable set movement structures and thus favored the necessity of working with the synergy, transparency and permutability of an open form to give dancers the freedom to use *their* intelligence by implementing strategies for making choices in performance that in turn made transparent to the *viewer* the simultaneously available processes and principles of assembling the configurating structures of composition. Choreography could be replaced by a computer program or digital screen— enabling those within and without to observe the branchings of compositive phrases and the assemblage options for configuring steps, patterns, placements and bodies as they transform the kinelexic (per)mutabilities and locution of spatial design.

The audience reads the fluidly emerging signs and signals of open choreography differently from a fixed, predetermined dance. This process of *dancemaking* virtually rules out or redefines mechanically rote counting since sequences can synchronistically reconfigurate and segue into one another while also being interrupted, rerouted and diverted. (This paralleled the death of the author and the automatic aspects of composition that writers like Gertrude Stein and Jack Kerouac employed.) Eventually I devised three basic geometric grid structures to orient dancers' spacial options for moving in and through a continuum with an automatic digital awareness that I likened to a kinetic radar, so as to be able to execute choices smoothly while fielding a variety of sign(al)s and decisions, so their bodies would know how to navigate fluidly amongst each other without interrupting development or continuity and be able to deflect collisions by revolving on their axis and rotating around themselves on a moment's notice to prevent forceful accidental impacts. Critics eventually commented that they couldn't tell what was (pre)set and what wasn't; the dancers couldn't always tell either. Though this digital processing of *movement* and awareness occurred in the decade before personal computers, it mirrored and prefigured many of the systemic processes of multiple signal relay that increase the capacity to move between the integers of signs and bodies, as between screens, icons and programs. The body *can* and does process information telemimet(r)ically, a relevance that will increase in coming decades.

The Web's interactive kinetic topologies promote intracompositive processes of kinelexic *reading* and programmatic interfacing simultaneously while their permutable trans- and infrareferential chains and parameters are intricately crossindexed and telereferenced. Thus the (ap)perception of intersecting sightlines and the virtual (inter)extensibility of their vector matrices and manifolds synthesize axes of intradimensional projection that hyperflexively concatenate tactically complex informational mixes whose highspeed transmissability breaks through to paracognitive awareness. The one-dimensional mentality of TV sitcoms and manipulated news formats are easily surpassed by online interfaces of instantaneous, multisourced investigative reporting.

Even though McLuhan envisaged an electronic age of information in the 1960s as a shift from book print to a hypervisual TV culture, three decades later the sociopolitical impact of TV still seems to lag far behind its potentiality. Why, for example, have telephone and computer not replaced or been added to the procedures of polling, voting and elections and other modes of public referenda? Inflexibly entrenched centralized governments with hardline hierarchical structures will undoubtedly continue being destabilized by the decentralizing, immediately accessible momentum of the Net. Politicians come on as hot, autocratic and fascistic, hence the perennial scandals, in contrast to the power dissemination of the Net, which is cool, pluralistic and democratic. This rift causes public and private to implode in weird, wild and unaccountable ways (e.g., President Clinton's bizarre 1998 sex and impeachment imbroglio).

The uses, applications and possibilities for information exchange to transform perception and develop software interfaces, intelligence and culture are ultimate questions that proceed apace in discontinuous waves and fitfully asymmetrical socionomic phases. The Net augurs a tremendously diversified social transformation that challenges the limits, parameters and applications that differentiate private and confidential information as it tests existing personal formats, a task that is usually the given prerogative of artists but has now gained incredible and autonomous technological momentum. (Technology calls the shots, but artists presage perception accordingly.) The Net's initial paradigm during the 1960s was the military's ARPANET nuclear monitoring back-up program, developed to insure the survival of network coordination for strategically linked computers throughout the country and for global surveillance in case of a national attack. That has now been preempted by additionally complex ethical issues having a planetary dimension. News groups and services (over 28,000 at present), chat rooms and online links converge the globalization of space and issues by tapping the power of anonymity with special interests. On the wackier side of the Web, McLuhan's celebration of tribal rebirth can now be rekeyed to the expanding laterality and literality of our postconsumerist specializations—the "id" side of the Web—a wide spectrum of available lifestyles sites, bizarre burgeoning businesses like porno sites for proliferating fetishes, which have become the iconoclastic antidotes of isolated hedonistic lifestyles (in extremis) to accommodate the insatiable vectors of omnivorous desire, subversive tastes, x-rated products and secret practices.

On the cusp of the new millennium the high-stakes shift still involves the merger of all media and institutions into a greater collective enterprise that combines telephone and telecommunications networks, data banks and online services, commercial and cable televison stations, libraries, post offices, etc. Fiberoptics promises the expansion mergers of stations, bandwidths and user groups with more speed, interactive programming, databases and infomatics capacities. (Eventually all appliances will be wireless; electricity will be transmitted in pulses the way communication signals currently are.) The shift from a service and consumerist economy to a digitally driven mediaocracy also presages a cultural implosion that will challenge the capacities of people's belief systems. Restricting factors are imploded by rapid change, information overload, unpreparedness, fragmentation, specialization, and environmental factors such as population density, pollution and toxicity that create catastrophic crises requiring rapid, radical tactics (AIDS, cancer, multitoxic syndrome, etc.), hence the unprecedented necessity of hybrid venture thinking.

Turing's ideas about the possible conception of machines and their intelligent neurointerface capacities were stymied in part by the limitations of the prevailing science and doxa of the then embryonic technology. Science, unlike art, is less likely to court the fantastic, impossible or impracticable—one reason a significant portion of Turing's (or Nikola Tesla's) ideas still seem farfetched. The future fusion of media will accelerate the interface of mnemonic systems capacities that will increase memory access technology and biosoftware resources, just as supplemental documentary and textual information with interactive video, sound, music and film clips will increase thresholds of cognitive transmissability. Digital eyeglass attachments, tiny earpieces with microdigital sensors might one day make a larger symbiotic continuum possible between brain, body, culture and computer to interface an array of extra-sensors, memory enhancement and body links (e.g., for medical surveillance, monitoring and biofeedback) with virtual and collective memory access capacities to take Turing's idea of artificial intelligence to another threshold. As Gertrude Stein said, when I close my eyes I see it. Today the wor(l)d, tomorrow the N'yet . . .

(1999)

Duchamp's attempt to rethink the world
rests on two supports: the machine,
the image and incarnation of our epoch,
and chance, which for our contemporaries
has de facto replaced divinity . . . He was
going even beyond our own time, which
still persists in wishing to adapt the
machine to man. Duchamp was trying to
imagine a state of affairs where man
would humanize the machine to such an
extent that the latter would truly come to
life . . . What if the machine, stripped of all
anthropomorphic attributes, were to
evolve in a world made in its image with
no reference to the criteria governing man,
its creator? . . . According to Duchamp, the
machine is a supremely intelligent creature which evolves in a world completely
divorced from our own: it thinks, organizes
this thought in coherent sentences, and . . .
uses words whose meaning is familiar to
us. However, these words conspire to
mystify us . . .

For
Edmund
Husserl

—*from the introduction to* SALT SELLER
(The Writings of Marcel Duchamp),
by Michel Sanouillet[2]

The Telaxic Synapsulator:[1] (The Future of Machine)

THE TELAXIC SYNAPSULATOR

TELETROPOPONENTS

DIALS	Selection/Modulations
	SYNTHNEXIOSIZER
EIDEOSCOPE	telethele(c)tics
(EIDEOSOSIS)	SYNAMBULATORICS
	pararamarizer
	PROTOTROPIZER
	tototronizer
	SYNAPSULACTRICS
PHONONOMOSIS	syncthizer
	PHONONOMOSTICS
	teleth(es)izer
	THEOTHETICS
	synecthisizer
	SYMBIONOSTICS
KINEMAT(H)ICS	syncromimesis
	SYNCHcinege(s)tics
	metatroposis
	PARANO(MO)STICS

THE TELAXIC SYNAPSULATOR is the first *meta-machine*.

"This is an are-y-o-u-r - e - a - d - y- for-this-(T - H - I - S) M A C H I N E ! "

The RAW IDEA (The Idea invents itself): *"THE (B)LINK IS ON THE BLINK!"* (Get it?) THE TELAXIC SYNAPSULATOR is *inventing itself;* it's about intercepting the telemimetic actions of blinking the eyes, and the emerging symbionostic science of electronic reflexion called: P H R E N O E L E C T R O G R A M I C S.

"THIS is a TIME TRIPPING SPACE SWITCHING INTERVAL ENHANCING T-R-A-N-S-F-O-R-M-I-N-G MACHINE!"

THE TELAXIC SYNAPSULATOR is an *electron-onostic* b l i n k e r l i n k e r. Blinking as a *techtol-ogy.*

"THIS is a SPECTROBOSCOPIC SPACETIME FUSION MANIPULATION MACHINE!"

The "derivation"–t e l e t a c t i c

t e l a c t i c

T E L A X I C

*WHAT HAPPENS WHEN WE BLINK OUR
EYES?* (How is seeing ((watching dancing, reading, looking at art, perception, apperception,
etc.)) a b o u t the "effects" of a f t e r -
i m a g e s ?)

"What's an after-image, anyway?"
"What's IN an after-image?"
"What's in it *after* images?"
"OR: what's *i t* (OR IN IT ANYWAY) *AFTER
AFTER-IMAGES?*"

–How is (or is) perception itself a kind of dialectical interplay of image and after-image (or,
dialectical interplay of signal, sign, impulse, precept, percept, picture, sensation, impression, gestalt, word, semblance, archetype, etc., and after-
images . . .)? (HOW DO AFTER-IMAGES AND
e s s e n c e s [co]CORRESPOND?)

How do speaking and dancing "play" with the
neuroacoustics of the interval and the eidetics of
the blink-apparatus (words and movements,
phonemes and gestures), like an invisible kind
of trigger or SWITCH?

THE TELAXIC SYNAPSULATOR is an *eclec-
trononostic* LIE-EATER (lighteater); a phenomenological anecdote for civilization's overload.
("BY THE YEAR 2020 e v e r y o n e will be able
to *OWN HIS OWN!*")

THE TELAXIC SYNAPSULATOR is not *not* a
real invention, i.e., one d o e s n ' t need the
(eventual) hardware to make use of it NOW. It
changes the frequency of the human body and
thereby alters the symbioses of field, ambient
and perception. *THE WORDS TURN IT ON!*

**"THIS is a DO YOURSELF A UNI-
VERSE (U-N-I-V-E-R-S-A-L) MA-
CHINE!"**

**"THIS is a SEEING PICTURES IN
YOUR HEAD (H-E-A-D) MACHINE!"**

**"THIS is a CINEMIMETIMATIC WHAT
COMES AFTER MOVIES (COUNTER
M-O-V-I-E-S) MACHINE!"**

**"THIS is a TELETROPAIC OMNI-
RETINAL FUTURE-SEEING (FUTURE)
MACHINE!"**

Kenneth King & Dancers in *Dance Spell/The Telaxic Synapsulator,* premiered March 1978 at the Brooklyn Academy of Music; choreography and text by Kenneth King, music by William-John Tudor, projection photography by Kerry Schuss, lighting by William Otterson, Synapsulator construction by Stephen Crawford. Dancers: front left, Megan Walker; upper left, Diane Jacobowitz; running center from the right, William Shepard, Daniel Lambert and Charles Dennis; center from right, Carter Frank and Kenneth King. © Serge Gubelman

THE TELAXIC SYNAPSULATOR will redefine, modify and (t)extend the concept-horizons of all corpor(e)al media and all cyberspectronic hardwares, since it virtually combines and s y t h n e x e o s i z e s application *technics* that neutralize t e c h n o c e n t r a t i c mind control.

"THIS is a BRAIN TO BRAIN AND MACHINE TO MACHINE DIGITAL ELECTROSYMBIOSIS TELETRANS-FERENCE MACHINE!"

–Hypnosis, autosuggestion, biofeedback, drugs, electromagnetism, radiology, art, electroshock therapy, propaganda, movies, mass media, cyberthetics, etc. obliterate in their own ways and drastically remodulate the blink-interval and consequently the neurothetic interface capacities of, for and between perceptual overlays, nano-transferences, interpenetrating modalities and remote access viewing of shape-shifting phe-

"THIS is THE WORDS ARE THE PARTS PARAMIMETIC DANCING MO-TOR MACHINE!"

nomena by using THE TELAXIC SYNAPSULA-
TOR to monitor the intraception spectra of mimetic impulses, signs and signal analogs.

((It is as if the Magic Lantern were turned
around—or inside out, so to speak—allowing
us to see directly into our own minds as well as
into the past; into the pictogrammatic and di-
morphic spaces and gradients between intervals,
words, letters, matrices [phonemic integers and
morphemic valences], between lin(e)s, margins
and parameters of texts; between images, patterns (and their contiguities), gestures, objects
and phenomena—psychomimetically and phy-
siognostically enhancing the animation ratios
and field-extensions of our brains to extend the
teleperceptual and mnemonic interface options
of the continuum of consciousness. Rather than
being positioned externally and passively before
prepared programs regulated by public media-
protocol, this is the "other," two-way bi-
bicameral development of the movie projector.
It is a glimpse of the future of technology: the
Destiny of Electricity!))

"THIS is a HUMAN BODY AS FIELD
INTERPENETRATING F-I-E-L-D-S
AUTOMONITORING MACHINE!"

Instead of a screen or visual surface, a high-
speed mirror reflective cylinder symbionotically
electrifies and amplifies the field extensions of
one's corporeal and perceptual ambient. It monitors the visualization of one's *own* s u p r a -
c e r e b r a l, preconceptual, intrapsychic and
intersubjective fields, (re)sources and informations, as well as bioenergetic rhythms via
transpersonal, t e l e t h e t i c continua p r o t o -
d u c e d, regulated and adjusted by the T E L E -
T R O P O P O N E N T S *and ensuing technics* of
TELAXIC OPERATIONS, condensed below.

"THIS is a DO-YOURSELF-AT-HOME/
HOME-HORIZON EXPANDING SYN-
APSULATING MACHINE!"

It is becoming possible and feasible to commu-
nicate telelexically and *telethetically* by transfer-
ring mental impulses, data, signals, gestalts,

"THIS is a PSYCHOMIMETRIC IMAGE
SUSPENSION PHANTASY INTERRO-
GATING MACHINE!"

ideoglyphs, pictures, images, eideograms, etc. directly b e t w e e n minds and machines, machines and machines, minds and brains, brains and brains, brains and machines, etc. *without* hardware as we now know and conceive it.

MANIFESTO PRESTO: (how it works, what it does, and does not *not* do; its functions, instructions and claims: (*"IT DRAINS THE BRAIN'S STAINS AND STRAINS!"*)

1. Its psychotropical use: as an anecdote and anodyne against fragmentation, separation, alienation, overload and paranoia—this is its ultimately therathetic use and paranostic application: BLINK CONSTANTLY, consistently attend to the synchronization modulations of the retinal shutter, PERSISTENTLY o-p-e-n and shut eyes with shudder-like rapidity to retrieve and field information, access data, cool out overloads, blow-outs and process peak experiences of the C.entral N.ervous S.ystem. "THE (B)LINK IS ON THE BLINK." LEARN TO BE *ON* THE (B)LINK!

2. SUPERHYPE: *"It cleans the 'lint' out of the interval."*

THE TELAXIC SYNAPSULATOR can be used to monitor the interception, irruption and interruption of the interval and the interstices of configurative matrices, mimetic transparencies and autoperceptual mosaics of the human gaze.

METATROPOSIS—A new range of metatechnics: watching, looking and seeing become: WATCHING WATCHING, WATCHING LOOKING, WATCHING SEEING; LOOKING AT WATCHING, LOOKING AT LOOKING, LOOKING AT SEEING; SEEING WATCHING; SEEING LOOKING, *SEEING SEEING* (METANOMOSTICS) . . .

"THIS is a BOUNDARY-PROBING, OPTION-SCANNING, SUPER DIFFERENTIATING MATRIX-INTERFACE MACHINE!"

"THIS is a HOLOTROPIC PROCESSES AND SYSTEMS S-Y-N-C-T-H-I-S-I-Z-I-N-G MACHINE!"

"THIS is a SEEING IT ALL AT ONCE POTENTIAL REALIZING MACHINE!"

"THIS is a YOU GUESSED ID THERE IS NO MORE YOU (Y-O-U) MACHINE!"

(Metapsychologically, what happens when we blink our eyes, viz. with respect to the "structure" of the ego? (IF ONE IS *NOT [NOT]* ATTENTIVE DURING THE BLINK THE EGO STILL HAS "A" STRUCTURE.))

During the blink-interval, r e a c t i o n s, images, pictures, AFTER-IMAGES, impulses, impressions, ideas, percepts, etc., are fired, processed, assimilated, digested and subliminally (re)routed. The ego *is* reaction; art: ACTION. Likewise, the purpose, function and applied use of any metapsychology is to stop behav(ior)ing or reflex it back upon the subject's awareness (electrometanoia). (Remember Freud's pioneering theoretical studies were case studies *toward* a metapsychology [1913: the three preliminary studies on sexuality])) . . . Hence why some dancers spin for long periods so as to seem to step out of existence or TIME . . . And why the body needs sleep—dream imagery processes perceptual data snagged at subliminal levels, because during daily experience it is not possible to "clear," neutralize or complete the side-effects of sense perception and the accumulated residue of impressions. ONE CANNOT MONITOR ONE'S AFTER-IMAGES THAT, OFTEN UNKNOWN TO THE SELF, TRANSPIRE BELOW CONSCIOUS THRESHOLD, hence sublimation and repression occur as well as the operations of the subconscious. A child doesn't "have" a subconscious until he or she acquires language . . . symbolism as a psychothetic currency . . . repression likewise isn't just "caused" by thwarting conscious contents, motives, desires, and promptings, but by the hidden activity of AFTER-IMAGES as well . . . Hence why Krishnamurti maintains that one would not need to dream if fully awake and aware. Also see *META-GEXIS*: the double negative can be used as a

"THIS is a VOID (AND AVOID VOIDING) ANTI-PROPAGANDA MIND CLEARING DOXA TRANSPARENCY MACHINE!"

"THIS is a PARAMIMETIC MULTIPLE FOCI SUPER ELECTRONONOSTIC F-O-C-U-S-I-N-G MACHINE!"

"THIS is a PARASYMPATHIC GENDER RECIPROCITY EMPATHY CONVERSION A-N-D-R-O-G-Y-N-Y MACHINE!"

"THIS is a SWITCHING POLARITY (POLARITY SWITCHING) AUTOTROPAIC AND TELETRANSFER MACHINE!"

technic to rectify ontogen(et)ic knots and con- tradictions: AFTER-IMAGES ARE NOT *NEC-ESSARILY* (in the context of the dialectic of the perceptual field) the "OPPOSITE" of images or impressions per se, as a negative is to a photo. There is a tacit, third category: a TRIALECTIC, needed to recircuit duality and contradiction. ((The Other is not not an after-image . . .))

3. MEDICAL APPLICATION: for flushing out radioactive contamination and overcharges, clearing psychopath(et)ic and nucleated poisons from the body, the CNS and environment. This involves several telaxic modulation processes; alternately running the Synapsulator backwards and forwards extremely rapidly. THE TELAXIC SYNAPSULATOR WILL BE THE FIRST OF A SERIES OF KINDS OF HYPERVIRTUALIZED EQUIPMENT-INTERFACE INSTRUMENTS THAT WILL HELP CANCEL AND ALLEVIATE THE LETHAL SURPLUS EFFECTS OF RADIA-TION. (Mention too Wilhelm Reich's pioneering work and the fact about the orgone boxes: since Hiroshima and the atomic bomb orgone therapy boxes act in reverse, that is, they a b s o r b radioactivity rather than cancel bionic contamination.)

4. P H R E N O E L E C T R O G R A P H I C S *P H R E N O E L E C T R O N O G R A M I C S* In coming decades drugs will be replaced by more advanced, exact methods and means of psychotropic alteration, including direct access to electromagnetic, solar and cosmic power (re)sources. Drugs will be considered naive and "inoperative"—"clearlight" is an energy re-source, not a "drug." It is a solar wave or cosmic beam of sorts. Acid is an (al)chemical agent and psychomimetic catalyst.

The eideopsychic extensions of consciousness through teletronic monitoring methods (OR:

"THIS is a KARMATROPAIC UPDAT-ING SPECTROANALYSIS DATA SCAN-NING AND SYNTHESIS SYNCHRONIZ-ING MACHINE!"

"THIS is a LEFT-BRAIN RIGHT-BRAIN SYNCHING UP (S-Y-N-C-H-I-N-G) SU-PER TOTOTRONIC TELESYNCHRON-IZATION MACHINE!"

"THIS is a MULTIPLE INTERFACE SYNCROMIMETIC PROCESSES SIMU-LATING AUTOREFLEXIVE MIRROR SCANNING MACHINE!"

"THIS is a RECOMBINABLE RECI-PROCITY INDUCING INTERSYSTEMIC FISSION FUSION MACHINE!"

THE TELAXIC OPERATIONS) involve access to secret, advanced equipment presently concealed by such governmental agencies as the CIA and NSA (National Security Agency) that produces *p s y c h o s i m u l a t i o n.* The coming science of electrotot(r)onic reflexion of consciousness is PHRENOELECTROGRAMICS, whose typographemizing function is comparably postvideo and parahologrammatic, doing away with external screens and thus metatechnically unifying the reciprocal dialectics of inner and outer perspectivity shifts that monitor and (re)modulate the human biogenomic field, which, when adequately charged, acts as a semiosymbionotic receiver-transmitter of messages, impulses and codes in blip rhythm polyphase transfer.

PSYCHOSIMULATION: the exemplification of "intelligence gathering means" means that when the human body changes its biofrequency capacity it can act as technomostic transducer, enabling the subject to inhabit an extended electrified field that boosts psychic and mnemoeidetic reflexion capacities of consciousness as and through post/meta/super cybernostics. (Reread what Marshall McLuhan said analogically about electronics, ESP and synesthesia.) ExplORAL-oration and expansion of applied biofeedback techniques, remote viewing and transmedia interphase supersystems hook-up options to monitor and amplify the virtually extended, interpenetrating, simultaneous and s i m u l t i m e - l e s s processes and operations of human consciousness.

Technics will replace techniques. THE TELAXIC SYNAPSULATOR, being not *not* a "real" invention, is a self-initiating concept and paraoperative, teletactic extension of technology (into *techtology*). (The idea of paranostics can be

"THIS is an ONEIRIC NEAR AND FAR DISTANCES BRIDGING AND COLLAPSING TELEPORTABLE D-R-E-A-M MACHINE!"

"THIS is a DISAPPEARING-REAPPEARING REALITY SWITCHING DENSITY DIFFERENTIATING AUTO-RHETORICAL ORATORICAL MACHINE!"

"THIS is a DELUXE PSYCHOMIMETIC INTERIOR EXTERIOR SWITCHING INFERENCES AND INTERFACES MIND-ALTERING MACHINE!"

"THIS is a METASCIENCE FICTION NEURONOMOSTIC EIDETIC PARARA-METER SCANNING (HYPERFICTION) MACHINE!"

traced back to 1913, when Edmund Husserl, founder of phenomenology, published *IDEAS*, a treatise that inaugurated the first meta-methodology for paraocular explorations and for coordinating all compossible, concurrent, simultaneously extended, interpenetrating and ontogenetically correlative processes, procedures, systems, structures, methods, tools, methodologies, disciplines, doxa, discourses, instruments, essences and metasciences, etc.)

Different *technics* (psychomimetic, cinemimetic, teleaural, metalinguistic, parasemantic, kinesiotheric, semiosthetic, pictORAL, etc.) extend and combine separate domains, discourses, methodologies, logics, typologies and p r o - g r a m s used in conjunction with THE TE-LAXIC SYNAPSULATOR, just as this meta-machine itself can be used in conjunction with cyberthetic applications as a kind of master adaptor to intercept, transmit, explore, enforce, aid, examine, develop and extend other technics and equipment-media interface options.

A *technic* is a means or method by which the operative parameters and limits of applied technology are scanned and calculated (e.g., PAR-ARAMARIZER, TOTOTRONIZER, PROTO-TROPIZER, PARANOMOSIS) to elicit compossible programmatic interfaces that can comprise hybrid hypersystems. Husserl's term KINEMAT(H)ICS can be applied to the phenomenology of motion and the kinesiology of systemic body explORALoration to distinguish the kinelexic differINFERENCES between orders, ranges, ratios, modes, registers, topologies, axiologies, kinetic dialectics, etc. (THE TE-LAXIC SYNAPSULATOR IS DEDICATED TO EDMUND HUSSERL [1859–1938], who introduced the basic seed concepts of his new mental or eidetic science as an epoché, or suspension of

"THIS is an EXCHANGING REALITIES PURE PHANTOM KNOWING (KNOWLEDGE) MACHINE!"

"THIS is a LONG DISTANCE INTER-GALACTIC TELEINPHOFOMATICS TIME RELAY TOTAL INTERCOMMUNI-CATIONS MACHINE!"

"THIS is a HISTORY (PROVING H-I-S-T-O-R-Y) IS JUST ANOTHER APPARI-TION A-P-P-A-R-I-T-I-O-N) MA-CHINE!"

"THIS is a DANCING THROUGH ALL OF SPACE GALACTIC HYPERSPACE S-P-A-C-I-A-T-I-O-N TRANSFLEXION MACHINE!"

the perceptual subject and field *without* the loss of the subject and/or field.)

Jean-Paul Sartre subsequently spent at least one third of *Being and Nothingness*, over approximately 350 pages of his *magnum opus*, rigorously examining the ontothetics of just what happens in and through the gaze and the perceptual field (horizon). Apperception depends on the eyes blinking and interrupting the gaze.

THE TELAXIC SYNAPSULATOR can monitor the trans-infra-and telesynaptical options/operations of human consciousness. Its components are virtual functions or TELETROPOPO-NENTS, WITH THREE MODULATORS: EI-DEOSCOPE (VIRTUAL SIGHT), PHONONO-MOSTICS (VIRTUAL HEARING), KINEMAT(H)ICS (VIRTUAL MOTION TRANSFLEXION); AND SEVENTEEN IN-TER(PH)FACE OPTIONS. THESE WORDS ARE THE CONCEPT KEYS THAT CYBER-NOSTICALLY ACTIVATE THE INTERACTIVE PROCESSES THAT WILL EVENTUALLY HAVE REAL EXTENSIONS AND HARDWARE . . .

ANY MEANS THAT ENABLE ONE TO ISO-LATE, REVEAL, INTERCEPT, AMPLIFY, (T)EXTEND OR (CO)COORDINATE MULTI-CONCURRENT AND INTERPENETRATING SYNAPTIC OPERATIONS WOULD BE A *META-TECHNIC*, SINCE THIS WOULD EX-EMPLIFY AND REFLEX THESE SIMULTANE-OUSLY ONGOING ONTOMIMETIC, MNEMONIC AND PARATHETIC PROCESSES: PSYCHOTROPICALLY, AURALLY, (TELE)KINETICALLY, ENABLING THE NEU-RONOSTIC A P P E R C E P T I O N OF ITS POLYPHASE SYNCHRONIZATION SELEC-TIONS. THE TELAXIC OPERATIONS WILL

"THIS is a SYNOPTIC PURE IDEA/ I.D. EAR AMPLIFICATION COMPRESSION HEARING EVERY-THING AT ONCE MACHINE!"

"THIS is a BIONICALLY REPLICATING BICAMERAL RELAYING BORN AGAIN BARDO ACTIVATING TRANSCEPTION MACHINE!"

"THIS is an EXPANDING SPACETIME COMPRESSION DECOMPRESSION BLOW-OUT MACHINE!"

"THIS is a THERE'S MORE TO SOFT-WARE-HARDWARE THAN HARDWARE-SOFTWARE EXTENSIONS MODULA-TION MACHINE!"

CHANGE THE CONCEPTION OF CONCEP-
TION, PERCEPTION OF PERCEPTION AND
PROJECTION OF PROJECTION; WHY IT'S
FEASIBLE TO COIN TWO NEW PROCESS-
CONCEPTS: I N T R O I N J E C T I O N AND
P R O T O J E C T I O N . . .

USING TELETHELETICS, THE TELAXIC OP-
ERATIONS will monitor SYNAMBULATORICS
and permit the subject to pass into an "electric
sleep" without having to lose consciousness to
rest, or go through a dream phase for physiological renewal. One can use SYMAMBULATO-
RICS IN CONJUNCTION WITH CERTAIN
SYNCROMIMETIC processes, for example to
learn foreign languages, to recall and decode
dreams, for inducing telethetic states, for elec-
trotonic reading and decryption, for making
subliminal mental processes conscious as well as
turning the user into a telepath.

Art too can be a *technic*. A technic is a means to
explore the conjunctivizing compossibilities and
unifying thetic principles for enacting and entraining the perceptual foundations underlying
any given method, means or other technic. A
technic provides the user-witness with boundary
scanning navigation coordination within and
amongst other available programs, strategies,
schemas, disciplines, equipment-resource-
instruments and media interface modulation
linkages. Thus THE TELAXIC SYNAPSULA-
TOR is a hybrid cross-breeding and intrareferential indexing modulation of:

techtonics
technotics
TECHNOSTICS

The "subject" we are now describing is *e i d e o -
s o s i s*: the virtual transparency, trans(re)ference

"THIS is a PENULTIMATE COSMIC
C.B. RA-DEO WIRELESS UNIVERSE
U-N-I-V-E-R-S-E) DECRYPTION PENE-
TRATION MACHINE!"

"THIS is a TELELEXICAL LEARNING
LANGUAGES WHILE YOU'RE ASLEEP
(S-L-E-E-P-I-N-G) WHILE AWAKE
AUTOMONITORING TRANSCEIVING
MACHINE!"

"THIS is a THERE'S MORE TO
THINKING THAN T-H-I-N-K-I-N-G
ELECTROCOGITO MACHINE!"

"THIS is a C-O-N-C-R-E-T-E ENERGY
CHANNELING INTERSYNOPTIC
TRANSMISSION MACHINE!"

and reflexion interphase modulation of sight, visualization, envisagement, eidetics and paracognitive states between mind/mind and mind/machine; screens and hardware will be very much modified, later replaced entirely by direct teleprompting and remote-accessed eidetic relay extensions of and between visual, mimetic, mnemonometric, metakinetic and synchrotropistic phasing modulation of image, picture, gestalt and essence animation in a virtual field.

PHONONOMOSTICS—metalinguistic and parasyntactical technics proto(in)duced by the resonances of etymorphogenic and transphonemic sound source scanning split up and trace words and codes to monitor their transassociative teleeidetic relay routes and reveal their underlying systemic/schematic interdigitation matrix configurations via tototropistic autoreferencing modulations; monitor concurrent components comprising any message, context, content, event or form of communication. Phononomostics, or sound recognition transference, also progresses by word bungling: "word splits and bits" that can *s y n c h n o s t i c a l l y* activate pictures and total psychosthetic recall from intramediated sources, data banks and virtual scanning resources. McLuhan: we're changing "from bird watchers to WORD BOTCHERS . . ."

Phononomostics reveals the underlying syntactical matrices of codes that concurrently comprise the digitation, message transference capacity, pixilation osmosis and systematic synchronization of telenostic structures and systems. *SYNAPSULACTRICS:* monitors the interception relays of all pictogramm(at)ic coefficients and pixilation valences of ideas, words, images and codes. The Synapsulator *s y n c t e t i c a l l y* atomizes morphotropic units and etymolexical root tracers of language to (re)circuit and ser-

"THIS is a DEEP SPACE FARMEMORY RANGING REARRANGING RELAY-DELAY PROBOSCOPIC MACHINE!"

"THIS is a TELENOSTIC BOUNDARY INTERCEPTION BORDER CROSSING TRANSFER SIMULATION MACHINE!"

"THIS is a BEYOND SYSTEMS STEADY-STATE S-T-A-T-E-L-E-S-S-TELEREFERENCING AND AUTOCOMMUNICATIONS MACHINE!"

"THIS is a T-I-M-E BUSTING TELE-TEMPORAL TRANSPARENCY CONCATENATING END OF TIME MACHINE!"

vice the audiophilic circulation of all precognitive, anagrammathic and metalinguistic flow routes.

HENCE: *E S S E N C E S P I O N A G E*—spying on the modes, codes and essences that activate, modulate and maintain the interface/interphase options between two or more fields, bodies, ideas, subjects, disciplines, agents, minds, ambients, systems, etc. Codes are made transparent and decrypted teletheletically using the PARARAMARIZER and phonotropaic functions. Even parapsychological processes can be monitored using it along with PHONONOMOSTICS, TOTOTRONIZER, SYNEXIOSIZER, ETC., MAKING IT POSSIBLE TO TRANSFER CONSCIOUSNESS/DATA BETWEEN MINDS, BRAINS AND MACHINES *WITHOUT* CONNECTIVE WIRES AND HARDWARE, THUS CHANGING THE CONCEPTS OF *PRECEPTION* AND PROTOJECTION; "INNER" AND "OUTER" WILL BECOME REDUNDANT. (INTROINJECTION AND PROTOJECTION BECOME CONCEPTUALLY METAPHORICAL AND METAPHORICALLY CONCEPTUAL, I.E., INTRAEXTENDABLE—"IS SEEING NECESSARILY VISUAL" OR: WHO NEEDS A CRYSTAL BALL WHEN YOU'VE GOT A TELAXIC SYNAPSULATOR!)

S Y N A P S U L A C T R I C S: the paraprogrammatic transception and synergetic intrarelation of all factors, data, valences, integers, orders, units, modules, registers, teleidetic coefficients, typologies and modalities of words, ideas, concepts, pictures, images, motifs, schemas, codes, etc.

The *EIDEOSCOPE* (eideososis = seeing seeing, the reflexion of reflexion, the metaphor of the metaphor)—sight surveillance, analog analogiz-

"THIS is an INTRASYSTEMIC MULTIPLE PERSPECTIVES AUTOSCANNING AND SIMULATIONS OVERLAY MONITORING MODULATION MACHINE!"

"THIS is a TELEMIMETRIC TRANSFERENCE THRESHOLDS CROSSING, CONSCIOUSNESS RAISING MACHINE!"

"THIS is a DOXIC LIBERATION YOU ARE BEYOND ORGANIZED RELIGION AND BELIEF METARELIGION MACHINE!"

"THIS is a TELETRANSFERENCE MOVING THROUGH ALL OF SPACE S-P-A-C-E CONNEXION MACHINE!"

ing and image suspension control modulation for eidetically tracking virtual semblances and analogies as well as all paranomic correlatives, making essences and gestalten transparent, telesynchronous and [co]copresent. For seeing similarities and unsuspected relational analogs between diverse and seemingly unconnected phenomena, events, structures, etc.

PHONONOMOSTICS—technics generating intraprogrammatic options to make the phonolexicological and code circuitries of sound, language and speech phenomena simultaneously transparent to their multiple interpenetrating registers, orders and layers with entity transference translation schematologies.

KINEMAT(H)ICS—the semiotropic gauge for monitoring, regulating, analyzing, super-(im)posing and transpos(it)ing motion register transparencies coordinates between simultaneously extended and/or interpenetrating orders, ratios and kinetropic interphase correspondences of animative processes linking the modes of (tele)kinesic exchange: shapes, contours, trace(r)s, marks, isomorphs, glyphs, objects, bodies, concepts, semblances, gestalts, words, ideas, analogies, symbols, structures, etc.

The *TOTOTRONIZER* scopes the whole from the part, scans the summative, relational and teleothetic operations and projections that inform and unify elements, parts, units, modules, regulative concepts, data, principles, premises, presuppositions, assumptions, operations, processes, etc., linking the projected totality of an event, phenomenon, program, entity, system, etc. to provide instantly updated assessment-appropriations of all data-valence/transfer-inter(ph)face sources and routes as new informations are fed into the concatenation and

"THIS is a YOU COMPLETE THE WOR(L)D IN YOUR HEAD (HEAD) MACHINE!"

"THIS is a PARANOMATIC FAR-MEMORY SUPER SIMULATING AND TELECOMPOSITIVE DETAIL CORRELATING MACHINE!"

"THIS is a PARANOSTIC TIME TRAVELING SPACE WARPING TELEMIMESIS ACTIVATION MACHINE!"

"THIS is a R-E-F-L-E-X-I-O-N SELECTION FLUX FLEXION ENTITY OSMOSIS TELEPORTATION MACHINE!"

ongoing scanning of its operations, including detail overlay and fractal osmosis.

PARARAMARIZER—scans the outer margins, horizons, limits, assumptions, preconceptions and eidetic fringes, technical and conceptual thresholds of words, sounds, fields, programs, texts, disciplines, phenomena, events, etc. so that as new or unfamiliar elements or data transpire, interrupt or displace each other's place in the total dialectical schema or sets of available relays options, perspectivity-modulation selections can be instantly surmised, monitored and reevaluated.

PROTOTROPIZER scans the possibly emerging spectras and modulating options for conveying and merging compossible data, programs, perspectives, disciplines, discourses, vocabularies, information, tools, instruments, vistas, events, etc.

There are at least three main SYNCt(h)etic interphase functions:

The *SYNCthizer* coordinates, adjusts and relates tracking interphase between two or more separate or a l i e n message, data or signal ambient/ systems; the *SYNECTHISER* monitors and intercepts processes, systems and (co)correspondences that are already in compossible interphase ambient modulation to reflect simultaneous patternings and pattern recognition coordination between typologies and topologies linking matrix differentials that exhibit similitude and dissimilitude, symmetry and asymmetry, continuity and discontinuity, etc.

The *SYNTHNEXIOSIZER* is the most complex synthetic, syncretic and syncthetic interph(r)ase modulation capacitor for coordinating and facilitating the transduction of systemic relays that

"THIS is a DREAM PROJECTION MACHINE, A TELELEXICAL DREAM DECODING MACHINE, A DREAM P-R-O-G-R-A-M-M-I-N-G MACHINE!"

"THIS is an INTRASYNAPTIC DUALITY ABSOLVING CONTRADICTIONS DISSOLVING PARAMATIC HORIZONS SCANNING MACHINE!"

"THIS is a HYPERMIMETIC BRAIN-TO-BRAIN IMPULSE AND IMAGING TRANSFER TRANSFERENCE MACHINE!"

"THIS is a RADIOACTIVITY ABSOLVING AND BIOGENOMIC CONVERSION NEUTRALIZATION MACHINE!"

autoreference divergent orders of program-
mat(h)ics, technics, ideas, concepts, discourses,
rhythmic and periodictic synchronization capacitors of codes, components, factors, infrastruc-
tures, etc. SYNCcineGISTICS is the analog animation super(im)position and analogies
tracking technic for coordinating teleth(el)etic
inputs from diverse systems including biogen-
omimetric transmedia.

The *t e l e t h i z e r* is a transmission transducer
and part of the *TELETHESIZER*—for systemically sending and transceiving various kinds of
simultaneous signal message/frequencies as well
as fielding conditions for telelexical and galactic
communications including telepathic and inter-
teletactic transmissions; used in coordination
with SYNAMBULATORICS; THE TELAXIC
SYNAPSULATOR functions as a cosmic telephone.

SYNCHROMOSIS (s y n c h r o m i m e s i s)—
telesynchronizing all virtual, mimetic and mnemonic interface capacities of words, images,
sound sources and information continua in simultaneously relayed streamings. For a pioneering meta-manual see John Cunningham Lily's
*PROGRAMMING AND META-PROGRAM-
MING IN THE HUMAN BIOCOMPUTER* (the
first meta-theory).

(But, really, it's possible to bypass all instructions!)

5. P R O T O T R O P O S I S
P R O T O T R O P O E S I S

P R O T O T R O P T I C S—scans the visibility,
opticothletic and semiomorphic configuration
parameters of potentially emerging mosaics, teletemporal, omnispacial and paramorphemic
factors, data, systems, bandwidths and loci to

"THIS is an OBSESSION COMPUL-
SION DISSOLVING INFERENTIAL DIF-
FERENTIAL PARASYNTHETIC INDUC-
TION DEDUCTION MACHINE!"

"THIS is a PHOBIA FADE-OUT OB-
SESSION DISPERSION EMOTION
SPECTRUM INTERACTION PHASE-IN
PHASE-OUT CATHEXION MACHINE!"

identify alternative futures. (THE TELAXIC SYNAPSULATOR CAN BE USED TO *SEE* THE FUTURE . . .)

6. SYMBIONO(S)TICS: BIOINFORMATIC COORDINATION AND SIMULATION OF DIVERSE TECHNOLOGICAL INPUTS, MACHINES, SOURCES, DATA FIELDS, AGENTS, SUBJECTS, BRAINS, ENTITIES, STORAGE BANKS AND GALACTIC STATIONS WILL BE ABLE TO BE CONCURRENTLY ACTIVATED, ENGAGED AND ENTRAINED AS WELL AS PROTOJECTED INTO THE ELECTRIFIED, VIRTUALLY SPECTOTYPOGRAPHIZED BIO-GENOMIMETIC CONTINUUM.

7. THE TELAXIC SYNAPSULATOR is a cosmic, autoperceptual, transeidetic, paranomostic *REFLEXOR*.

metatrosis

metatropics

METATROPOSIS: transference strategies to scan the conception of c o n c e p t i o n (cf. Alfred North Whitehead, *Science and the Modern World*—this was a pivotal meta-key and panascop(t)ic invention of twentieth-century scientific methodology). See also Marcel Duchamp's notebooks: "See, one can look at seeing, but one can't hear hearing." ((—Why not? The m e t a p h o r of the metaphor: one *can* see seeing . . .))).

THE TELAXIC SYNAPSULATOR LETS ONE S Y N E X T H E O S I Z E the concepts of conception and the ideogrammathics of ide(a)ology (hence the metapolemics of teleeidetics and paranomostics). The metaphor of The Machine: the metaphor alone triggers a virtual action like a kinemathic motor that turns on the ability to scan televirtual compossibilities, teleeideticized (co)correspondences, analogies, typologies, meta-

"THIS is a TRANSCARNATE INSTANT ATTENTION PSYCHIC GALVANIZATION COMPRESSION DECOMPRESSION ACTIVATION MACHINE!"

"THIS is an INTEGRATED INTRASYSTEMIC TELESOMATIC ENERGY CONCEPT COMPRESSION BIOAUTO-GENERATING PROGNOSTICATION MACHINE!"

"THIS is a M-I-N-D BLOWING MIND-TO-MIND AND MIND-TO-BRAIN SYMBIONOTIC PARASYNCHRONIZATION AND TELETRANSFERENCE LIBERATION MACHINE!"

"THIS is a PERIPHERAL VISION BOUNDARY STRETCHING PRECEPTION PERCEPTION AUTOLINKING (APPERCEPTION) MACHINE!"

technical options and intrasystemic cross-trans(re)ferences.

8. THE TELAXIC SYNAPSULATOR can meta-kinetically monitor, kinematically and parami-metically coordinate (and co-coordinate) these protonomial states:

WATCHING   LOOKING   SEEING

(Watching, looking and seeing now have extended metaptropaic extensions generated by the synergetic action of their double autoflective combines: watching watching becomes an onto-genic correlate for the state of OBSERVATION; watching looking = RECOLLECTION; watching seeing = RE:COGNITION)

    looking (at) watching = perception
      looking (at) looking = apperception
        looking at seeing = discernment

    seeing watching = apprehension
    seeing looking = appropriation/assessment
    seeing seeing = COGNITION

Double correlatives s(t)imulate intrapsychic, transsubjective and suprapersonal ontogenesis. Metalogically THE TELAXIC SYNAPSULATOR is especially adapted to develop technics to amplify apperception and cognition manifolds (which are usually considered to be outside the domains of both art and science, though tacit to both, thus requiring t e c h n o s t i c innerventions).

9. TELETHICS
   TELETHETICS
   T E L E T H E L E T I C S
   TELETHEOTHELE(C)TICS)—systemic modulation surveillance and instant transference/translation options for synoptically seeing and assimilating intraextendable similarities, sem-

"THIS is a MAGIOELECTROMAG-NETIC MNEMONOMISTIC META MANTRA MATRICULATION MACHINE!"

"THIS is a CHANGE OF STATE AND STATE OF CHANGE TRANSGENERA-TION MACHINE!"

"THIS is a HANDY ALL-PURPOSE RE-DUCTION TO ESSENTIALS (ESSEN-TIAL) TELECOMPOSITING PARA-CRYPTION TRANSPOSITION MACHINE!"

"THIS is an ENHANCED CELLULAR CODING AND DECODING REGULAT-ING DEREGULATION PARAEIDETIC INDEXING MACHINE!"

"THIS is a SEEING-IT-ALL-AT-ONCE MACHINE!"

blances, correspondences, analogs, analogies, correlatives, programs, paradigms and transcendent connections between what is known and what is not (not) (un)known:

PARANO(MO)STICS: making the factorialities of spacetime transparent to themselves; meta-knowledge.
METATROPIZER: intrasystemically scans eidetic blueprints, simulated mode(l)s, datalogs, teletextual transferences, cyberthetic principles, genotypes, autoprobes, isomorphs, systems relays, introprotogenic and interface configurations, paradigms and transfigurative options for simulating compossibilities combines.

S Y N C ^I_E N E G ^E_I S T I C S: Metascanning reciprocity analogs for negotiating and adjudicating transferences between ideas and concepts. (Ideas are like steamships; concepts are tug boats—necessary to steer them into port.) THE TELAXIC SYNAPSULATOR IS A PARA-EIDETIC PROTONOSTIC TECHNOSTI-SCOPE.

How can an image be a concept?
How can a picture be a metaphor?
How can a gesture be a concept?
How can a word be an idea?
How can an idea be an image?
How can an image be a percept?
How can a gesture be a metaphor?
How can an idea be a metaphor?
How can a metaphor be an idea?
How can a metaphor be a sign?

How can an idea be a picture?
How can a picture be a gesture?
How can a gesture be a sign?
How can a word be a concept?
How can an image be a gesture?

"THIS is a SEEING-IT-ALL-AT-ONCE SEEING S-E-E-I-N-G MACHINE!"

"THIS is a TOP SECRET CLANDES-TINE SURVEILLANCE SECRET(S) PENETRATION MACHINE!"

"THIS is a SYMBIONOTIC INSTANT EMPTYING OUT MAGIC MANTRA IN-DUCING MEDITATION MACHINE!"

"THIS is a STAR MACHINE!"

"THIS is the ULTIMATE MACHINE!"

"THIS is a SYMBIOBIONOSTIC EC-STASY INDUCING SUPER TRAN-SCRIPTION AND TELEFLEXION MACHINE!"

How can a concept be an image?
How can an idea be a gesture?
How can a sign be an idea?

THE THREE MAIN DIALS AND SEVENTEEN
MODULATION/INTERFACE OPERATIONS
AND SELECTIONS/OPTIONS ALLOW FOR
UNLIMITED USES AND EXTENSIONS . . .
THESE WORDS TURN IT ON!

"THIS is a BEYOND CONCEPTS (SU-
PERCONCEPTUAL) MACHINE!"

"THIS is a M-A-C-H-I-N-E MACHINE!"

"THIS is a M-E-T-A-MACHINE!"

Spring 1974, revisited 2002
NYC
K 11.14.17

[II]

Since its inception and mass popularization over forty years ago, television has held the promise and potential to bring the performing arts into one's living room. There are special technical and esthetic difficulties for video to bridge and transpose the actualities of performance—transmitting living presence, dramatic impact and palpable spatiality that often are greatly diminished, if not entirely abrogated. But when that translation *does* happen, and the work is a large-scale operatic multimedia spectacle of total collaborative cohesion, the accomplishment is doubly overwhelming, euphorically so. On Wednesday evening, May 26, 1993, PBS/ Channel 13 broadcasted a brilliant hour-long film (1992) of Igor Stravinsky's neoclassical oratorio *Oedipus Rex* from Japan's Saito Kinen Festival, performed by the Saito Kinen Orchestra, conducted by Seiji Ozawa and directed by Julie Taymor (both stage and film version; she also designed the masks and sculpture and acted as one of the film's editors, with Gary Bradley).

This unique production, soon commercially available on videotape, is a genuine crosscultural, multiethnic, artistic fusion. Just under an hour, it telescopes an epochal expanse with assured mastery and exemplary grace; its enchanting complexity deservedly inspires fervid, even enraptured reverence. Its revelatory transmissivity of quick changes between multiple perspectives, synoptically varied, angled views with fluid aerial panning, enhanced close-ups, and radical shifts of dimensionality magnified its stunning visual power and elicited spectral gradients and poetic nuances not perceivable even for a theater audience. It afforded a rarified reflexivity and heightened condensation, first by distilling a stage production, translating it into a film presentification experienced as broadcast video and then, astonishing for the virtualization of an intricately integrated dramatic experience, illuminated a timeless mythic power with intense ritual fascination and transcendental mystery. A multimedia video production that becomes a self-contained, iconic artwork raises additional, innumerably intriguing aesthetic issues about the capacities of digital synthesis to coordinate an electronic fusion of forms.

Stravinsky composed *Oedipus Rex* between 1926 and 1929; its libretto, by Jean Cocteau (translated by E. E. Cummings but performed in Latin— a language beyond language), significantly abbreviates and condenses the original Sophocles. This performance featured Philip Landridge as Oedipus, Jessye Norman as Jocasta, Bryn Terfel as Creon, Harry Peeters as Tiresias, Michio Tatena as the Messenger and Robert Swenson as the Shepard, with the Shinyu-Kai Chorus, directed by Shin Sekiya, and the Tokyo Opera Singers. It was choreographed with constant kinetic surprise by Suzushi Hanayagi and performed by the Saito Kinen Festival dancers with featured Butoh dancer Min Tanaka, whose multiple doubling of the roles of Creon, Tiresias and Oedipus transformed the formidable ritual drama into a kinetic mystery play.

This landmark production of *Oedipus Rex* is architectonic, immaculately conceived and directed, hypnotically gripping at every moment; the intensely engaging camera choreography shuttles recompositively fluid angles of presentation in lyrically rhythmic counterpoints to the orchestration, and translates transliteral transpositions that synchronize its volumetric proportions, ranging, and raising, its inherent, transhistorical spectra from a timeless archaic ritual to a modern, monumental multimedia spectacle, suggesting a crossroads of worlds vivifying dimensions and forms spanning the ancient and futuric, timeless and immemorial. The floor of the large, spacious, multi-tiered stage resembled a giant curved rake with jutting prongs protruding like a frozen steel wave to embody realms beyond earth, life and death, where gods, mortals, creatures, phantoms, demons and animals cohabit and commingle. (Other

contributors included set designer George Tsypin, lighting designer Jean
Kalman, production supervisor Paul King, technical design and fabrica-
tion by Michael Cunj.)

The cameras rarely showed the wings or boundaries of the stage, further suspending the scenic placements, parameters and transitions of the
action while heightening its structural agility and existential grain. In the
first few minutes enormous dimensional transformations and spatial super-
impositioning dazzle eye and mind. Julie Taymor's direction is daring,
powerful, visionary. The play's epic, starkly archaic Grecian authenticity
is reinforced and transposed by the pristine sparseness of its Japanese
sensibility and augmented through superimposed scapes and cinematic
cross fades, using puppetry and intriguingly auspicious, oversized
sculpted constructivist implements: paper-machéd hands and totemistic
headpieces with dietistic heads and quasi-Mesopotamian masks[1] for the
protagonists, sculptured body appliqué armor, huge machéd vulture-like
birds, globes with bright, fibrated colors, Butoh stylized make-up of
blanched, cracked skin and holocaust tatters for the plague victims of
Thebes, highly imaginative lighting, costuming, and decor at times suggesting an underground, or underworldly, cavern or catacombs, groves,
and a palace. (Primitivistic and neomodern design elements seemed intraexchangeable: costume design by Emi Wada; make-up design by Reiko
Kruk.) Suzushi Hanayagi's choreography contrasted, magnified and disembodied the essences of its telemimetic narrativity, transforming the
stage into an actively engaging ritual dance drama doubling as a mystery
masque noir to heighten its overall dynamism as grand operatic spectacle.
Having the seer Tiresias, King Creon and Oedipus' final blinding all
sung, danced *and* mimed simultaneously, overlapped with subsequent,
recurrently reiterative phases within a simultaneity of mimetic and mnemonic modes, created highly unusual and unique harmonic counterpoints within the formidably bountiful, powerful musical production.

The opening introductory shots, like the whole production, borrow
Butoh's starkly stylized, white body painting techniques—a ptomaine
apocalypse with chalky, cracked skin and leaden, impassive expressionism;
the opening credits are superimposed on dead bodies, plague victims
with living eyes—living corpses—whose parched exteriors are exquisitely
painted, dramatic body masques suspended in the surface of a still, blue
river, as if caught, or arrested, in a membrane of molten lava. The open-

ing sequence begins in black and white, with a closeup of the Speaker, a dynamically captivating Japanese actress (Kayoko Shiraishi) who functions as an intracessory storyteller-announcer interposed between scenes, stopping the action with her forcefully clipped, sharply accented, declamatory or accusatory pronouncements that anchor and inform the action in advance of it occurring. English subtitles help provide another dramatic distancing technique, separating the discursive action of the printed, spoken and sung language, supplying, then suspending, literalized meaning, disassociating and disembodying its multiple *scursivities*, allowing the music its stirring autonomy, unfettered from syntax, and catapulting *reading* the diversity of elements and modalities, and the spellbinding, mysterious mythicality of the entire production, into a high-caliber impact. As the camera initially pulls back, the vectors of perspective vibrate, shrink and miniaturize space, showing the Speaker placed before a large, blank proscenium; using multimedia animation and film projection techniques, a huge, white, dove-like, mythical bird with enormously extended wings flies portentously in suspended superimposition across its expanse. Drawing a knife, she penetrates its surface and slides it upward; as the paper tears, the splendorous, colorful stage action is revealed to the full orchestra's overpowering, opening sonic crescendo.

Thebes is dying of a plague. Suspended in mid-air and mid-stage above the chorus is a huge disk, and projected upon it a highly stylized, agonized plague victim, lying prone, connected at the abdomen to a long, red-ribboned umbilical cord, writhing slowly, helplessly—an everyman (Min Tanaka), covered by form-fitting, sculptural armor with segmented, appliqué *accoutrement*—the first cipher of dance doubling as a proxy puppet making implicit meanings and actions explicit. Corpses litter the landscape and riverbed; fear and hysteria predominate. "Oedipus, the plague has come . . . From the plague deliver us," the chorus intones, incants and pleads. This large circular disk display magnifies the continuum of affliction; huge, scrawny, purple paper-machéd vultures on poles swirl ominously in a multitude as they are carried through a choric dance descending over the scape. (Birds were formally used in divination: "birds of prophecy birds of death circling his head," Sophocles.[2] Disk = planet, globe, sun-moon, Zeus, circle, womb, tomb; contexts shift images, and images contexts . . .) The choric victims are tattered like war victims, their skin flaky, in bleached rags, blocked in anxiously collectivized configurations of stalwart solidarity, and they circle dynamically in a blankly impassive, impressive *ballet de morte*.

The disk then ascended out of view. (It reappears as a huge solid surface, like a planet, behind King Creon, authoritatively delivering the message of the gods as a large fibrated globe with intricately burnished and blended colors—yellow, oranges, burnt hennas. Later Min Tanaka, first a background proxy for Creon, also becomes a mute double for the seer Tiresias atop it.) Behind this dire, opening choric scene of birds, appears the first, mysteriously commanding presence of Oedipus: "My children, I shall deliver you . . . I shall free you from the plague . . . I, illustrious Oedipus, love you . . ." Oedipus takes imperial responsibility, not realizing that his prescient, double talk innuendo also decrees a prophetic, terminal fate.

"How, Oedipus, will you save us?" asks the chorus. Creon, the brother of his wife, Jocasta, Oedipus tells them, has been sent to Delphi to consult the oracle. Hands folded over his chest, Oedipus declares: "I await Creon . . . Hail Creon." Creon appears, a pale yellow rectangle of paint framing his face; like all the characters, he is dressed in a long formal robe. His aria, an ingeniously fluctuating counterpoint with thrilling, melodiously melismatic bravura—and a double tessitura—rapidly shifts between high and low registers, liltingly punctuated by trebled reeds and piped syncopation alternating with booming basso percussion, while he auspiciously points and commandingly traces large circles in the air with the oversized index finger on each of his puppet hands, gesticulating with added portent, "The murderer hides in Thebes." King Laius's murderer must be found and punished: "At all costs he must be discovered." Oedipus, whose heroism and mythic power originated from having solved the riddle of the Sphinx, rallies courageously to this impending challenge, even though many years have elapsed since the (unknown) patricide. The chorus cowers before this scene and the brilliantly illuminated sun globe power disk. "Purge Thebes of its stain." The tremulous, contrapuntal weaves of harmonic, operatic waves surge with fortitude and authoritative gusto: "Apollo, the god, has spoken . . ."

Hands over his face, the disk now golden, Oedipus remonstrates, "You cannot right this wrong . . . It is I who shall cleanse Thebes." The layered resonances activated by melodic fields of choric interplay sonically accrete as intensifying intonations suggest a mass deliverance: "You must have faith in me—I promise to carry out this task . . . I shall drive him out of Thebes. The ancient crime shall be avenged." The god has been answered; the circuit ignited. An apparitional, winged creature, part puppet, part floating constructivist sculpture, like a tutelary spirit (most probably the dead king as the phantom of the plague), is carried aloft auspiciously on poles and hovers etherically with fragile, wispy, tissued wings, moving circularly and circuitously through and over the stage, then splits apart; another armored figure is sighted in the background atop the globe holding staff or wand—the dancing double of the seer Tiresias (mythically hermaphroditic). The premonition *of* a premonition; a most austere foreboding.

Oedipus, apprehension aroused, accuses Creon of coveting his throne. Tiresias, called to interpret the oracle, refrains from speaking: "To speak would be a sin. Oedipus, I cannot . . . Allow me to be silent . . ." But silence is accusatory. Oedipus, obliquely accused, angered, stonewalls and in turn accuses Tiresias, who is very reluctant to parry. The murderer is in their midst. "The slayer of the king is a king," he blurts out cathartically. This axially pivotal moment erupts like a deadening, prophetic flare; large eyes traced on the back of Tiresias's puppet hands punctuate this undeniable, oversized portent. Blindness is an acute second sight that gesticulates cogently and veridically. The circle closes in, as the chorus, treading stealthily with branches (propitious offerings), parades, swirls, lines up ceremoniously, leaves falling and scattering. They circle Oedipus's dancing double, whose shadow-proxy figure on a raised gold dais upstage center executes a kind of mechanically mock regal pantodance; the chorus salutes him, whirls ecstatically en masse, falls to the floor, gracefully rebounds. "Envy hates good fortune . . . All praise Queen Jocasta." Apprehension swells ominously with drum rolls. The queen is about to appear to shame the crowd for quarreling. (The role of Tiresias, both sung and danced in highly stylized double relief, adds dramatic cargo for those who have appreciated Martha Graham's dance, *Night Journey* and invites a curiously supplemental comparison. Graham's dance erotically physicalizes the sexual encounter of Oedipus and Jocasta with shocking libidinal sinuosity, but it is Tiresias's presence that marks, seals, and explodes the bondage of their karma; all spaces transpire together, conspiring and converging ominously.)

Another anticlimactic interlude transpires with the presciently charged reemergence of the Speaker, who urgently passes behind Jocasta and then invisibly among the frozen phalanx of chorus citizens, fitfully delivering, almost hectoring, a nearly shrill, calamitous presentment. *Be forewarned* is her strident foreboding: Jocasta *will* vociferously counter belief in the oracle! The Speaker is both a foil and galvanizer, a sign and cipher, tremendously effective as lightning rod and stillpoint combined.

Jocasta is imperious, smooth and fierce, sinuous and hypnotically erotic; aureole-like spokes protrude from her crown. She, too, has been blinded, or she blinded herself spiritually; the chorus surging with tumult rumbles to this apprehensively subterranean, internecine undertow. Jocasta rebukes them for their clamoring. "Are you not ashamed to raise your voices in a stricken city? . . ." she cajoles, shrewdly manipulative under a heightened pretext of concern, approaching Oedipus. "Nothing is proved by the oracle . . . The oracles have always lied." Her *fait accompli*— she abandoned her child to assure the prophecy could not be fulfilled; King Laius was murdered by *thieves* (her alibi). Her recitative quivers and rebounds with darting, plaintively staccato reverberations: "Never trust the oracles . . ." Her eyes are fixed, insistent, penetrating. Jessye Norman's virtuosic artistry and monumental bearing mike the registers of a unique performative intensity. (Seeing her recreate this role ten years from now could prove even more amazing. Martha Graham's creation of Greek heroines such as Jocasta, Medea and Clytemnestra occurred in her fifth and sixth decades, and it was her seasoned maturity as a dramatic dancer that brought forth these figures' formidably forbidding power.) "Nothing is proven by the oracles . . ." In profile, stoically concentrated and self-contained, Jocasta's each stylized step is weighted and presciently measured; by its mechanical meter she must conceal the inevitable even from herself (so it will concede itself, too, for after all, it has been *deigned* and foreordained). She sings with unctuously exaggerated precision, the musculature of her mouth forcefully overproducing the outlines of words, stretching their articulatory shapes with a fanatical motor compulsion, as if foreswearing and repressing some other, momentously incredulous realization. Something is surely coming undone. Oedipus will never return to Corinth.

Suddenly, above the stage, an omen is (re)enacted, as chorus members gather to position a wheeled vehicle, a miniature chariot, which appears from the horizon of the wings with a small erect figure of its driver to reenact King Laius's fateful day at the crossroads of Delphi. "Laius," Jocasta shrieks in high register, as if confronted by his ghost. Memory becomes more than memory, like the sea turbulently swelling its crest, or the dark, effervescent hood of a wayward wave rearing to regurgitate a terrible secret. A woman from the chorus unreels long, taut, continuous swathes of a blood-red ribbon with smoothly elongated, gliding strides, tracing, retracing, crossing and crisscrossing the girth of the stage, staking out its vectors in the shape of a triple X in sharply angulated, apprehensively sinuous passage. These are the forgotten bloodlines becoming visible, the veins of time, ties and truth lines that tremble and bind, damned crucible of a macabre fate upsurging and usurping, conscriptions for constriction, hazardous portents of imminent disaster. "Suddenly I am afraid, Jocasta!" Oedipus confesses. Slowly, like an oracular procession, the vehicle's wheels slide precipitously forward, beginning their inexorable progression over its anxiously ribboned course—an ominously staged imprecation. The queen's increasingly unsettled ostinato reiterations punctuate her agitated aria, again in a desperate effort to deprecate the oracles. "I killed an old man coming from Corinth," Oedipus blurts out. Cathexis is a suddenly blinding maelstrom of inconceivable, convoluted realization.

Jocasta tries to vanquish this revelation; her irrevocable instinct to obliterate the long-sublimated dereliction of her infant son is belied at an unguarded moment by the heaving mimetic traceries of her attempt to restrain a breathless choking. A duo aria: "Let us return home at once . . . There is nothing to know," she bridles insistently. "Jocasta, I must know." In panic, Jocasta flees. Delirium quivers at the boundaries of an escalating circuit of recognition. A messenger and shepard appear.

The messenger has dire tidings. "Dead is Polybus," Oedipus's (adoptive) father. "He was not Oedipus's father." The shepard discloses the clincher—he rescued the child abandoned on the mountain, his feet pierced by spikes: "This should have remained concealed." Oedipus: "What are these monstrous tidings? I shall find out my true lineage . . . Jocasta is ashamed of me . . ." The puppet figure becomes proxy for that abandoned child; the superposed, winged dove reappears.

The truth is out. The oracle has been fulfilled; vengeance's sting snags like venom: "Unlawful was my begetting, unlawful my marrying, unlawful my shedding blood . . . all brought to light." His incredulous eyes stare searingly; passion implodes. Inevitability confronts itself; inevitability turned abomination—love vilified.

Jocasta has locked herself in her room. She reappears center stage and walks forward to its edge, as if before parapet or precipice. Red ribbon descends, choric assistants wind a noose on the ancestral, totemic headpiece above her real head; she flings open her robe, screams, the headdress severs, flies skyward, symbolically decapitating her, as she sinks to the floor in the enactment of ritual suicide. Almost in shadow, the dancer-double reappears, intercedes, removes the golden pins from her hair, and with his back to the audience while dramatically held under the elbows by, and drawn toward, Oedipus, stabs and lances the eyes on his doubled, sculpted, totemic head. Turning frontally into view, having exchanged roles and *become* Oedipus, thick, red painted rivulets adorn the agonized plastique and drained, empty pathos of his blankened gaze, eyes symbolically gouged, blinded and bleeding; he gropes his way disorientedly. The chorus is surging to a near militaristic, steadily pounding dirge whose droned, thumping overtones produce rocking crescendos with thudding, deadened repetition; exile ordains itself. Blinded, this Oedipus becomes (again, in another mode) a themic double of Tiresias; the circuit has doubled back on itself yet again, one last time, ignited and burning itself out, it leaves the chorus to solemnicize, "Farewell King Oedipus, we loved you . . ."

During this climactic, self-inflicted saturnalia, this double, unclothed Oedipus staggers, falls, slides downward, descends, and slips under the frontal lip of the stage, where underneath (the underworld) the chorus squats as silently alert witnesses and displaced or uprooted citizens, poised on their haunches in a shallow, reflective pool of water, viewed through crossbeam supports, reminiscent of an ancient underground aqueduct. In an instant antihero has become outsider and pitiful pariah. (In Sophocles' text, Jocasta and Oedipus have four children, two grown sons and two small daughters; Oedipus gathers the latter to him, solicits and entrusts Creon with their care before departing.) The chorus's heads are craned upward toward the invisible sky. The camera pulls back. A long-shot view of the entire stage reappears, showing a teeming sheet of rain, a wall of water cascading torrentially over the backdrop like a celestial upheaval or release from above. In one glorious moment, a sudden wave of healing releases all the magnificent, puzzling and contradictory tensions that have built fiercely, frenetically and inexorably. The gods have completed their mission.

Philip Landridge, Jessye Norman, Bryn Terfel and all the singers gave outstanding, compelling, haunting performances, amplified by the excellent production, choreography and direction, supporting cast and chorus, and impeccably integrated design elements. Most mesmerizing was the collaborative fusion of art forms that catalyzed the grandeur of a chthonic transfiguration of magisterial operatic magnitude and that transcended the language of dramaturgy, but that also lifted and poetically liberated it, and its narrative import, to a theatrical hyperdimensionality of incommensurable, performative impact. The totemic accoutrement of oversized sculptured hands and headpieces for the protagonists magnified their being, virtualized their karma, and reindemnified the action, transforming them into cosmic agents of supernatural personage, dexterously reanimating the static tradition of opera to deliver up its immense mythic power, impossible dilemmas, and timeless ontological lesson.

Incest is the secret of secrets, the final taboo, cathecting the unspeakable and unnameable. The knotted convolutions of this perverse parental transference cross the thanatrophic threshold that intersects with the underworld: "I must know who I am, know the secret of my birth."[3] and later, "What man has ever suffered grief like this?"[4] Being's first, primal transference occurs through maternal bonding; Jocasta caused a triple rupture by defying child, deity and self. Because the Delphic oracle prophesied that Oedipus would murder his father and marry his mother, Jocasta's secretly attempted abandonment of her infant had to be thwarted and backfire as an ultimate, histrionic incendiary. Myth needs exceed narrative, tendering its irreconciliables to extend the ambiguity of paradox while plumbing poetry, cauterizing dreams, and reassembling the veridical scramble of signs that will decipher its indemnifying karmic codes—kaleidoscopic shards of elided (and eluded) clues, and fragmented, mnemonic memento mori—buried deep in invisible, (intra)cellular-genetic, collective recesses. The logoic net and mythic catharsis must be sunk deep as a psychoprobe to excavate truth through the illumined numinosity of poeisis. The breaking of psychoanalytical encipherments of sexuality unleashes a libidinal dam and stormfire of desire as the most rigidly guarded and fateful of humankind's taboos (Oedipus's blinding is also an obvious proxy for castration). His childhood abandonment, a virtual, would-be infanticide, anointed his and her doomed, hyperontological *rite de passage;* Freudian analysis could only hit pay dirt with Jocasta's narcissistic, psychogenic disclaimer: "Why should the thought of marrying your mother make you so afraid? Many men have slept with their mothers in their dreams."[5]

The ethical dilemmas dovetail and ensnare one another in labyrinthine complicity—*why* did Oedipus kill King Laius? Why did the oracle and/or gods decree this gargantuan debacle of human error, suffering and fratricide, unless as a cosmic lesson for mankind for all of time? Isn't Oedipus, as an entity of mythic agency, the eternally potent allegorical paradigm for archetypal ethos and the etiological enforcement of ultimate taboos? Isn't the ambiguity of Oedipus's ordeal that, though a mortal, he sustained a god's trial, a scabrous fate sustained by devastating forces of circumstance that reduced his sovereignty to that of an unpardonable criminal pariah through blind victimization—with unprecedented sorrow and occluded, circuitous retribution? "I have been saved, preserved, kept alive for some strange fate, for something far more awful still."[6]

From the opening moment, the poignancy of eerily uncanny present-time parallels flash by, e.g., the plague devastation is not unrelated to our presently harrowing struggle with the global AIDS pandemic; psychiatrists and psychotherapists compile surveys showing greater incidences of incest than heretofore suspected or reported; and a precocious sexuality, erotomania and power-preoccupied century has stormed the gates of taboo, etc. But ravage and revulsion transformed by art and poetry become symbolic and prototropaic; the unspeakable is hypostatized, transfixed, virtually transfigured—justice expended by exile. Greek mythology cathected a theogonic, supernatural reciprocity of worlds, realms and beings whose interactive agencies were transacted through convoluted ritual hypostases and whose axial, libidinal intertwinings celebrate a complex, superworldly, retributive ethos. Tiresias says, "Oedipus is a plaything of the gods"; myth embodies strange concatenations, an immortal and immoral eschatology of mortality impacted by oracles, invisible agents, seers, demons and phantoms to reconsecrate a tale that can never die; karma presages a furtively harbored and festering histrionic comeuppance. The quarantine of complicity even silences the priesthood: "but Apollo refused to answer me."[7]

A high-voltage production and complex collaborative endeavor of this magnitude magically summons ineffable essences and indelibly timeless traceries; its charged emanations even exercise a virtual *dialexis* (two simultaneous, contrapoised *readings* in time and across esthetic countertemporalities) reminding one of how far aesthetics has come through its circuitously historiotrophic, now televisual routes to entrain other, elided, primogenerative modalities since its incipient ideal of beauty fixated the classical canon (now replaced, or extended, by technics of ethics, ethos and transvaluation). The fusion of media via the transmissibility of film and video affords the veridical power of digitated fissionings of imagery made electronically hyperflexive, mixing its synergistic imports with transhistorical supports. Art transfigures even myth, supercedes dialectics and analysis and holistically re(com)posits the pluralities of identities that generate an alchemical suffusion and resolution of forms and being—an enhanced, cogently rarified conception of beauty exceeding the corporeal and physical. This production reconfigured the presentational matrices of the classical ideal, expanding ethos to encompass even the forbidden and undesirable—lust, incest and murders actual and intended (fratricide, matricide, infanticide), plagues, death—the ultimates—transgressions and afflictions that stymie conceivability and riddle existential resolve while stretching the paralogical (and pathological) parameters of time and history, psychology and being through allegory and music.

Myth promulgates an implicit, double-tiered, even paradoxical ethic through poeisis: the plague has a supernatural cause; retributive justice is a complex pact between gods and mortals. Just as Iphegenia was the world's first loss, Oedipus, too, holds up an inverted redemption for mankind; pathos, too, is salvation. He augurs the incipient and consequential injunction against incest as the ultimate transgressive power of love, and the love of power. He is the gods' exemplar and interdiction for all of time. The virtual redemption of *Oedipus Rex* is an ironic, timeless allegorical saga—a purposely convoluted, agonizing embroilment of hypertrophic proportions fretted with ambiguous causality, transgression, the fitful entanglements of fate, and the catastrophic ethos of affliction that reflexivizes the primal essentiality of myth to create its double—redemption through art. This exemplary production and televised dissemination integrates and synthesizes all the arts. (Even Wagner could not have dreamt of a *Gesamtkünstwerk* made electronically *transmissible*.) The injunction at the entrance to the Delphic Temple, GNOTH SAUTON (know thyself), could be transliterated as "Man, you will die." Myth is the ontic absolution of this existential predicament, and myth is transcendental and paracursive—its primordial intimations and interpretations are autogenous and eternally permutable. Oedipus *is* redeemed— *myth* is redemptive. Music pierces these deeper currents and cathects the substrates of myth's formidable secrets; dance exercises the motoric and chthonic forces of ritual expatiation; decor and light illuminate and enhance the vicissitudes of vision; and their combined realization is a *language* deeper than language, thus intoning the poetry *of* poetry—song, whose rainbow bridge (opera) excoriates the snares of fate and bestows the beatified amplitudes of destiny. Pathos, too, is salvation . . .

(1993)

On occasion, extreme and improbable opposites offer tantalizing, atypical cross-correspondences and asymmetrical correlatives that serve the function of linking and aligning highly unusual events, situations or people. Reading Maurice Blanchot's *The Space of Literature* occasions some fortuitous, furtive thoughts about the practices of writing over (and overwriting) history, which gets curiously irrupted by, and transassociated with, some cursorily contrasting reflexions about—Jackie O., to illustrate the ontology of solitude and absence.[2]

Maurice Blanchot is the highly influential French writer, *philosophe* and *littérateur* who greatly impacted several generations of thinkers including Sartre, Batailles, Foucault, Derrida and many others, infiltrating and informing their practices. He's a mystery figure of the writer incarnate (and disincarnate)—a writer's writer and intellectual's intellectual, a master polemicist whose hermeneutical wizardry negotiates strategic border exchanges between literature, philosophy, criticism and theory— whose seminal importance revolves around formidable distillations attesting to a perspicacious ontological precision, a reflexivity that sharpens and enhances a radical objectivity able to situate itself inside and outside of itself simultaneously. Blanchot mirrors language's deep, autonomous, paraontical structures, doubles them, turns them inside out, makes language's *being* speak, interrogate and flex itself from inside and outside its givens, its conceptual parameters, contexts, and, above the contours of any intermediary. Blanchot absolves the (psychologically constituitive) positionalities of subject and author. What could seem to be more improbable than conceiving these two dissimilar personages in tandem? (Even *if* there's an end of history, there's never an end to theory, at least in France!) Blanchot's texts play with concealment; he refuses to be photographed, shuns publicity, focuses resolutely on his work.

Photographing Mrs. Onassis, on the other hand, is an unceasing, frenetic tabloid industry; her pictures are arresting for their tacitly guarded, surreptitious solitude. They constitute a glamour institution and public factorium of couture imagery whose celebrity allure is saturated with regal remnants displaced by a fascistically commoditized democracy. She remains a durable national icon whose fascination is the preserve of her (usually mute) image frozen over hyperdistances of silenced innuendo with commanding implications. History has been written and rewritten, and it has overwritten itself upon her. -Jackie has been memorialized in and by the present, her presence sealed, further shielded behind oversized trademark designer shades and concealed under signature scarves, sighted on Fifth Avenue with her grandchildren, or caught by tabloid telephoto spies, her still slim, sixty-plus model's body captured changing seductively into a bikini at her Gay's Head retreat before a swim, or surreptitiously by a television crew as she emerges coyly from a stretch limo saturated with gamey, slo-mo mysterioso innuendo, avoiding (or trying to avoid) the shutter while flashing the lens a gracefully cool, impassively teasing glance before disappearing behind a door or impenetrable facade. Her pictures reinforce a being enshrouded by ultimate secrets and sycophantic solitude, a fixation on privacy (but a *theatrical* privacy, since her image is constantly being captured) indicating an unbreachable silence whose image alone *suffices*. Not without irony, Jackie is a quintessential image of essential solitude . . .

Blanchot has written about the ontology of solitude and of writing over- *(of the writing over of)* history, doubling the *(doubling of)* practices and removes that later provoked Foucault and Derrida; the latter supplements and reinscribes this signatory prowess. But unlike them, Blanchot seems to have kept a strictly enforced strategic distance from the iconic limelight of the French intelligentsia while exercising his pivotal role as a kind of prophetic secret agent, the cogito incognito. By keeping concealed, he's accessed the more reclusive recesses and essential foundations of his art. More than being a celebrity, he's galvanized the magical lacuna of anonymity, catalyzing its secret harbor of invisibility, and converting his labor into a prodigal production that exceeds tacit boundary ma(r)kers. For Blanchot, authenticity and action are certified by invisibility, concealment, anonymity.

Since leaving the White House as our iconic, preeminent First Lady, Jackie has kept a distant reserve from its subsequent inhabitants. It seems she hasn't set foot or been photographed there since being shrouded in long dark widow's veils. Her image confirms what cannot (not) be known, especially when plentiful revelations surface about JFK's notorious promiscuity in tabloid reportage, pulp thrillers and Hollywood blockbusters like Oliver Stone's cinematic exposé, which entertains clandestine conspiracy theories behind the assassination. But since last fall's presidential campaign Jackie has quietly received, and reportedly had low-key private luncheons with, newly elected First Lady Hillary Clinton. Last week (summer 1993) Jackie's long-time beau, Maurice Templesman (a married diamond dealer who supposedly turned her twenty million into over two hundred million), had the Clintons and Kennedys out on his yacht during the President's highly publicized August vacation in Martha's Vineyard. Hostess Jackie received them privately below board; later all were decked out on deck for the requisite low-key but nonetheless high-profile photo opportunity. Its prominent, front page placement on the *New York Times* showed a jovial President Clinton standing center beside a seated, puffy and aged Senator Ted Kennedy and his new wife; Jackie was discretely shaded, standing partially, and very carefully concealed, off to the side behind a white mast beam, choreographed for sterling background fascination. Message is innuendo and scripting is image. Blanchot: "Whoever is fascinated doesn't see, properly speaking, what he sees . . ."[3] Jean Baudrillard: "Fascination, in my opinion, is that which attaches itself to what is disappearing. It is the disappearance of things that fascinates us."[4]

Jackie protects by projecting the mirror image of herself as herself, a being whose glamour is eclipsed by disappearance; the theatricalization of her presence doubles itself, its media impact assured by unrelenting paparazzi. Unusually photogenic, her mystique one-ups Hollywood's; she need not act, just *appear*. The mystery of her near-perpetual silence can certainly be traced to that shattered moment in Dallas when she cradled her husband's bloodied head after his assassination and during the infamous, high-speed motorcade to Parkland Memorial Hospital, further memorialized by Andy Warhol's pop-cult *Blue Jackie* silkscreens of her disembarking from Air Force One in bloodstained suit with JFK's casket upon returning to Washington as indelible national hypericon. Since then, the tacit immutability of death and disappearance have haunted her presence, a doubly inscribed presence that also resonates as absence, of one who not only knows too much, but who has seen everything, been everywhere. (There was scant surmise about her personal and political safety after the assassination, which landed her in Greece as the wife of shipping magnate Aristotle Onassis.) What opportunities and destinies the nation lost on that infamous day now seem inscrutable in the allure of her sphinx-like gaze, both open and gracious, but indelibly concealed, like a sealed vault, a national, mnemonic crypt of what cannot be disclosed about clandestine histories coveted behind the national facade, and those famous oversized shades on that forever fateful day. With or without reincarnation, Jackie's our Catherine de Medici; the heraldic bounty of fascination revolves around a mute coat of arms, emblematic of a silent enigma—absence by presence, and vice versa.

Curiously, in contradistinction, the English translations of Blanchot's books contain no biographical information about the reclusive author (who must be in his eighties); surely he must have been engaged in or appeared for public occasions, and if so, it seems by a carefully perpetrated absence or disguise. Blanchot is a final cipher for a whole circuit of modern cultural history spanning existentialism, phenomenology, structuralism and postmodernism. Let's face it, the French have turned thinking into a glamour industry; they furnish the latest *trompe de textes* or *topos logos du jour*. And more specifically, marketing *difficult*, abstruse thinking freighted in sparkling, complex rhetoric that stymies in the effort to liberate itself from *ontometaphysics*, it ends up being even *more* paracryptic. They've refined, defined and redefined the exigencies and border turfs of modern philosophy, poststructuralist exegesis, cryptoanalysis, and non-narrative narrativity. They resurrect and exergeticize Descartes daily, jousting with a Cartesian cottage industry on the scale of the Taj Mahal! In *A Step Not Beyond* (1973) Blanchot adapts a camouflaged

Derridaean rhetoric while developing essential, shrewd insights from
Pierre Klossowski about Nietzsche's Eternal Recurrence and the paradoxical ontology of temporality; his writing adeptly works over the her-
meneutic play of attenuated methodological trans(re)ferences whose
conceptual amplitudes realign and refocus all doxic and cognitive polarities. *The Writing of Disaster* (1986) might be situated in a suspended
realm or vertiginous zone after the closure of history and philosophy
proper—the outside of otherness, a remote time in a rarified terrain.
Blanchot has been the invisible catalyst for transforming the end of history into the end of knowing/knowledge, an original supralexical cognitive (pr)axis that opens up the enterprise of hyperontological reflexion
fusing literature and philosophy by leaving subject and author ga(s)ping
in the dust. His astonishing commentaries on death and solitude in *The
Space of Literature* (1982) have been distilled from studies of Kafka and
Rilke. *Foucault/Blanchot* contains a 1963 essay by Foucault in tow and
homage, and an essay by Blanchot (1986) surveys Foucault's career.
(Blanchot notes that he only met Foucault once, during the 1968 university uprising, though Foucault did not know who he was.) There's a
liberating deceptive double play on historical innuendo: death and anonymity, duplicity and otherness, become ultimate proxies and confidential witnesses for tendering and contending the adjudication of the
irreconcilable reciprocities between public and private, celebrity and
scholarship . . .

Photography layers images, plays with recollection, amplifies memory
and enforces mythology. It entwines sight with multiplicities of temporalities, extrapolates their intertwined densities of associated details challenging eye and mind to scan bundles of eidetic saturations as they wind
through neuropathic expressways entraining cortical typographies, con-
tributing to collectively haunted, surrealistic cultural conflations while
also jumping oneiric fissures. Writing extrapolates and layers over the
presciency of intersynaptic digital resonances of images that are not yet
visual or that become transassociatively hypervisual, or whose components are both above and below limens of (re)cognition, yet exceed
(re)presentation. And reading authors, one likes to believe that one *can*
imagine them factually and existentially, aside from their being supplemental registers of an invisible virtual entity. The disclaimer: a text can
be in excess of, or liberated from, the specificity of an identity; it fix(at)es

and refocuses the virtuality of the literary (pr)axis and accesses knowledge by concatenating historical contextures, analogous to the paradoxical state of subatomic particles in the realm of quantum physics that jet-
tisons having any concrete placement or actual positionality while
moving through relative waves of shifting spectra. Before Foucault's virtuosic exegesis of the death of the author, Blanchot had already vetoed,
blotted and subtly sabotaged the knowing subject in favor of a surreptitious cognitive *f(r)isson*. Because only a portion of his writings have been
translated, the reader is left to ferret through the available selections and
relish their sublimity through a sort of ontophilic absence—being's subversive ruse . . .

Time writes over time, history writes over history, time writes over
history, history writes over time, writing writes over time writing writes
over history, history writes over writing; history writes over time writing
over writing, etc. The virtual interprecessions of such moments, movements and meta-moments constantly obstruct, redefine, obliterate, transform and liberate identity through a subliminal polyphony of ontotropic
modes that constitutively transform the spectrum of lexicality's recombinant registers. Blanchot's cogent metaphilosophical gambit has been the
adventure of reflexion in a suspended hypertemporality, exposing and
counteracting the indemnity of time and (recorded) history by reworking
the subject's dialectical leverages within the reciprocating double movements of anteriority and posterity, cause and effect, cohesion and dispersion, similitude and difference, continuity and discontinuity, psychology
and ontology, being and nothingness, philosophy and literature . . .

Three days ago, May 23, 1994, Jacqueline Kennedy Onassis was buried
in Arlington National Cemetery beside JFK after a six-month battle with
non-Hodgson's lymphoma. (She died on May 19 at the age of sixty-
four.) Rereading the words written above eight months later impacts with
an incalculable edge; they could not be penned now, pressing a realization of how they manage to eclipse and supplement other meanings and
histrotrophic dimensionalities. Her passing suddenly consecrates a theat-
rically telescoped cloture that precludes the open horizon that the "end
of history" frames as an (un)containable play of double reflexions, whose
vectors of visibility and transparency are, and can be inscribed only by,
writing, a writing that must be written over itself and oneself, since lexi-

cography too becomes a final metaphor for being and being (being) writing (writing) over *itself.* The histrio(s)trophic denouement of being and temporality interposes irrevocably clandestine contradictions whose political parameters camouflage uncanny subliminal currencies, parsing state secrets and subterranean unknowables elided and eclipsed by public relations subterfuge. Has Jackie indeed prepared a manuscript culled from her diaries as reported in the tabloids and will a posthumous book be forthcoming with her secrets revealed? Ha! For her, bearing and appearance were palpably silent; enforcing a double curiosity too since she refused all interviews but one (about being an editor at Doubleday) and said little all these intervening years, nothing about JFK except the inaugural speech for his library. She never commented on the assassination, whose drama and images inscribe her mighty myth and its surreal aftermath, nor on the possible reasons for her marriage to Aristotle Onassis, which might in part have been for her and her children's security. The unquenchable enigmas of time and writing pivot how and what can be seen, *said*, written and known before, during and after an event, or lifetime. Blanchot's seminal double reflexions on time, history, solitude and death seem (re)collectively mirrored in the overwhelming public response to, and sorrow for, Mrs. Onassis's passing. Being larger than life magnified her mortality. (Not just the end of an era, the "Camelot" metaphor for the expansive 1960s, but the retrospective fact that at the end of her path she once again pulled a double disclaimer by becoming Mrs. Kennedy forever, lying next to her first husband in perpetuity in Arlington National Cemetery.) Like a high magician, Jackie's charismatic flair for fashion and her supernatural grace accomplished more for the appreciation and expansion of the arts during her White House years than any other public official then or since.

Blanchot: "you cannot write unless you remain your own master before death; you must have established with death a relation of sovereign equals. If you lose face before death, if death is the limit of your self-possession, then it slips the words out from under the pen, it cuts in and interrupts ... Kafka feels deeply here that art is a relation with death. Why death? Because death is the extreme. He who includes death among all that is in his control controls himself extremely. He is linked to the whole of his capability; he is power through and through. Art is mastery of the supreme moment, supreme mastery."[5] Here, perspicaciously distilled, is a concentrated matrix of quintessential insight that only Maurice Blanchot could conceive. Jackie's mystery, in part the indelible stigma etched in public consciousness since the profound theatrical spectacle of her husband's funeral, doubles over itself, herself and ourselves with her passing. Jackie's presence is an enduring art (and industry) of mastery in the face of loss and public grief; her own demise symbolically reinvokes, convokes and doubles historicity's upsurge. And, given the circumstances, extreme control over her own death as it was enacted during its ritual public expatiation with a simplicity that continued to shield the privacy of her persona, it too seemed prechoreographed. (Her remains never left her New York City apartment, her closed draped casket was viewed only by relatives and close friends in a spare private room followed by a private church service and brief ceremony at Arlington National Cemetery with President Clinton delivering a concise eulogy.) Just as Blanchot delivers unusually penetrating illuminations about death, so Jackie's regal legend bestows an empathetic reciprocity of charged relations in its virtually hermetic, collective semblances of cloture, supernatural power and extremity consecrated by the magnetic presences of myth and paradox, suspending time by the anguish and dramaturgy of disappearance . . .

(1993–1994)

Dreaming is forever mysterious and inexplicable. Reading Aristotle's *On Dreams* (*De Somnis*) and *On Prophesying By Dreams* (*De Divinatione Per Somnum*), I'm reminded of two rather recent though quite dissimilar sources that shed a considerably different light on this subject (which will always elude theory). First are Susanne K. Langer's insights ranging throughout the three volumes of *Mind: An Essay on Human Feeling*, based in part on her research into art and neurophysiology, with regard to the many cortical regions traversed by electrical impulses as they entrain neuronal networks and jump intrasynaptical junctures in concert with rapid eye movements whose mimetic pixilations cathect an upsurge of fantastically discontinuous passages, sparking unusual juxtapositions of oneiric imageries fretted with illogical (dis)associations. These (tele)somatic impulses perhaps start all the way at the base of the brain stem or are activated by physiological motor impulses remaindered from the day or occurring during sleep (Aristotle maintained the latter).

A second insight comes from theoretical physicist Michio Kaku's explication of string theory, a comprehensive fusion solution of quantum physics' breakthrough epistemic of ten-dimensional hyperspace—the vibratory pulsions of hyperdimensionality offer a new paradigm for the synergetically intersecting dimensionalities of mind, perception and the phenomenology of dreams.[1] Just as the unitive, holistic complexity of the human body is comprised of intrasynchronous processes and biosystems, so too do intracortical and physiogenic functions and actual, virtual and irreal dream transparencies interfuse to create phantasmagoric hybrids often so unusual one cannot believe or fathom from where such dreams come. Obviously the motivation of dreams, how they surpass comprehension, and their eccentric weaves of compositing, fissionating imageries are more mysterious and complex than the simple reduction to wish fulfillment (or fantasy) initially posited by Freud.

The intricate intracortical labyrinths of impulse generation, diffusion and transmission engage simultaneous branchings and network firings whose (co)extensive dendritical tributaries activate improbable and fantastic dream collages that permutate recollected, but often greatly altered, representations of place, scape and identity. Dreams spin out televisual velocities and paraeidetic amplitudes that intimate travel, astral flight and the apparitions of mythic beings, possibly resulting from the irruption of fleeting bits of memory, shards of past circumstances, latent wishes or unsuspecting motor activity, which rescrambles the riveting emotional cathexes of conflict, consternation, (dis)belief and fear in bizarre and incredulous ways. When one realizes the vast storage capacity of data, traces and substrates imprinted in the human brain's huge, complex (genetic) storehouse, and how this constitutes its neuropathic, teleassociated retrieval system, the strange otherness(es) of dreaming may seem more plausible. Freud's therapeutic breakthrough was the understanding of how images cathect and stand proxy for entire mental constructs—repressed memories and their tracer trails buried deep in the psyche—and how dream images can be icons, ciphers and symbols of and for phobias, compulsions, obsessions, etc. In the celebrated case of a hysterical young woman named Dora, Freud discussed how psychoanalysis learned to understand and penetrate the occluded regions and encrypted layers of the unconscious mind, which can be simultaneously active but not always accessible to consciousness until the analyst decodes the patient's language for reporting them in order to unmask true feelings and childhood traumas. Simone de Beauvoir on Freud: "The hysterical patients who came to see him had not been raped by their fathers as they claimed: they had dreamed of being so raped and that was far more interesting."[2]

The parallel, now omnipresent artistic technique most applied to and

taken for granted to mirror the dream work is collage, whose discontinuous visual amalgams fracture, simulate and recombine discrete elements
that shift the proportional alignments and (il)logicality of modes, orders,
materials and placements. Collage's mimicity overlays, leverages, recom-
bines, transects and disembodies place and figure and thus simulates
combinational oneiric analogs composited by association/dissociation,
radical juxtaposition/condensation, substitution/inversion, displacement/
intrusion (of foreign or illogical elements), and distortion and bifurcation/
bilocation of plane, figure, space, scape, sequence and locale, including
scalar transformations, teletemporal shifts and reversals, etc. Collage, now
a given, is actually one of the most comprehensively transforming inventions of mankind, one that only became an official genre at the turn of
the twentieth century, first invented by artists, then usurped and coopted
by advertising, television and cyberography. It has enabled us to reposition, overlay, supra-and super(im)pose different orders and inventories
of imagery, reconfigure constellations of perceptual elements, and envisage alternatives, options, connective matrices and compositional possibilities between atopical categories, happenstances, events, eras, topologies,
disciplines, systems and worlds. Because dream imagery occurs exceed-
ingly rapidly and can be entrained in and by the fleeting flexions of rapid
eye movements, the uncanny momenta of elided and concatenated vistas
of dream collages elicit an implicit sense of completion or closure by virtual telescoping, mimetic cadencing, ephemerality and transitivity.

Collage breaks up surfaces, shatters continuity, interrupts narrativity,
and discombobulates the given mode(l)s of readability and meaning by
scrambling the codes of assemblage and order, selection, focus, placement and context. Some direct precursors of collage were Symbolist poetry, Cezanne (whose art embodied the prefigurative emergence of cubism), and Freudian psychoanalysis, especially its archeoeitology of dreams
but also the daguerreotype and early cinema. The inventions of the tele-
graph and camera initiated the cultural atomism of signals and images,
isolating and delivering up pieces of vision as ultimate units as well as
inaugurating the binary transmission codes of messages and language.
Before the collages and assemblages of Kurt Schwitters and Max Ernst
and the art of Picasso, Chagall, Magritte, etc., Cezanne's starkly muted
geometric transformations shifted, unmoored and uprooted the planes
and alignments of perspective, mass and object gestalten, unlocked the

three-dimensional placements of scape and pried apart the facticities of figuration and object(ive) space, generating the initial possibilities for the emerging style of cubism. A psychotropic fragmentation and irruption of the elements and isomorphic components of form emerged, skewering and repositioning the angles and vectors of their multiple perceptual and presentational foci by the simultaneous slippage of planes, flattening and foreshortening objects, abridging or elongating sightlines and telegraphizing vectors and matrices, all the while distancing and reconfiguring the sense(s) of gestalten, their imprint, alignment, focus and (re)presentational impact. In short, cubism caught the world at a tilt between the restless counterpoints of easel and tripod and introduced the skewed emergence and kineticized palpability of the decentered axis, the bifurcation of recombinant registers and multiple indices of polysemiot(r)opic realignment.

Dreams break all the geometric rules of perception and sequence, jumbling the virtuality of sightlines by abrupt abrogation and fitful clotting. The transformational juxtapositions and paraassociated principles of dream images resemble the omnivectorial relays of the gaze that apprehends the (re)configurative schemas of collage, because the actual interplays between, and rapid jumps of, vivid ellipses and eidetic transpositions, in byte-sized increments or discontinuous intervals, more often resemble a hyperpixilated mosaic. Joseph Cornell's shadow boxes and collages created an enchanted alchemical poetry through their unexpected arrangements and strange junctures of found objects and materials—the multidimensional dialectics and techniques of collage break through to, and thus can combine or supersume, montage as well. MTV and other pop video ad techniques manipulate a pulse-driven, steadystate synchronization that frenetically and televisually collages a syncopated mosaicization of image relays, overlaid in discontinuously dialectical concatenation with after-image delays that mirror the haphazard, fitful fluctuations of onierically stimulated rapid eye movements.

Collage quickly penetrated and influenced the other arts. Not strictly a self-contained (i.e., in-itself) form but rather a renegade amalgamation of forms, the hybrid interface capacity to activate an interpenetration of figures, vistas, principles, senses, modes, textures and meanings makes dreams and collage hypermorphic, metadoxic, trans-and telepermeable, not by changing them into (and *inter*changing) one another, as eidetic

transferences and pictorial transpositions, but by converting the isomor-
phy of structural valences and mimetic coefficients through proximic similitude with multiplanar and transspatial bifurcation.

Collage is also, in retrospect, the precursor of the mid-century experimentation that mutated the boundaries between art forms, which began
occurring during the 1960s and is now full-blown as multimedia—the
digitated (inter)mixing of formal principles of presentation and proliferating as the overdetermined industry of cyberwares, CD-ROMs, etc. Collage's precinematic harbinger, the magic lantern, was also an important
early kinetimatic source—*motion* itself extrapolated, juxtaposed, wrested
and arrested imagery, disembodied and unmoored it from stationary
placement and created multiple, kinelexically virtualized registers of
iconic and canonic synchronization, mimetic dissociation and figural dissimulation. In music, Charles Ives's collaged melodic fragments interspliced with tonally dissonated themic extracts of popular folk motifs,
while Igor Stravinsky's compositions collaged textural discontinuities,
warped timbres and the cacophonic relay of overtone overlays. John Cage
pioneered a more anarchistic, radically discontinuous concept of collage
by mixing and programming random and discrete sounds, sources and
scores, utilizing (during the 1940s) sparse elementary melodic structures
punctuated with noise and sustained silences, then later orchestrating
densely interpenetrating continua using radios, appliances, electronics,
voices, ensemble mixes and multiple samplers, including computers, etc.
Merce Cunningham's dances and Events are collaged synchronies of interactive ensembles, sections, modules and parts performed as high-
frequency, simultaneously interpenetrating hyperdimensional continua.
Late-twentieth-century theater, after Happenings (also beginning around
1958), eschewed narrative and psychological motivation and began collaging unlikely combinations and sequences of objects, bodies and props,
disassociated scenes, nonsequiturial language and random actions by performers, creating alternative modes of non-scripted stagings that broke
the codes of, and reinvented, dramaturgy's presentational logic.

Another parallel development that supplemented the principles of collage and intraleveraged its virtual connexions with oneiric reflexion is
montage. Montage iterates the pictorial rhythmicities and lyrical momenta of sequential, free-associated imagery and undoubtedly owes more
of a debt to the art of photography. Montage depends upon specific de-

sign schematas to interconnect the visual parameters of its passages, sightlines and contexts and to intercut its assembled modes and telesynchronized topologies of image repertoires, though montage is probably now deemed more a cinematic technique. Robert Rauschenberg's early use of silkscreen images collaged from popular culture, later incorporating his photography, layered mixes of intragraphemized media gradients and extended the virtual registers and lexical parameters of painting, stage decor and photomontage.

The discontinuous relays of vectors and sightlines that implode the logicality of sequence and concatenate visual thresholds implicit in the plurivalent readability of collage enable the eye to scan multiple registers and read several simultaneous pictographemized structures or levels, because the saccadic scanning motions of the gaze have a built-in lexical/mosaicizing retinal action. That oneiric imageries conceal and are concealed cryptomimically in the unconscious in and as language was Freud's seminal realization. In *Dora: An Analysis of a Case of Hysteria*, he noted that syntax is not able to capture all of the simultaneous levels that constitute the interdimensional, topogenic totality of the mind's operations.[3] Later Jacques Lacan developed its linguistic and theoretical extensions to magnify an analysis of language's pervasive action in and as the unconscious. But syntax is a one to one operation; in order to process text, the eye must proceed sequentially word by word; even poetry that ventures into experimental, typographemized terrains has to be followed sequentially as it builds, accretes or concatenates the tonus of its virtual multiplicities. Gertrude Stein started it; she was involved with finding literary analogues for the techniques of the cubist painters. In books such as *How to Write*, and in her extended experimental prose, poetical works and plays, she scored word salads and syntactically scrambled collages that combined alogical, pre-Dada free-association to layer grids that could push the structural, compositive possibilities of fiction and literature beyond narrative syntax. E. E. Cummings was one of the first American poets to seize, transfer and apply the discontinuous abruptness of the cinematic rapid jump-cut and the detritus of advertising and popular culture to reconfigurate quixotically transmutable topoi whose implicitly fragmented *sign*tactical mosaics intracollaged images and rhythms into high ironic relief with a brisk, brilliant bite. By the 1960s, William Burroughs headed off the intertextual goldrush by several decades by em-

ploying various registers of paraliterary collage using cut-up and fold-in
techniques that assimilated mordantly surreal and often outrageous sexual phantasy infiltrated by fantastically alien weaves of hallucinatory, hypertrophized narcophilic and necrophobic narratives, further enhanced
and layered with loaded campy irony.

Thinking and cognition of course can also proceed haphazardly by
techniques of association that outstrip logical progression, thus having
analogies with collage. The conventions of writing conceal this from the
reader, who accepts the illusion of the permanently articulate or grandil-
oquent author proceeding, or able to speak with, unfailing logicality or
literary noblesse. The neurotropic flexions of reading too are first a collage of words that cohere by radical association and lexical strategies that
assemble sense, schemas of context, logics and meaning. Philosopher
Jacques Derrida's essays operate on the margins of topoanalysis, decon-
structing pivotal themic parameters by etymological polemicizing to realign the cognitive sightlines and excavate experimental conceptual thresholds by sometimes positioning multiple columns of text that, ideally, are
meant to be read in tandem as a unitive exposition.

I am thinking again about one specifically uncanny, arresting dream
that collaged images, scenes and perspectives. (It occurred about fifteen
years ago and was obviously fraught with multiple meanings that, whenever recollected, do not seem to exhaust or outrun themselves.) Certain
rare dreams (after Bachelard) seem to be more poetic and to encapsulate
permutable matrices of reflexion.

> I am prone on my stomach, slowly inching forward on a raised mound of earth
> in a wooded area where I played as a youngster. The mound is a large raised ridge,
> resembling the protruding above-ground path that an earthworm makes while bur-
> rowing, only it's much, much bigger. Suddenly I am similarly prone but poised
> high above, on the sheer edge of an overhead precipice, looking down from a con-
> siderable height and observing far below a very clear, completely translucent reser-
> voir; I can peer into its depths. The reservoir is completely bound by high, angular,
> constraining mountains. A strange, elongated fish emerges from the depths and
> ominously swims into view, moving stealthily along the edge of the basin just be-
> low the surface. It seems to belong to a species between a catfish and barracuda,
> arousing my voyeuristic trepidation. Suddenly birds appear high in the air, swoop-
> ing in curvilinear arcs, diving downward and hitting the water's surface, where-

upon they are instantly transformed into fish, recalling M. C. Escher's paradoxical pictorial transformations of inverted forms in double perspective. Then I notice that just below me on the right, standing on a grotto-like ledge or lair cut out of the side of the mountain amid exposed slabs of rock-like shale, is a huge creature, half-human, half-serpent, whose dark back and skin are exposed; he has wooly, close-cropped black hair and is dressed in a tank top. He seems preoccupied, talking with someone just out of my field of vision. The top part of his body is human, very muscular, with a broad back, but the lower half is entirely serpentine, with a large, brilliantly colored, scaly tail coiled ominously behind him. A wave combining fear, surprise and awe sweeps over me, being so near to yet undetected by this creature; the close proximity jolts or shocks me . . .

The wild, vivid impact and mythopoetic dimensions of this dream exceed that of most others and seem to outstrip even its obvious herpetological, phallotropic, ophiolatreiac and psychoanalytical meanings. Crawling slowly along the earth on my stomach places the solar plexus in sustained, direct visceral contact with the earth. Recollected, this image was brief but telescoped a sense of longer, incremental advance. The solar plexus is the physiogenic center of emotions, especially those that are tenacious, moody and earthy as compared to feelings, which are more rarified and more often associated with the heart or heart center. (Whether the raised mound, which was a track, was the remnant of the serpent man's tunnel through which he burrowed to his lair only occurs to me as I write up the dream.) The vista of the lake or reservoir that suddenly loomed into view and was observed from a great height, though large and spatially extended in the dimensionality of the dream, was also a contained nature scape, not a wide open immensity. Near the several-acre wooded area behind a lake where I grew up and played as a youngster was a "hidden lake" concealed behind the first, publicly accessible one. This locale was obviously transposed in the beginning of the dream. What was startling and unusual about the shifting terrains of this dream collage was the telescoping of time and the visceral impact of the radical juxtapositions—being suddenly displaced, incredulously confronted by a preternatural view from a dramatic height after close protracted proximity with dank soil, and counterpoised as a solitary witness to the suspended sense of beholding strange sights unfolding, an aerial view of nature's secrets being revealed. The clarity and impact of the dream (why I deem it poetic or allegorical) seemed reinforced by the pristine translu-

cence of the water below and the lone, strange fish surfacing from unimag-
inable depths, then the aerial display of birds diving the vectors and being instantly transformed on impact into fish, archetypally connoting the
intracontrovertability of nature's being in its metamorphizing plenitude,
as well as a virtualization of a symbolic shamanistic transference.

The serpent man greatly intensified the dream's magic and mystery, an
unsettling, riveting, forbidden creature—could he have been the prophet-
ically empowering, giant Pytho (from which derived the Pythia or Pytho-
ness of the Delphic Oracle), or a hybrid serpent-satyr chthonically and
phallomimetically incarnated? The serpent of course is often misunder-
stood—typically demonized rather than daemonized—a formidably powerful, archetypal source, an Ur-image of wisdom and prophecy that inspires foreboding and reverence, since it is a creature that can penetrate
the strata of the earth, and it moves swiftly with silent, deadly stealth.
The Kundalini, on the other hand, is the forbidding, transforming serpent fire power known to yogis that arises in states of meditation at the
base of the spine and travels upward to the top of the skull. It is associated with rapid, radical transformation, instantly opening all the chakras,
and it is akin to the Tantric practices of Tibetan Buddhism. There are
also parallels with Wilhelm Reich's analysis of character armor in his
seminal *Character Analysis*; muscular armor, the striated zones of repressed energy that isolate fields of tension and split mind from body,
becomes momentarily dissolved by any undulatory (i.e., serpentine)
movement that passes through the vertical bands of constricted muscles
bound by psychic rigidity (or by the undulating wave of the orgasm);
that is also experienced by dancers as a primal movement releasing
bound energy—as, for example, in Haitian Vodoun dance and drum-
ming ceremonies.

In the dream collage, images are also pictomimetic proxies for forces
of nature that convention tends to anthropomorphize through myth and
art; these transliteral, one-dimensional conceptions may actually limit
understanding by preventing us from conceiving them unbound from
the dualistic thinking that conceptualizes in either/or categories such as
good and evil, dark and light, positive and negative, animal and human,
while their analogic action might be more akin to the conversion image
of the birds rapidly transmorphizing into fish as part of nature's oscillat-
ing plenum. Their power might resemble M. C. Escher's double form of

paradoxical perspectival transformations, which is why, as images, they cathect more than literal or hermeneutical meanings. Mircea Eliade's researches also come to mind—his studies of comparative religions synoptically analyzed the ranges of archetypal knowledge that different societies and mythologies ascribe to dream animals, and that can be a fusion of totem, symbol, cipher and fetish as psychomimetic figures of shamanic transformation and psychic empowerment. Seeing only the back of the serpent creature compounded the mystery of the final image, formidable and mesmerizing, as I was unable to fathom what he was, what he looked like, his identity; obviously he was also a cipher and symbol for sexual mystery . . .

Collage of course is as ancient as dreaming. Its thetic leverages of pictorial overlay, superimposition and radical juxtaposition, which made similarity and dissimilarity palpably vibrate, were evidenced long before Plato's parable of the cave. Early proto-man's primeval atelier resided in the deep prehistorical solitude of underground caverns like those at Altamira in Santander, Spain, or in France at Font-de-Gaume in Dordogne, Lascaux, or the recently discovered Chauvet cave in the southern, Ardèche region (December 1994—thirty thousand years old, according to radiocarbon dating), where those first primordial artists took what we now deem to be primitive instruments, possibly flint, charcoal or mixtures of staining juices from wild berries, to paint incredible collages on the walls and recesses. For a long time an even longer line of scholars, historians, anthropologists, art historians, philosophers and critics have puzzled out these phenomena, wondering and surmising what might have been the original motivation to create what still proves to be prodigal, awe-inspiring panoramas.

On the walls of the Chauvet cave (still restricted to experts, not yet open to the public) over three hundred animal images dance in silent, suspended animation to astound the eyes.[4] Some of the walls are densely populated scapes of collaged and overlaid hoards of bears, lions, horses, bison, elk, mammoths, rhinos, owls, and a half-human half-bison creature. It could be the primordial site where dreams might have first been harnessed and broken through to what we now deem to be an active imagination, thereby inaugurating a ritualized interfusion that entrained the prehensile agility of motor capacities that coordinated the brush-

strokes, instruments and technical artistry with an emerging sensibility—
the desire to capture the likenesses (if not spirits) of so many animals in
such diverse, startling arrays, often unmoored from gravity or floating in
air, layered with exacting similitudes and dynamically interactive presentational contrasts. These early artistic processes served to conjoin the over-
stimulated psyches and hypervisualization of the dream state with an
oculomotor ritualization of presentation and representation, resulting in
these incredulously extraordinary collages that captured the animals' inimitable grace, power and movement. The motor reflexes that entrained
a complex prehensile dexterity obviously engendered an empathetic rapport with the untamed forces of nature, whose acts of becoming rendered
dered in paint exemplified what we now deem a natural chiaroscuro and
whose compositional finesse evinces complexly modulated registers with
finely honed intraconfigurated gradients deploying a full range of carefully conceived and executed mimeticized figures.

Certainly those early acts of adorning underground vaults amounted
to more than *making* a painting, i.e., capturing an image or making a
vast mural, though the capturing function, as a symbolic proxy of, or for,
food and power, may indeed have been a visceralized factor of their nascent, sacralizing process. More likely, those developing brains of the primeval foraging artist shamans, while exe(o)rcising their might of battling
the elemental profusion of their life world, also gave birth to presentational symmetry. What still astounds today is the veridicality of their eidetic traceries and the dynamic reflexivity of vectors, trajectories and
sightlines that still bestow wonder in their beholders, as well as their
makers' symbiosis with being in the Being of the world, probably well
before language or the inauguration of any symbolific function. Art may
well have entrained and coordinated motor and cerebral functions by
connecting dreaming and imaging capacities with the emerging enterprise
of visualized ritualization that became the medium that broached
(pre)conception as a very early forerunner of the cogito, just as, by analogy, Susanne Langer traces the evolution of language to the motor activity of early ritual dance, which activated the development of the frontal
lobes of the brain and prepared for this capacity.[5]

But the spectacular prodigality, sheer visceral impact and esthetic
power of their cave compositions still overwhelm and surely evidence the
birth of a genuine paraeidetic capacity that transcended whatever consti-

tuted proto-man's early life world. That they made their collaged murals in the deep, dark recesses of caves, away from the terrain of the hunt, or daylight, raises fascinating questions about how they harnessed their imaginations. Also enigmatic is the origin of their tools, their materials, their preparation, and their use of fire and method of illumination (many of those works mysteriously adorn high ceilings that appear impossible to reach). The interconnective relationships between dreaming, imaging, imagining—the precursors of symbolic mentality, language and intelligence—and whether a certain threshold of pent-up psychotropic imagery preceded presentational mimesis must remain a mystery. Also unknown is how much of the retinal and cortical actions of dreaming had to have reached a certain threshold or overload in order to be able to break through to the motorically and mnemonically consummated act of painting, while reflexing still another unexplainable paradox—that their art appears to have sprung fully realized, with no record of development, evolution, practice or trial and error—also, could painting have preceded language? Merleau-Ponty: "The first painting opens up a world, but the first word opens up a universe."[6] Like dreaming, this locates the paradox of time and history, where before and after as (tele)temporal categories or measurable registers become schematically reduced to being a set of redundant dualisms that the act of painting eclipses and/or transcends. Before and after become coterminalities of a huge mimetic crescendo exercised by an unprecedented merger fortified by the release and containment of the power of dreaming into presentational mimesis.

Collage objectifies the mimesis of oneiric configurations and unlocks the keys to dimensionalizing how many strata of brain, mind, being and world resonate simultaneously, thus moving representation beyond representation and thereby telescoping cognitive and systemic transferences. Susanne Langer: "Dimensions are conceptual principles, which require symbolic presentation to let them emerge as spontaneous elementary abstractions."[7] Collage provides a key for reseeing and reconceiving historical works and periods in a new way; it contains a perceptual fulcrum for processing multiplicities—of signs, styles, cycles, pictogenic schematas, isomorphic constellations, etc. Dream and collage mirror the construction of different ranges and interpenetrating registers of topologizing—of dream scapes, imaging capacities, figures, configurations, veridical textures, objects, symbols, places, structural and temporal interconnections, historical styles, spatial modalities, eidetic spectra, locations, etc. The visual and virtual flexions that initiate closure (completing any perceptual circuit) actually engage an open system of looking and seeing, of tracing with necessarily haphazard, darting and arbitrary flexions of gaze, then processing (consciously, subconsciously and/or intuitively) the relay of vectors, pictorial indexes, image transparencies, isomorphic transpositions, transstructural and symbolic valences and intraconfigurative schemas. The shift of registers, illogical and disjunctive alignments and placements, creates mirrored reflexions, contragenic equivalences, co-relations, correlations and a unitive holistic symbiosis. Aristotle: "In dreams, too, we think something else, over and above the dream presentation, just as we do in waking moments when we perceive something; for we often also reason about what we perceive. So, too, in sleep we sometimes have thoughts other than the mere phantasms immediately before our minds."[8] Collage thus becomes the instrument or agent for the estheticization of the cogito.

Collage catalyzes multiple semiooptic morphologies (and morphot(r)opologies) of images that layer eideographemic matrices of (auto)perception, as well as the subliminal isomorphic refraction and defraction of intraschematic reflexions. Entrained within the (tele)associative relays of reading (and reading *seeing*) and tracing out these topogenic, constellated combines uniting disparate, diverging and interconnective retinal vectors, sights and sightlines is a double helixical weave of semblance and resemblance. The reciprocities of their concrete (intra)extensions and conversion principles systemically transform and translate parallel likenesses and transferences of isomorphs and signs, images and concepts, metaphors and analogies into and through one another. As conversion currencies, the mimetic relays between these topogenetic double transferences perpetrated by dreams and collage make transparent the enciphered relationships of visuality to language, and dreaming to thinking. Art raises questions about the deep structures of cognition; conception obviously depends upon imagination harnessing extended modes of envisagement. Thinking could not have developed without the psychically assimilative autoscopic (and autot(r)ophic) function of dreaming; the preception, perception and apperception of modalities involve complex transferences between forms, senses, images, concepts, references and inferences. Dreams and collage translate and transfer the rarified, reticulated filaments of our image manifolds, feelings and perceptions. In Gaston Bachelard's vernacular, they are the brokers of immensity.[9]

(1997)

Ciphers supply the keys for cracking codes, usually the job of cryptana-
lysts, intelligence agents and spies. A code reveals how signs that configure information are encrypted, interconnected and converted, laying
bare their hidden logics or presuppositions. Psychoanalysis, too, depends
on finding certain pivotal words and images to unlock a mental circuit,
block, neurosis, secret or phobia. Even movement has codes; artworks
too. A dance is active with signals, signs, images and codes. In puzzling
out a work's impact and associations, one is often unconsciously hunting
ciphers, which are structural and systemic.

The structural, polemical and practical breakthroughs afforded by semiotics have extended the parameters and horizons of signs and ciphers.
Semiology and structural linguistics have propagated numerous new disciplines with hybrid philosophical thresholds. *Ideo* merged with and
through computer digital technics inaugurates the *programmat(h)ics* of
the idea, surpassing any specific ideology. (One wonders whether art or
ideas can ever be free from ideology, overt or tacit.) Multimedia and the
hyperkinetics of intertextuality move the boundaries of and between different forms and disciplines, permitting multiple exemplifications, extensions and transpositions for the isomorphisms of ideas and opening up a
grammatology of codes and ciphers. The systemic scripting of signs

might be called *semiographemics*, and the inventory of the electronic superhighway's emerging frontiers of transreferential, parallel-processed, digital cognition *ideoprogrammat(h)ics*.

Isomorphisms are the structurally isolable factors and elements that coordinate the larger organizational codes and modes of articulation within a given form or format; in painting and dance, for example, the areas of a canvas, parts of the body and sectors of space isolated rhythmically work with and against each other as delays and interactive parts to coordinate as structural variables. Isomorphisms are the morphogenic keys of transformation. Undoubtedly the root idea comes from evolution theory—conceptual gradients shift as structural registers focus new alignments of forms, species and phenomena. Ciphers are the clues for reading signs that at first may seem enigmatic or unreadable but that can also be multisemic and polyvalent, building up multiply interpenetrating orders of isomorphisms.

Gestures were the first ciphers, the keys for unlocking ritual. In dance, both in the performance of complicated rhythms or arrangements of movement phrases, as well as in the perception of all the *geomimetrical* variables and kinelexic axes that compose and recompose watching and reading, the moment-to-moment structuralities underlying composition involve a highly active continuum of kinetic ciphers. For example, it is the totality of corporeal isomorphisms in Martha Graham's *Medea* that makes the powerfully tragic, mythopoetic essence of one "guarded by a serpent" appear as an image on stage. (The image is an archetype, but an archetype is more than an image.) Archetypes are engaged, retrieved, summoned and manifested by ideospecific motor-mimetic isomorphisms. Their operation—how they configure (the matrices of) ideosigns that structure import and networks of association, perception, meaning and cognition—is a genuine philosophical problem.

The codes and ideosigns of intertextuality promote continuously mimetic, transactional exchanges among shifting spectra of logics, discourses, arts, disciplines and programs. Basically, a code regulates the grammar of how and why signs configur(at)e, the logic or schematic of their arrangement. Observing one's responses and gauging and processing the overload of reflexions of ambient perceptions involve a continuous remodalization of ideosigns, linking precept and percept, sign and signal, image and afterimage, and their intraconvertible and transmissible codes

and ciphers. The ways that dancers move and articulate, rotating and extending all their joints and limbs in rhythmic counterpoint, generate
more kinetic isomorphisms than most athletes (except perhaps gymnasts
and figure skaters). It's also true that some dance styles have greater
ranges of isomorphic development and deployment than others; also,
paradoxically, fewer isomorphisms can be more expressive than a profusion—think of Isadora Duncan in contradistinction to a conventional
ballet. The whole body picks up signs and signals, amplifying sight. Art
too invites a more (trans)personal or subjective reading of ciphers, since
it invites multiple interpretations.

Ciphers in motion and motion ciphers are fleeting, read differently
from discursively identifiable, discrete units, and they are more often registered as mimetic effects and affects, as impulses, signals and qualities.
Art *is* ideotropic: elements, semblances, motifs, principles and structures
culminate in and as perception, whose (para)sympathetic actions realign
junctures and ratios between inner and outer, continuous or discontinuous, concrete or abstract modes, or whatever the strategy or dualistic
counterpoint. After decades of incessant dance experimentation, how
much *information* there is in movement still seems to evade many of its
practitioners. For example, ideokinesis is a discipline that *images* movement, first to locate the psychomotor elements that motivate enactment,
performance and projection, as well as entrain the reading of its kinelexic
indices. *Ideoprogrammathics* extends the systemics and kinetrics of multimedia threshold interfaces of computer and media in and through digital
transformations by activating hyperdimensional links and extensions of
virtualized signals and signs while creating interpenetrating plays of perspectivity.

The ultimate digital isomorphisms are the coordinating bytes and pixels
that kinetically and kinelexically structure the programmathics of signs
and the matrices of codes that create symbols, icons, programs and events.
(Electronics and genetic engineering will transmute and manipulate what
we now deem *ultimate* codes, the biological scripting of species and gen-
era.) The hypersystemic densities of syntax, images and information made
possible by electronics, postdeconstructive philosophy and metatheory,
television, conceptual art and computers build up complex, interactive
fields composed of implicit, synergetic grids that catalyze and sustain
intraexchangeable ratios between seeing and saying, making and doing,

sensibility and cognition—art and science. The compossible transferences between discursive and nondiscursive forms, between isomorphisms and ciphers, metaphors and analogies, art and cognition, as well as the spectrum of media interface options, are generating emerging, inclusivizing translations and transreferencing capacities that computers—and bodies— have begun, and will greatly continue, to enhance and sustain.

The motion arts—dance, film, video—process multiple orders and registers of visually flexed and reflex(ion)ed signs with concatenated bundles of highly condensed, psychomimetic images in passage. By analogy, electron physicists are fond of reminding us laypersons that subatomic particles have virtualized positionalities, i.e., no real or specifiable location except in the *act* of positing them; still, they sponsor real functionalities. Discontinuity catalyzes the apperception of multiple temporalities, and/or the multiplicities of timed elements, in the sets or sequential parameters of perceptible movements, motion and the momenta of events. The discontinuous interrelationships of isomorphisms situate a work, experience or event within a field or continuum of processes whose discernment may require multiple, concurrent and synchronistic phases. Isomorphisms catalyze the structural and systemic correspondences that permute to make all (p)arts resonate and become cohesively transparent to one another, activating metaphor and analogy and their enciphered extensions. The isomorphisms that language coordinates— from vocables and phonemics to the compositive logics of rhetorical structures and intrasyntactical correspondences—seem infinitely more complicated, since they structurally reflex all of perception, knowledge and experience.

The isomorphisms of the voice and writing build up (often simultaneously) tactile, conceptual, kinetic and somatic streams of ideosigns, making them (intra)transmissible, ensuring that a multiplicity of signifiers generates polysemic vectors of connotation constructed by and across grids of denotation: tone and plays of pitch color the harmonics of punctuation and create semantic emphases, while specifically stressed words engender omnitrop(h)ic shifts of context, references, messages and meanings that accrete and accrue within the still larger momentum of dialogue, passage and cognition.

The translations and transpositions of and between isomorphisms and ideas, and their exemplifications through language, art and media, in-

volve conceptual pivots combining metaphor and analogy; ciphers and
ideosigns branch and link up plastic, pluralistic orders of interpenetrating, polyvalent logics whose seamless, dialectical weaves engage and synergize matrices and constellations, themselves engaging the codes that
supply the correspondences and electrical counterpoints for what we now
deem digital—that is, automatic (and automimetic), transactional exchanges and intraconvertible rates and *ratios* of cognitive currencies that
I call *semionostics*.

The isomorphisms of images involve first level, axial plays and overlays between contrarieties that set up a virtual, eideomimetic dialectics—
M. C. Escher's intricate, delightfully baffling drawings that figurate the simultaneously double perspectives of visual paradox are a good example.
Thinking in, with and through images and their isomorphisms, as well as
imaging and imagining the processes language makes possible by (multi)-
media, furnishes hyperdimensional shifts between structural registers that
instantaneously autogenerate ideoprogrammathic technics and techniques
for decoding and translating systemic referents. Cipher and gestalt—one
figure, image or picture embedded in another figure, image or picture re-
sembles the mimetic conundrums of Chinese boxes-with-boxes; as, by
analogy, cryptanalysis or critical theory can contain keys for deciphering
their autoreflexive processes. The way in which ciphers are clues to the
"subtexting" processes just beneath the threshold of a work and its
meanings, especially in the nondiscursive realms of art, is constantly intriguing. The pioneering psychoanalytical work of Nicholas Abraham and
Maria Torok on the cipher, secret and encrypting in the psyche, have
philosophical extensions that Jacques Derrida and Avital Ronell have
treated at length.

Motion and movement of eye and ear, seeing and hearing, constantly
convert and converge reciprocities of codes and ciphers via language and
perception into our conceptual and cognitive currencies. Now that history and art are over, *why* can't a dance be a high-density digital crystal
or chip that condenses writing, kinetics, information and dramatic impact as *scursis*, while also being both praxis and theory? Hey! The whole
body changes frequency, picks up signs and signals, amplifying sight, and
ciphers.

(1995)

Shadow boxes become poetic
theatres or settings wherein are
metamorphosed the elements of
a childhood pastime [blowing soap
bubbles]. The fragile, shimmering
globules become the shimmering
but more enduring planets—a connotation of moon and tides—the
association of water less subtle, as
when driftwood pieces make up
a proscenium to set off the dazzling
white of seafoam and billowy clouds
crystallized in a pipe of fancy."

—*Joseph Cornell (1948)*[1]

A jump into the blue—Joseph Cornell's visual alchemy—a seraphic transfiguration and *dialogue* of eye and mind. Celebration of the Great Paradox: miniature metatheaters that are exemplary art *and* metaphysical praxis; in fact, Cornell's entire opus flexes philosophical puzzles—vision beyond the retinal image, concrete visual conundrums cosmically (un)bounded; galactically transfigured cognition. "And poets and dream-ers find themselves writing things upon which metaphysicians would do well to meditate."[2] Like Gaston Bachelard, Cornell reminds us what an enchanted imagination *is*.

Joseph Cornell, who invites the philosopher's fancy, could be con-strued as an heir and modern exemplar of Emerson's transcendentalism (with regard, for example, to the lyrical ideality of nature imagery in art), and, following Marcel Duchamp (a good friend), as *after* the retinal im-age (perception to make transparent apperception). Aristotle: "For the thinking soul images are like objects of sensation . . . Hence the soul never thinks without an image . . . The thinking faculty then thinks of its forms in images . . . whenever the thinking faculty is involved with im-ages, it is moved . . ."[3] Wittgenstein: "For the play of images is admittedly the model according to which one would like to *think of thinking*."[4]

Sartre: "What happens simply is that a complete world appears to me as an image by means of the lines of the book . . ."[5] The image *is* con-sciousness, and Cornell's uncanny compositive flexions sunder the barri-ers between objects and images; their equilibration and dimensional and mosaicized placements punctuate multiplicities of paracryptically interac-tive modalities with sublimely suffused mimetic gradients. Each of his magic boxes or "habitat worlds" offers a complete cloture but an open scape—a multicontextual, paraliterary and hyperreal semiosis—an esca-lation of the harmonic resonances of eidetic tonality (totality) whose am-plification of mimeticized frequencies celebrates the inseparability of the real and unreal.

This appreciation combines an ongoing meditation on Joseph Cornell with regard to the eye and *eideolexis* by collaging some episodically ex-tended musings on two series of habitat boxes: *Celestial Map* (from the soap bubble/galactic star map series) and *Aviary* (and others from the cryptonymic parrot habitats). The parrot *sanctuaries*, giddy and enig-matic, spoof the mundanity of their immediate givens (including the per-ceiver) and, when contrasted to, and with, the transcendental expanses of Cornell's galactic scapes, create a delirious virtual antipode, a hermetic dialectic completely contained, engineered by, and residing within the parameters of a box! (Lexicality releases the ordering, scoring and se-miomimetricality of words and images, pictures and (e)scapes; and how they can be seen and *read* simultaneously.) Thinking *of thinking*—a free-floating *field* whose transassociative plays and pivots of signs and ciphers (and thereby images and ideas) evokes a fluid, hyperbolic exchange cele-brating the inscrutable permeabilities of retina and stargate.

As to the need for a philosophical appreciation of Cornell and his compositional paradoxes as exemplifications of a pure visual poeisis of sublime wonderment: cf. Maurice Merleau-Ponty's seminal essay "Eye and Mind" in *The Primacy of Perception*—a germinal ontoaesthetic pro-toanalysis of painting via aerial insights into Cezanne;[6] also Michel Fou-cault's long, prodigal, analytic semiosis of Velázquez's *Las Meninas* in *The Order of Things*, and *This Is Not a Pipe*, on Magritte. One cannot help but wonder how Merleau-Ponty might have responded to Cornell's *oeu-vre*, following his protoreflexive aesthesis of painting in "Eye and Mind," *The Prose of the World* (specifically the essay "The Indirect Language"), and the posthumously published (and unfinished) *The Visible and the In-visible*, certainly among the finest phenomenological ontopolemics of eye, envisagement, vision and (ap)perception's reflexively intertwining axes, noetic and concrete . . . Why not engage a (mock) metaanalysis, *but in the parrot terrain*, to sketch an ontology of visual paradox, rebuses and conundrums, where the ironic perchings, duplicitous placements and avian posturings (e.g., *Aviary*) are contrasted with starkly nonsequitur ambient *accoutrement* (racks of miniature drawers, clocks, preserved pages of old posters, placards and antiquated books, parched antique theatrical memorabilia, tight wire spirals, silver rings, string, coils, corks, etc.) to transform the paraliteral into metareflexive presentifications of *tableaux vivants* (and tableaux *of* tableaux: double reliefs and sprung vistas duplicated by virtual removes—gradient displacements with elegant slippages), into consummate, farcical *fables* supporting interlevitated compositional conundrums. Merleau-Ponty: "What interests us in these famous analyses is that they make us aware of the fact that any theory of painting is a metaphysics . . ."⁷

A categorical paradox: Cornell isn't "officially" a painter or sculptor, but, alternatively, an alchemical poet of the imagination, adept at shy, sly ontolexical puns. He creates hallowed habitats, magically charged ambients, specular tableaux, charmed idylls and *secret* scapes opening onto, and outwardly toward, galactic vistas—hermetic, lyrically mysterious and uncannily, even supernaturally charged. In his inimitable transference(s) of materials (found memorabilia; bygone relics; delicate, poignant objects; chipped paint; granulated or vermiculated wood; clay pipes; colored, prismatic cocktail glasses, etc.), the dancing dialectical counterpoints between real and unreal intimate and reflex hypervirtual perspectivities (perspectives of, and within, perspectives). Virtuality becomes synonymous with "blowing soap bubbles . . . the dazzling white [of] seafoam and billowy clouds." His ballet homages, too, surprise with their elegant realization that a solitary spectator just might happen upon a splendorous private spectacle, an intimate encounter that bestows poetic vastation. A beguiling sleight of hand (and sleight of eye) whimsically informs the nonsequitur slippages between configurative (dis)placements of scrupulously arranged, exquisitely selected materials that inscribe their tactile alignments with deft strategic cloture and magical finesse, and reverberate like the resonant overtones of effervescent metaphysical puzzles. This bemusement heightens the transpositional play of fascinating, intricately decoyed dimensional shifts spanning geometry and cosmology that camouflage the intervallic keys, arcane liberation and crystalline transferences of *illumined* seeing.

The eye dances over Cornell's prescient visual conundrums in order to scan and scavenge the covert moves implicit between interstitial gradients connecting expanses that open and vibrate *between* dice, goblets, cordial glasses, star maps, suspended rings, clay pipes, shards and yellowed samples of antique bibliophilia, globes, etc. Their enigmatically subliminal actions sanction the co(s)mic disclosure of the wor(l)d's secret substrates in high exotic relief, overlaying the lyrically arcane with schematically eccentric, almost surreally dissociative juxtapositions reminiscent of incandescent dreams. Some examples: *Habitat Group for a Shooting Gallery* (1943) contains four colorfully plumed parrots on multileveled wall perches, each with appliqué numbers: 78, 23, 43, 12; *Untitled (The Hotel Eden)* (1945), connects a string from the parrot's mouth to a framed box-within-a-box of tightly encoiled concentric circles, a transposed juxtaposition suggesting a secret alliance with a purely epigrammatic, conceptual dynamo; *Untitled (Parrot and Butterfly Habitat)* (c. 1948) features a parrot with its back to the viewer, looking coyly, quizzically and nonchalantly over its shoulder, while juxtaposed in the adjoining compartment is a tall, transparent tank of exquisite butterflies suspended in hyperborean flight; *Grand Hotel Semiramis* (1950) contains a single wound coil and a second coil fragment extending from the parrot's head and beak; *Aviary* houses a parrot perched within a recessed compartment surrounded on three sides by racks of miniature drawers, with a curiously placed coil poised beside its mouth, as if the parrot were echoing or conversing with its invisible *other*, intimating further its own tacit or silent voice or the collusive symbiotic contour of such a potency; *Untitled* (1948–50) fixates a cartoon parrot placed amongst several banks of clocks that belies making some seemingly definitive, but nonetheless silently incalculable, heady "statement" about "time" (fools all?); *Toward the "Blue Peninsula"* (1951–52) reveals an empty habitat cage with open window, blue sky, sprung lair, suggesting liberation, escape, desertion, flight; *Isabelle/Dien Bien Phu* (1954) places a cartoon parrot under a broken glass cover as if splintered by gunshot and sniper penetration (a shooting gallery?), with splattered paint (blood) on the background; *Untitled (Hotel Beau Séjour)* (1954), whose interior is lined with the aged yellow hotel placards of yesteryear and also with a ring, perch, and cork sphere lying on the ground, covets an implicit alignment and indubitable certainty of an *as yet* undecipherable hypothecation.

Assembly-line parrots—the breakthrough of repetition techniques (before Nevelson, Rauschenberg, Warhol, etc.): replicating squares, insigniated boxes, multiply reproduced portraits, found trophies—coins, rings, marbles, drawers, clay pipes, spirillae, rarified nature images—as *re*collectable (re)iterations—the virtualized iterations of reiteration too as paraocular echos: seeing beyond sight. -Imbricated details: rough-hewn edges, aged cracking paint, chipped or crumbling surfaces . . . *tactilized seeing.* Metaflexions of collaged elements too, transfigured and illuminated: assemblage made reflexive, "constructivist constructions."

Exquisitely poised, poignantly arrested (esse)scapes—spectral image valences thrown into theatrical relief by purposely concealed or deflected pictorial coefficients whose positionalized latitudes enhance *inter-* and *trans*similitudes—enchanted scenes (alchemy for the virtual eye) suggesting and simulating a site like that seen through an imaginary celestial telescope. The soap bubble series flexes hyperdimensional, cosmically resplendent scapes: *Untitled (Soap Bubble Set)* (1936) presents a background with a detailed classical illustration of a moonscape labeled "Carte geographique de la Lune"; *Soap Bubble* (1936) displays clay pipes in various positions against lacquered pages from rare books (intersection of reading and dreaming); *Untitled (Solar Set)* (1956–58) sports a hanging "sun" (a suspended, upside-down cup with the decal of a fiery mythological face) placed amidst rings suspended on a rod above a line of five cocktail goblets or cordial glasses containing colored marbles— imbibing, by proximity, vectorial transferences and equatorial exchanges, the intoxication of cosmicity; *Untitled (Phases de la lune)* (1957–59); *Sun Box* (1956) contains a backdrop picture inset of planetary rings, creating an immense cosmic scape behind a spherical cork ball; *Untitled (Space Object Box)* (1958) with the correlated figurations of cosmic-astronomical animals: dog, giant serpent, giraffe; *Birth of the Nuclear Atom* (1960) with molecular-like, minutely patterned, speckled and particalized circles. Sartre: "To be able to imagine, it is enough that consciousness be able to surpass the real in constituting it as a world, since the negating of the real is always implied by its constitution in the world . . . Consciousness as a fact has many other ways of *surpassing the real in order to make a world of it*: the surpassing can and should happen at first by affectivity or by actions."[8] And elsewhere: "because the whole of the real is surpassed in order to make a world . . ."[9]

Transcendent surprises and beatific perspectival transpositions (e.g., twin goblets in front of astrological mappings of the galactic firmament—scalar transferences between planets and marbles) convoke infradimensional slippages (closure by immensity: gradient correlatives telemimeticized by fantastic contrasts and intrasymbolical shifts between different natural orders, scales, objects, pictures and virtualized image valences), which necessitate, in turn, that the perceiver's eye(s) engage composites of congealing mosaics by scanning and (re)assembling apperceptive transferences from secret image repertoires (a head classically sprung from a white wooden shard, glasses and rings against the starry celestial firmament, etc.). -Mirrors placed at odd angles around obstructed sight lines yield multiple, transactional perspectives—multiplying vistas, e.g., a parrot concealed and revealed only through, and by, mirror reflexions. -Compositional coups, transfigur(at)ed idea(l)s, optical tropes: *sheer* enchantment (and by ornithological contrast: and the owl boxes—mysterious, chthonic epiphanies; haunting, gothic reflections).

The irrepressibly exact interpression of harmonies, qualities, textures and color schemes galvanizes televisual volleys whose axial provocations elicit silent ontical queries, paralexical probes, novel idea(l)s, sublime connexions: cosmic insights (cursive carriers) that merge with image valences whose mimetic impact is reflexive of tomes (discursive redemption). Also, fretting these philosophical transparencies recollects Susanne K. Langer's insight that artistic composition parallels Freud's dreamwork, but here as ontoaesthetic, psychotropistic clues with the simultaneous cohesion and dispersion of imagistic and structural isomorphisms, oneirically transfigured. (By analogy, some unusually vivid dreams can be easily recollected to become mental art works, virtual interior eidetic displays.) Cornell's visionary breakthrough unifies art and ontology—*makes* ontology art. Sartre: "The problem is therefore extremely different: the object of the image differs from the object of perception in that it has its own space, whereas there exists an infinite space which is common to all perceived objects . . ."[10] (Object and image: mercurial differentials with intraexchangeable valence transpositions.)

The galactic Cornell: virtual infinitivities reflected and reflexed through the sublime calibration of interdigitated details. Each meta-theatrical box is informed by sublime compositional leverages whose plastic analogues operate behind a galactic matrix of supralogical similitudes. Their noetic axes spring paralexical visual parameters congealed by the cloture of the figurative and configurative, image and symbol, sign and cipher, and release crystalline mimetic gradients bestowing a *metathetics of illumined seeing*. Also, these mystically impenetrable virtual space scapes exceed and supercede their containment in and by a box, creating ricocheting *infinitivitites* (microminiaturized interstitialities)—the sense and bounty of limitlessly "sprung" totalities. Their concatenated vortexes, disembodied vectors and supraspacialized ambient reflexions are analogous perhaps to that inimical relationship reflected (and deflected) by, between and beyond temporality and duration; then (in a double movement) between duration and timelessness.

Parrots (as mimetic sages) act as doubles—and *double agents!*—they become doubly reflexive, slyly ironical and impassively expressive while wryly mimicking humans at *loaded* removes; con artists and jesters all! And the indubitably mimical reflex is caught in a bind: the parrot's eye and gaze (not *not* the same!) instigate a tacit house of mirrors effect (in the viewer) whose reciprocating reflections become *your* eye (mind), seeing *your* eye (mine) *seeing the parrot seeing you, and seeing the parrot seeing you seeing it (seeing you seeing yourself, seeing seeing,* etc.—deliciously and deliriously deceptive minted ontical metaphors mined (*mimed*) recursively as doubly sprung reflexions (alchemical *currency*: recursivity—a double scursis). Here God has facetiously turned himself into an ersatz parrot, who becomes, in turn, an "absolute" proxy in Cornell's felicitously farcical fancy! Jacques Barzun: "Darwin himself was bothered by the eye, which needs so many separate parts neatly put together before it can see."[11] And elsewhere: "Think of the eye, too busy to see how it performs its own seeing..."[12] ("[B]ecause the whole of the real is surpassed in order to make a world..." might also be parsed "because the whole of the real is surpassed in order to make of *it* a world"—the created *beyond* the created.)

The *(g)lance* of the parrot's gaze might recollect Wittgenstein's rejoinder: "And nothing *in the visual field* allows you to infer that it is seen by an eye . . ."[13] Also consider Jacques Lacan's cryptonymic shard: "the (c)ode of the Other" might be evoked to hint at an unconscious obliquity that belies the function of art: the themics of illumined ontothelectics—being's ruse (i.e., being no one—an ode to disappearance, at least on the part of the subject!). And an (c)ode too attuned to the optical closure of realms—the "same old story": forfeiture by animals, beings, elements, elementals, spirits, devas, deity, etc.

Cornell's redoubled magic unravels (and unreveals) the concealment perpetuated by the deflection of artfully staged appearances—the constructivist's ruse—etherealized assemblages whose vision involves ideality transpositions that delightfully scramble (and bilocate) concatenated image combines that t(r)ip the re(p)lay of their spatially isomorphized registers by intraprecessing presentational principles that surpass and transcend their modes, methods and staged strategies. His boxes mosaicize interleveraged axes as his collages perform surprising planar and isomorphic transferences through the disembodied valences of imaginal transformation (cf. Husserl: the ontology of reflexivity is the real *subject*). But then, Cornell's ontic resolutions involve a fusion rendevous that revolves around the invisible, imagined reciprocity between the real and unreal whose ethos extends into the *hyperreal*. The parrot is a cavalier and natty caricature *of* a caricature, reminding us how we, too, are but masks, disguises, decoys and foils to and for each other and to ourselves (certainty as the revelation of the unreal, recalling Nietzsche: "A sage too is a fool . . ."[14]). Its habitat is a given, closed, confined, framed space, a lair (liar) bordered by vertical racks of drawers, many partially and mysteriously open just enough to peer into, revealing children's tiny accoutrement: dice, jacks, balls, marbles, whose di*splay* is a surreptitiously reflexed invitation to make perception an enthralling game of make believe.

William James: "A successful piece of mimicry gives to both bystanders and mimic a peculiar kind of aesthetic pleasure. The dramatic impulse, the tendency to pretend one is someone else, contains this pleasure of mimicry as one of its elements. Another element seems to be a peculiar sense of power in stretching one's own personality so as to include that of a strange person. In young children this instinct often knows no bounds . . ."[15] The parrot is the imitative animal par excellence, precisely because of the elevated irreality of its (implicit) "voice," which has substance and (double) credence only in the duplicitous curvature and dissimulating closure of man's, and who thus becomes a deceptive double mime (dopple ((dopey)) mind, mined)—loaded dice—*loaded metaphor(s)*. The parrot also becomes a mercurial ontolexic cipher for the human double—and thus (presto) the visual made audible, a paravocal duplicative—*redoubtable* transference (and redactable, too), bestowing by sight the multiple reciprocal indices of reflexed ontical metaphors. (Paravocal: the parrot as its own Other.) Parrots thus become subversive proxies for self, shadow, double, Other, etc., by whimsically mirroring their sportive, imitative flexions, (re)doubling the *subject's* own mimesis. (Slippery prestidigitation—shadow and double can invert, and transvert, reality and irreality, and one another.) In *Aviary*, the locution of the spirillaic coil next to the single perched parrot implicates the space of the *Other's* mouth, cadencing a double *double* play (the parrot as proxy for the duplication *of the* duplication of the Other, and the Other's double too) . . . an official sublime prankster mimic par excellance escalating the flurry of paravocal similitudes that flagrantly fly in the face of (dissing) *dissimulation*, fanned by their flamboyant plumage! *The v(o)ice gives f(l)ight even when wings cannot!*

In fact, (the cipher of) the parrot's (implicit) voice replaces flight, or becomes flight's salient, silent, autonomous *frisson*. ((The Other is implicit as the double mimed, caught in the crossroads mirage of the glance by an invisibly lanced paramimetic trans(re)ference.)) And the parrot's perch, his *authorial* placement, a virtual sovereignty anchored by aerial suspension, makes these compositions ingratiatingly but deceptively engaging, deviously beguiling and ontolexically hyperactive too, for, with a tiny tic or (hallucinatory) flective tilt of head, the parrot becomes patently ironical, circumventionally and comically seditious. Here we have it at last—the parrot parroting philosophy and inaugurating a mock philosophy of *parrotodoxes*—a furtive enterprise not (not) without inimic intimations of imitation, delivered with delectably cool, seditious hyperbole, and with an acutely attenuated, *fugitive* irony. (Here Cornell wears the fool's cap with the prestidigitated flourish of the mage.) The parrot as an ontological prophylactic, too, on probation: duplicity *against* duplicity itself! That ring emphatically suspended in front of its eye lances the uncanny alchemical clincher, the ruse of the wink (a knowing, almost invisible gesture)—a subterfuge conundrum embodying nonetheless a paralexical authenticity by the implicit absence, removal and solitary confinement (we're all parrots—conditioned, caged, habituated and over-extended by dissembling, mostly by words put in our mouths). The *theme* must be confinement and revelation!

Biting off more than one can chew and . . . *chewing!*—that's how the wor(l)d conspires against itself anyway! And am I overhearing someone? "The parrots are discoursing 'about' the plenitude of n o t h i n g n e s s and immutability." Cornell's whimsical eclat is artisanely alchemistic, his vision, seraphic; optical perchings and structurated lensings scry realms behind and over the visible, using the representational like a magic foil or pivot to eschew (*esse*chew—chewing essences) the transformations of its givens (inaugurating perceptual *metatropisms*). Cornell belies his co(s)mic duty—reminding us of the (para)poetic mystery and imagistic flexions of the logos—*its* eideolexic junctions that figurate, fissionate and punctuate indelible articulatory modes with subtle semiotrop(h)ic ranges; these picturated schematas accrue consummate amplitudes syn(an)ony-mous with *poiesis*. His works speak over and under a transcending dead-pan muteness (and whose transfiguring mutabilities become archly para-mimetic), a silent speech that also *moves* over, through and above an implicit, profound solitude, veridical remoteness and truncated silence—virtuality abbreviated by plurivalent transpositions that echo and bound over the shrill and thrilling, classically chromatic continua of a wonder rainbow. Cornell invented a lyrical concreteness for the pliant, transpris-matic plays of the fantastical, and, like the Symbolist poets, discovered the means to actualize, positionalize and (re)modalize a polyvalent poetic plastique—the masque-like theatricalization of (orders of) imageries raised to a sublime metaphysical stature, inaugurating a larger onto-allegorical enterprise, a metalexical dialexis, a double read whose sublimi-nally subversive schematic cant is innocently transfigured by *illusive fac-ticities* (childhood materials, delicate objects, magical scenes, fleeting signs, oblique references and rarified images), making transparent the ax-ial idealities of the figurative/reiterative.

This of course can only be an *intimation* of a parrot prolegomenon for a stuttering, surrogate semioanalysis of . . . the transfigured imagination belied by the itinerary of those enticing, partially opened drawers, arous-ing curiosity (categories? receptacles? concealed realms? imbricated spaces?)—intimate repositories of secret passage, telegraphed space, talis-matic objects, enchanted ideas, all saturated with far memories. The mnemonic miniaturization and reiterated condensations of space and suffused spatiality (not *not* two differentiations) provide an interesting parallel, too, to Marcel Duchamp's miniaturized "suitcase" museums— the scalar reduction of art works into condensed enciphered emblems intensifies their tautly wound, bound torsion of signs—what Gaston Bachelard converted into a protoanalysis of containment in the first part of *The Poetics of Space* and later folded over into a polemical poetics of immensity, rendering a blueprint exegesis for a phenomenological excursion through the esthetics of hyperdimensionalized domains. (The reflexions of multiple perspectives concatenate the matrices and frequencies of *inter*dimensionalities activated by the composite manifolds of constructivism's fusion of image/isomorph/space/plane/object/sign/symbol, etc.—a paradox physicists identify as "wormholes.")

It seems (seems?) that even within Cornell's vast repertoire of the imagination, (phenomenologically reflexed) vision becomes mimetically transmutable; eidetics breaks through to an *eideothetics*—seeing embodies virtual transparencing techniques—seeing that is more than sight. The roving eye's quickened autonomy *suspends* even its own (pre)conditionalities and habits and thereby reflexes and intentionally entrains a highly versatile verisimilitude of transschematic resonances, binding transcendental vectors and magical overtones together to see (the correlatives of) seeing in-itself (and in the act of seeing; facticity *hyper*hypostatized). Here eideolexis performs reciprocally calibrated double(s) operations as paradigmatic removes that shift the visual parameters to reflexivize *reading*, making it parallel with, and transparent to, seeing (and seeing to itself). These secret practices and hermetic apertures thus cathect a language of dreams, and perhaps above and below their numinal thresholds (the touchstone of an informing oneiric sense, and of a primal eideotropic intuition) is inscribed this entirely realized, resplendently occluded mythos of appearances. These double actions (flexions, actually, since their tiny mimetic impulses activate and cathect the gaze) reduplicate their presentational impact by deferred virtual removes that recoil on the viewer while apprehending the vibration of their parasympathetic sightlines. For a fleeting moment the eye is permitted to penetrate the cosmogonic grain, where the contours of visibility are inscribed, tracing and retracing the nimbuses of essences that arouse the metatropisms of figuration (the "hem" of the visible universe flexes the resonances of its invisible "hum"). Hence a *double* reflexivity of phenomena emerges in the retinal amplitudes of this illumined transfiguration, penetrating ontic strata, presences and paranomonic regions (drawers, hermetic crannies, mythic creatures, presences, animal powers, ghosts, zodiacal alignments, galactic transpositions, etc.), thus suspending doxa, too, whose lateralities simultaneously stretch, bound, interprecess and penetrate multiple modes, orders, registers, codes and dimensions.

Joseph Cornell's invitation to engage the philosopher's fancy attests to a cosmic grace. The X in and of the eye, lancing the blind spot, is equated with, and implied by, the ring placed in front of the parrot's eye, which also accomplishes *an anagrammatic framing of the frame* (EYE = i.d.(e)-eid-die-eon-eidolon). Here's the ontic "goof": the parrot (destabilizing themic pivot in the twenty or so habitats of the series, the last being an empty aviary with a wide open window signifying escape) is nonetheless (still) watching us watching (it ((id))) watching! Being is being surveilled by *this* secret agent, a purposeful sham impos(i)tor provocateur ("goof" indeed—a double-sprung reflexivity, nonetheless).

The parrot becomes the uncannily pivoting *cipher*, the animal power that activates and instigates a sublime (subliminal) paradox, becoming ontocryptically the ruse of its own selfsame encipherment, as in those featured tableaux where the bird is situated too presciently behind the suspended ring (emblem of eternity) or poised behind or alongside the encoiled spiral (which frames the piercing eye that appropriates all, which, in turn, unwittingly concretizes these interdimensional transferences: the final mystery of passage, flight, transformation and *disappearance*). The symmetrically placed wound coil protomimetically releases the bound torsion of its enigmatic placement as it suspends its intercalated "coefficients" of signage, bestowing speechless clues that are nonetheless logophobic commentaries on appearances configured by paralexical sightlines! The extended filaments intertwining its imaged metaphors thus dialectically (and diatropically—by optical tropisms) pivot panoplies of transassociative compossibilities between eye and ear, seeing and hearing, visibility and invisibility in the direction of holy *he(a)res(a)y*—the heresy of the ruse (muse). Sturm clearance—with protean alertness the parrots' *hearsay* becomes hear-easy: the eye first sees lightning before the ear subsequently is seized by thunder. Here, logicality subverts the strategies of its own subterfuge, ma(s)king itself behind rueful foils that cumu-

latively (re)assemble (the ground) by nonsequitur and concatenated
(dis)plays (displacements) of imaginated contiguities whose paradoxical-
ity purges the eye of its enigmas—secrets wrapped in layered sheaths
round and wound, bound and unbound by pivotal focusing *flexions*—the
immanent (w)ink of the parrots' eye confirms this starkly liberating *ges-*
ture. The lyricism of Cornell's work doesn't prevent a conceptual gnosis,
either (the lair is sprung).

The intrigues underlying (t)his private game provoke the creation of a
spontaneous eidetic (t)ide and (e)ideolexic bridge that (re)connects
praxis and theory (with a semiomimetic exegesis and optholexic *theorem-*
ics, after Bachelard and Merleau-Ponty): a phenomenological reflexion of
the imagination that appropriates transparent conjunctions between any
given pairs of riven opposites through the deflection of their protoreflexive constellations—galactically extended intrapressions of signs, clues,
sights, imaged processes—languaged decoys whose mercurially paramimetic play of sign(al)s and ciphers pl(a)ys a perennially elusive *pas de*
deux with poetic ethos, a rapture (and rupture) of the sublime, attesting
too to the intertwining axes of conception and ideation.
   The surprise, (w)edge, and wonderment is that we are enabled to see
eye and mind visually reflexed by such paradigmatic ((*parrotdogmatic*))
puzzles that prove inseparable from their virtualization and (pr)axis: be-
hold this other (and thought's Other) *thinking*! I'm thinking again of *Avi-*
ary, with the spiral spring coiled enigmatically in front of the parrot's
keenly beguiling gaze, suggesting a kind of ratiocinating cartoon gestalt
whose tendered immediacy is reminiscent of boxed-in balloon dialogues
and funny book analogues—suspending more than its uncanny *signator*—
and, rather, by inaugurating a hyperscape raised to active performance.
Signs and ciphers explode sight, image, mimesis and v(o)ice, the haunted
and enchanted, the real and unreal, the visible and invisible in the soap
bubble opera, journeying though the extended realms of the microminiaturized, hypermimetic pluriverse, cracking the codes of visuality and literality (which must precede and supercede both visibility and logos),
perception and apperception, and spatiality itself to set up axes, pivots,
paradoxes, parapolarities. Pipe dreams? (Reality itself is a pipe dream!)
   In *Celestial Map* the symmetrically placed twin goblets hyperflex an
echo (re)duplication syndrome of replicating vistas, arrested televirtual-

ized firmaments, dissimulating proportional placement facings ratios (duplication of doubles, too); empty glasses with die at the bottom instead of spirits displace even cherries and planets; a co(s)mic conviviality toasts the intoxication of vision and vision's rapture; vision's *plenitude*, where even the purity of emptiness is offset, and renewed too perhaps, by loaded dice—loaded sights charged with charm and chicanery as *agents* of chance, and thus as agents bartering the universe's duplicitous fate (face). (Destiny remains the secret agency that guarantees Cornell's inner esthetic cohesion.) William James: "We may, on the other hand, construct a nervous system potentially adapted to respond to an infinite variety of minute features . . . We can never be sure that its equilibrium will be upset in the appropriate direction . . . In short, a high brain may do many things, and may do each of them at a very slight hint. . . . The performances of a high brain are like dice thrown forever on a table. Unless they be loaded, what chance is there that the highest number will turn up oftener than the lowest? . . . Can consciousness increase its efficiency by loading its dice?"[16]

Cornell, in figuring a "low brain" to catalyze the "high brain" in the *parrot's* panopticon, has indeed loaded the dice, upped the ante, spurring metatropisms of metaphoric image valences inaugur(at)ing the lodes of extended encipherization. -The ring (the circle concretized) extends the amplitude of spiral and circumference; thus speech and its double prefigure subject, agent and Other and become hyperflexed as plastic intimations, as symbiotically protean archetypical symbols inscribed *within the inscription* of totality and unity. The ring's presence (existential emblem of the arrested parrot gaze) is contrasted against these synergizing unitive gestalten and contraposed to the moveable "abacus" of silver metal rings in *Celestial Map,* whose inferred incremental positional markers delineate virtual placements on the overhead rod like a mysterious, unspecified metric gauge. Such tacit strategic transferences engage a double mimetic action of vistas projecting *into and out of* themselves surreptitiously and simultaneously—even simulating their simulacra (double removes ((of double removes))) of reciprocally mutating, telemimetrically coactive micro and macro exchanges (of semblances, proportions, ratios, scales, orders, codes, meanings, paradoxes, etc.)—the intoxication of project(ion)ed wor(l)ds extending the registers of (e)scape, scope and scale,

the outsides of the insides and the insides of the outsides—tran-
sposi(ti)ng proximity and distance exchange ratios while dynamically in-
terprecessing a devious dialectic of delivery and perception (deception):
seeing as beatitude and benediction . . .

(1987; 1992; 2002)

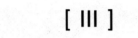

(Excerpts)

The idea for this piece actually occurred in 1972 while writing *Metagexis*. Instead of an autobiography, an *Autobiopathy*—after Zen (and semiotics) the *subject* . . . is supposed to *disappear*. Although I make notes and keep notebooks, I don't keep a "writer's diary" per se, hence this began as an open "ground" to try out, and write out, experiences and recollections in order to uncover their underlying formatory ideas. Since there is both a writer (W) and a dancer/choreographer (D), WHY NOT HAVE BOTH OF THEM TALK TO, AND INTERVIEW, ONE ANOTHER . . .

D: What are you doing now?

W: Writing an *Autobiopathy*—what else!

D: An *AUTOBIOPATHY*? What's that?

W: Well, everyone writes an autobiography; but this is an *Autobiopathy*.

D: Oh; perfect explanation. Is the subject the *disappearance* of the subject, *again*?

W: Uh-huh; and more than that, too . . .

D: *More*?

W: Yes, it's possible to write (ride) over oneself—we're just a collection of processes.

D: Oh, what an optimist! And another doubly reflexive entendre retort, too . . . The *technics* of disappearance?

W: Rather a writing out, over, and through experience—a survey of the transactional reapportionment of the subject's interprecessionary bioenergetic, perceptual, and cognitive processes.

D: Sounds like multimedia—not only the mixing of forms, but the mixing of processes, too . . . The dancer, likewise, tries to dance over himself (recollecting Nietzsche).

W: Writing can place a subject between "brackets" or under virtual x-rays . . . The problem (and challenge) is to move the ego past itself (i.e., subjectivity per se) so the autooperation (or synchronous remodalization) of these bioenergetic and psychophysical processes prehend and apprehend themselves, mirror and reveal a larger, holistic "circuitry." And a note about the word *interprecessionary*—I discovered it in R. Buckminster Fuller's two-volume *Synergetics;* it's a very useful, systemic pivot.

D: In an analogous way dancing reflexes the elements, referencing a larger totality, too. Like swimming—while one's body is submerged in water the intraleveraged equilibria of the double, elemental reciprocity gives it suspension from gravity and an orientation to another kinetic terrain: the watery. Similarly, while dancing one moves on fluidic ethers, electromagnetic currents and space circuits. "Dancing is writing in space"—and since *writing* is coextensive with all of language, so an Autobiopathy can be the merging of self with a greater field and flow?

W: Yes, and insight into sentience revolves around the f(r)iction or illusion that we, as subjects, are separate—appearing, experiencing, then (eventually) . . . disappearing (which one can do from moment to moment, too—transposing the metaphor of passage). Each cell has sentiency, is vitally alive, participates in awareness, and, like language, precedes and supersedes both perception and existence. We *think* that we learn, control, manipulate or fix language; but language is culturally and genetically an in(ter)dependent (meta)entity—its combinatory possibilities mean processes outrun ontology. Writing is not contained by a subject, but exceeds it; language too is a disembodied entity, and like a reservoir, potentiated and autogenic, i.e., beyond the parameters of any individuated intelligence. Language, no matter how accurately it mirrors mind, nature or world, is also autoreferential; grammar, style and rhetoric create a self-referential, synchronistic, reflexive continuum. And the same with dance—the intensity and (implicit) immensity of movement transport one past (one's) identity,1unused unused merging with a greater (sense of) being. The writer's fascination lies, in part, with the autonomy of language that in turn informs and connects all processes and procedures of perception and experience. Art is a means of emptying or refocusing the subject's *field*. And one doesn't know *what* one thinks until one asks oneself, or doesn't really know it (perhaps) until one *interviews* oneself, or writes it out. The game thus involves a double reflexivity.

b

D: -Or, of course, until it is danced out (or painted, sculpted, filmed, etc.), i.e., reflected through a virtual form. Likewise, there are some things that can be discovered only by dancing and that cannot be stated explicitly (or discursively), but that obliquely inform—at the margins and edges of b(B)eing (e.g., the mythic, spirit realms). Dancing is riding through space—all space; space is not only three-dimensional. Dancing takes one beyond what one can know, or what knowing *is*; then it becomes enjoyable puzzling (through dialogue) what it is, or means, or what its correlates might be in, with and *through* words.

W: Writing that concerns and engages me, though not always about dance, comes about because of dancing in the larger context of the ontology of motion—movement of phenomena, dimensions, orders, contexts; and the motion of words, thoughts, images, associations, worked over and through experience. And though I write at a word processor, it is not until we're home and dancing that I *hear* text, check sound and rhythms, edit or tighten syntactical structures, and launch the next probe. Perhaps not until the next century will the relevance of writing and dance (i.e., transmedia bridges across disciplines and bicameral potential) be realized; we've been making case studies ... (Hence, the writer must dance and the dancer write.)

Anyway an *Autobiopathy*—how (one's) being is an intersection of ideas, issues, personas, beings ... ("All my pieces are ghost written," I've exclaimed hyperbolically on occasion.) To (double and) remove oneself so as to be a medium, to transmute the personal into art, activity, action. The *idea* of an Autobiopathy requires a technic of writing to remove (absolve? make transparent?) the subject by exploring the foundations and underpinnings of ideas that (pre)figurate the weaves of the self, and that inform its works, processes, activities and projects as transactive, semiolexic puzzles with unexpected configurations and metaconceptual matrices flexing perceptual, apperceptive and cognitive muscles.

And after all, "Writer" and "Dancer" are just *processes*, separate but interrelated—and *intra*leveraged! (So what if they ((we)) share the same body, same house, etc.!) -Ideas also "dance" interactively, intraconfigure systemically, become embodied and entrained, but they are, nonetheless, always rooted in the mind of a specific identity (analogous to the way that any dance technique is always rooted in a specific *style*, there being no *pure* dance technique). The self becomes a site or scape as well as a foil for writing so the *personal* disappears; becomes reinscribed or *recircumscribed*. (And, unlike Bataille writing on the impossibility of observing death while experiencing it, disappearance—Krishnamurti reminds us—can be a cosmic mode of meditation and be virtually observable, transforming placements of the subject through metatheoria, and reflexivity, of hyperdimensional processes.)

Metaphorically, an *autobiopsy*, like the successively generated pictures and macroscopically circular slices of a magnetic resonance imagery system (CAT scan), magnifies the inner structures and principles anterior to, and transcending, personal particulars—*auto*nomic imageries that trace the automimetic trajectories of the passages of flexions and impulses. A bioscopy of one's dances and texts; being an artist duly engages one in a series of virtual removes, and distances oneself personally and psychologically from being simply (or only) a subject—what's necessary are virtual *biopsies* of being's action and activities whose interactive contexts autosimulatively splice together and weave microviews and metaanalyse, compositing a larger field and overview. Hence, "X" is a kind of meta-, transpersonal and/or *transreferential* subject—a reflexivized (meta)entity transmuting the impulses of ego and actions of self so that identity per se is recentered, de- and reconstructed, and transformed—by intrasynaptic processes, synoptic actions, renegotiable sights and hybrid languages that intersect, and interact, with it. (Jung's clarification: the *self* orchestrates the parts and functions of body, ego, libido, etc.) This clarifies "deconstruction" to mean making transparent the processes and technics of anal-

ysis and perception (by microanalysis of word, unit and matrix), and
the reflexions of those processes supraposed in assembling a larger
whole.

D: That's what happens too when the body moves either very quickly or
very slowly—other perceptually transpersonal processes transpire.
What are your insights about the connection and differentiation of
the *cellular* and the *genetic*?

W: Well, as a dancer you know that memory is not just neurological but
extends through the cellularity of the body. At the same time, transformations in the whole organism become genetically entrained, as
the "codes" underlying behavior and knowledge accrete and modify.
Noam Chomsky's point about the transformation of language
through generations—that linguistic capacity transfers automatically
between generations—is actually a genetic statement. The child does
not have to start at the beginning (e.g., with the rules of language);
generations pass information incrementally, i.e., genetically . . . Is that
another plié you're doing?

D: Yup. Then another and *another* after that. Thank goodness you're not
a dancer and spared this daily drudgery.

W: Ha! Try the umpteen zillion textual rewrites, and you'll change your
mind.

D: Do I detect cynicism? Cynicism arises either from excess of experience or insight into the pervasive ethical deficiency of others.

W: Well, whether you know it or not, I get inspiration and ideas from
you. You're my transmitter.

D: Really? How's that? You're the one that reads. -I get all my ideas from
you.

W: My point is that if I could write what are in your dances, I'd have
more than book or treatise.

D: Well then, get busy! My point is that if I had your words for all the
movements I do I'd be a millionaire.

W: Well, keep practicing, but don't get carried away. (Why I write texts—to be *done* with a dance! And so a reader might *feel* and *sense* them long after the fact.) Dialogue and dialectic—dialogizing exercises dialectic, i.e., multiple interpenetrating logics with transposable relation(s) . . . systems and systemics. Of course this is a dialogue.

D: Well, they're (we're) not (not) separate and not *not* two . . .

W: You mean, we're not not the same person?

D: It seems to amount to the same thing—anyway, ontology *in extremis*.

W: You mean, of course, we're not *not* the same person?

D: You mean, we're not not *being being* the same person again. But let's save the lesson on Gertrude Stein, the ontologics and *ontotheletics* of grammar, for later.

W: Exactly, *grammathics* again.

D: And riddles. And what could be more fascinating than . . . grammatological riddles!

W: Practically anything, including splitting hairs . . . *or* one's identity. Because our experiences of reading and using language double the ontological factor(s) . . .

D: You mean you're the right brain in this bicameral brouhaha?

W: And you're the left hemisphere?! No, that's too literal—there are two parts and two intrapenetraing functions to perception, reading, and being an artist; one part observes and reflexes everything (even the self that observes *observation*), and the concomitantly recombinatory, intraprecessionary processes of reflexion . . .

W: Explain why you assign a complex and important role to improvisation as a basis for process dancemaking and choreography, and the development of dancers.

D: Improvisation begins as movement play and spontaneous exploration. It can also be highly structural, formal, and systemic. Though it

is more a modern dance than a balletic phenomenon, it can combine
the principles and techniques of both. Improvisation reveals the
grounds and roots of ritual, showing that dance goes even deeper
than our bones, being bonded in our genes. Dance can distinguish,
then fuse, the digital and genetic: this might be its artistic horizon
and challenge in the next century.

Ritual and improvisation: when teaching dance composition one is
continually astounded to see (even with beginning students) how
deep the sources of ritualistic response are, like a kind of primal
grammar or genetic blueprint of automatic, prescient activity—and
seemingly as integral to genes and cells as to muscle and brain, activating passages and pathways of coded mimetic transferences between
bodies, extending bioenergetic fields to realms mythic and ancestral.

Because the moving, dancing body can systematically engage con-
curring, recurring and interprecessionary rhythms, patterns, structures and perceptual tracks (built up from concatenating chains of
entrained flexions and iterative impulses), one can also learn to watch
and see the semiotropic convergences of volleys of *signal* chains
emerging into *signs* (usually first as gestures), and constellations of
signs into structures. One sees symbolic transactions of movement
phenomena in a dance continuum extending the kinetics and somat-
ics of movement before and after form per se, as dreams break the
bonds and bounds of reality and perception.

Improvisation shows how the *dance is a text*—it synergizes the elements of kinetic syntax and factors of composition (line, structure,
form, exchange, spacing, rhythm, configuration, texture, import, etc.)—
the volleying of shifting delays of signals and signs permutes and realigns the relays of contexts, transformed by the tiniest change of temporal, corporeal, muscular or spacial detail.

Even the making of a very formal and finished dance work can
involve improvisational strategies at any stage of its creation. Improvisation is artistically prestructural, as images can be prescientific.[2]
Movement itself is a motor and motive phenomenon; dance, an art.

Improvisation is more integral to (post)modern dance because its
semiolexical deployments and structural principles are more fluid,
less determined; experimentation is at its core. The ballet lexicon is
basically a closed system, though any mode of movement can catalyze

and open the parameters of any other given technique or style. Modern dance, basically an *open* system, is akin in its free-form modes to the sketching, action painting, free-verse poetry and automatic writing of the painter and writer. The liberation of forms from representation, literality, narrativity and tradition was furthered by abstraction—abstract expressionist painting in the 1950s, happenings and performance art in the 1960s.

Improvisation loosens the boundaries between form(s) and content, styles and techniques, the set and unset, the continuous and discontinuous, the symmetrical and asymmetrical—creative antinomies, indeed—*and* between the known and unknown, contained and uncontained, bound and unbound, self and other, objective and subjective, visible and invisible, motivation and intentionality, because movement connects through, across, over and around polarities, spaces, landscapes and dualities. Dance can be so spontaneous and vital (even with beginners) that it leaves the viewer bewildered—complex kinetic exchanges, sequences and passages need not be (pre)planned, organized, or set. Thus improvisation recasts hierarchical stratifications; even virtuosic movement makes the watcher's eye sweep and scan the entire space and the configurative designs interactive with the other dancers, rather than holding a centralized (i.e., egoic) focus.

For observer and audience, improvisation generates different transactional modes of *seeing*, freed from expectation, presuppositions and assumptions—the simplest as well as an unexpected move or conjunction of gestures or patterned responses can surprise, connect, resonate or explode incredulously. Seeing, doing and making *can* be transactional and align modes by autoassemblage, where responses between bodies and dancers transpire faster, it seems, than the brain can think, presenting a new terrain and challenge. Improvisation reveals the spontaneous, organic dialectics of action dance-making; it is the bridge between *process* and product.

Thus improvisation creates a site for multiply interactive processes. Where do our ideas about process originate? Undoubtedly from biology and physiology, and the fact that numerous autonomic (automatic) processes are intrapressional—digestion, sensation, breathing, circulation, respiration, reproduction, etc. The processes of improvisation project dynamically interactive, virtualized orders of imageries.

There is also a larger, more inclusive *systemic* and dialectical relationship between process(es) and system(s). The interaction of different processes composes the human biosystem. (As a choreographer I do not give dancers only specifically set, repeatable phrases, though we work toward that too, but rather pieces of phrases and steps that *they* have to recombine and work into the ongoing development of permutable structural schemas. These automatically build up volleys of steps and patternation options that can be reassembled and reordered to operate as rapid volleys of signs—as in-process indicators and recomposable clues for ways to select and order an ongoing dance's materials. This assembling is or makes a kinelexic grammar of dancemaking possibilities.) Language too moves between systems of categorical differentiations and schematic orders (typologies) of combinatory and assimilable spatial topologies. It is the idea of the matrix conjoining several compossible and simultaneous processes, modular components, body logics and digital rhythms that allows for further system(at)ic transformations, and that points to a new compositional paradigm.

Improvisation can reflect, *reflex* and make the totality of human experience(s) transparent, as well as its own factors (of experience or motivity—symbolic or structural, also able to mirror its own *pre*-structuralities, rhythmic conflations, etc.). Improvisation can double back on itself to fold the accretions of the moving body into larger contexts. Improvisation shows that movement and dance can be self-reflexive of phenomena, mirroring essences. One need not start with "a" structure and construct or compose "a" dance—doing and making are reciprocally inseparable. This points to a kind of futuric ontology—dancing is *being being* seeing. Shiva is *before* the creation of the wor(l)d.

Some dancers breakthrough to genuine kinaesthesia, so spatial apperception creates fluent, fluid meshes between motivity, balance, form, alignments of corporeal and spatial isomorphisms, the harmonies of transspatiality ("geometry/typography") and the further ranges of transformative possibilities tempered by gradients of qualities plastic and/or emotive. Usually a dancer following rote choreography need never bother with decision making in performance (as Isadora Duncan did), nor with conceptual concerns (and concepts shift as our facts, feet, eyes and experiences change, realign or gather momentum); the entire (pr)axis of the (post)modernist matrix finds that its principles, lexical pivots, conceptual premises, structural and stylistic boundaries are indeed transactional—connecting forms, processes, impulses, flexions and realms with other disciplines.

Improvisation constantly explores (modes of) *compossibility* and moves between and through the first and last dance. There is comprehensive *systemic* play generating a continuum of spontaneously synchronistic processes, and dance invites semiolexical transpositions (and in Merce Cunningham's instance, engineered, formally repeatable synchronistic processes, arrived at by chance procedures!). Coordinations of discontinuous, automatic motor sequences process raw passages of signals patterned as multiplex responses that weave (inter)texturally with the steady gain of momentum. These semiotropic coordinations congeal into manifolds of concrete signs—readable indicators that make transparent identifiable, eidetically sprung traceries of line, design, structure and gesture that coalesce symbolically as import, impact, resonance, and meaning, and reflexive, too, of natural forces, energy fields and phenomena: rivers, eddies, whirlpools, waterfalls, vortexes, winds, currents, branchings, tributaries, etc.

The postmodern axis—or dance after Merce Cunningham—involves the (self-)reflexivity of movement principles and dance structures, breaking through to autonomous schematologies combining simultaneous logics and interactive body grammars. That these can be systemically open, observable and coordinative *in and through the acts of* doing, deciding, making, dancing and seeing is akin to the cognitive acumen necessary for creative problem solving, collectively experiential. (The idea that form as *performance* can be inclusive of interactive processes was polemically made explicit and extended by John Cage's pioneering, experimental music; in *Silence* he says why worry about structure—it's always there!)

There are motor-kinetic, tactile-somatic, and semiomimetic body grammars composing kinetic registers and kinelexic gradients—while reading, watching dance, film or television, even while talking, walking, thinking and seeing. The schematic complexes of "codes" that inform and navigate a dance's (or group's) course, and that coordinate the multiple dexterities of patterns, steps and configurations, are both sub- and supraliminal. A dance can also incorporate written, spoken or projected texts with spoken or recorded voice, (electronic) music, projections and film/video to program simultaneous (and sometimes synaesthetic) processes. Even disjunctive and discontinuous processes can build up new senses of continuity and totality. Yet just *how* the intense enactments of impulses and responses, the concatenation of rhythms and qualities by one or more dancing bodies, have analogues, axes and indexes grammatical as well as grammatological points to a further programmatic threshold utilizing multiple logics and pluralistic modes of intraprecessioning signal-sign assemblage. (Grammatological = orders of sign registers, schematologies of synchronous and asynchronous structurations. In the post-Cunningham, minimalist dance, simple everyday movement strategies structured in concrete, usually very repetitive and accumulative patterns, often with considerable systematic density, showed that themic and motific materials can be formally and contextually self-referential, and hence systemic within the parameters of its self-contained formal deployments.)

Meaning can be motor-mimetic and involve the play of gradients throughout an energy continuum; the eye can scan transliteral, kinelexic correlations and motoric-motive congruences, as well as polysemic structural schematologies involving multimedia principles and projections techniques, and interconceptual breakthroughs can eventuate in, and synthesize, new entrained orders of intrasensory ratios, logics and body grammars. Merce is the originary structuralist, and the diverse postmodern endeavors that ensued (which really expanded the complexity of the highly refined, balletically oriented lexicon) prepared the ground for a grammatology of performative modalities and performance techniques.

These kinelexically enhanced, programmatic extensions suggest a horizon of other *digital* (and *digitated*) formats whose principles are reflexively and compositively analogical; these extensions apprehend, then apperceive, further logicalities of electronic locomotion and passage, transversing the virtualities of space. This is proximally experienced in normal daily life when trying to unscramble the jumbled, partial and puzzling recollections of dreams, assaying their fractured asymmetrical sequences, dislocated transitions, or disjunctive juxtapositions of elements and orders with actual referents and intimations of concrete meanings. Dancing, too, is like scrying with crystal ball or palimpsest.

W: Before Richard Kostelanetz left for a vacation in 1991 he lent me the only copy of a manuscript for his forthcoming anthology of articles and criticism about Merce Cunningham, *Dancing in Space and Time*, which had just been readied for the publisher, and he included my long "Space Dance and the Galactic Matrix: Merce Cunningham, An Appreciation." While proofing the galleys for publication by A Cappella Press, I (re)realized the expansive, all-encompassing endeavor necessary to develop a terminology suitable for an aesthetic overview of his work required a pivot to connect the modern and postmodern. (I worked on my essay during a three year period—1988–91.) Just as there's a kind of transformative quantum jump moving a dance from rehearsal studio to stage, so too when moving an essay from manuscript to printed page. This was the first piece I wrote on the word processor . . .

D: And that *I* began typing on a temp job at Dean Witter Reynolds in the World Trade Center, luckily a do-nothing office job with plenty of "down" time! What readily amazed and became unexpectedly useful about writing on word processors were the time and labor-saving electronic options of cutting, moving, replicating, aligning and altering the text, which lets the writer readily learn editing techniques and spares retyping a piece in its entirety for each successive draft.

W: I started with that single, first paragraph. Like a kind of virtual replication it suggestively split into a second and succeeding paragraphs. I resist writing from outlines and choose to organize my thoughts by assembling preliminary notes, fragments, possible sketches and lists of issues. Sometimes the words come very quickly, requiring shorthand or, like a surgeon, very fast fingers. Writing is also cinematographic—contexts accrue without placement and scenes are "shot"

out of order; editing constructs continuity, focusing disparate logics
and senses. Until I actually begin to write, I'm not sure how contexts
will configure their specific wording, structure or the grain of meanings, even, materializing in the process what I do *not* know, since
hunches and the fleshing out of vague innuendo are part of any
writer's compulsive fascination; one follows the *sense(s)* of a context
or trails of an idea. Sketching a piece also begins to collect appropriate words and phrases, juggling and juxtaposing their possible syntax-
ing to (re)focus these emerging senses. The necessary modes of constant free and cross association intermix by throwing nets through
the grids and depths of mental topologies, thereby extending the parameters of word, sentence and the structures of conception, letting
eye and mind range and syncopate and giving a buzz and sizzle to
the act of writing. Writing is also like cooking—exotic spices and
gourmet sauces—adjectives and adverbial clauses further temper the
qualities and tensities and elaborate the alignment of modes, eliciting
possible transconceptual gradients and giving an inkling of its emerging totality. Then a larger kind of editorial process works over weaves
of contexts by pruning, rewriting, reordering, making concise; lastly a
fine tuning where a single change of word or the repositioning of a
phrase or sentence will complete a whole paragraph or piece.

Some days I write at length; other days I only work on a single
paragraph or sentence. Just as an oculist aligns multiple lenses, the
writer layers a multiplicity of references, inferences and networks of
associability; contextuation generates and realigns the summating accretions of complexity or completion. There's also the problem of
memory, history, and identity that further compounds the writer's
(and language's) transformation(s)—hence Husserl's (*Ideas*) and
Nietzsche's (*Ecce Homo*) reminders that truth is in the realm of fiction, albeit an elegant one. (Cognition is also a capacity to envisage,
envision, *see*.) And it may be impossible to report anything objec-
tively; writing transforms its contents and subject accordingly—the
word relativizes experience and perception. Writing must be a *transmissivity*, not just documentation. Facts hurdle themselves.

And as I'm finishing the final edit here, wondering about the
readers it might reach, I find this presciently evocative reminder in
Georges Bataille's *Inner Experience*:

I carry within me the concern for writing this book like a burden, I am *acted* upon. Even if nothing, absolutely, responded to the idea which I have of necessary interlocutors (or of necessary readers), the idea alone would act in me . . . the companion, the reader who acts upon me is discourse. Or yet still: the reader is discourse—it is he who speaks in me, who maintains in me the discourse intended for him. And no doubt, discourse is project, but even more than this it is that *other*, the reader . . .[3]

Writing is a continually challenging, probing process, and without doubt the word processor supplied its necessary next step. Between 1980 and 1983 I had written (that means entirely retyped numerous times) the long essays I was developing on Nietzsche, Susanne K. Langer and Maria-Theresa Duncan. And of course one can *look* inside old typewriters and see how they work mechanically, but the insides of electric typewriters and word processors are thin boards with microscopic transistors and multicolored, intricately coiled wiring. They're unfathomable, and their digital capacity instantly corrects spellings or moves one to a word or passage anywhere in a text with one or two keystrokes of a "search" key, or copies, deletes or replaces text (the software being virtually invisible). Word processors reinvoke, with a trenchant technological twist, the meaning of *wordsmith*.

W: How did you become interested in theater?

D: In kindergarten I had the lead as a farmer in a musical production and had to sing! It's a hazy memory and must have been dreadful! All I remember is the bustle of parents, the last-minute preparations, overdressing in two layers of clothes, a lot of straw, the final climb up the backstage stairs, then having to perform while holding a little girl's hand on the very narrow edge of the stage apron in front of colored footlights; the lights obscured almost everything else. A few years later I would have repetitive dreams that my bed was on that stage! Another curious memory (I must have been eleven or twelve) was going to see a magician (who was a friend of our family) perform a show of his tricks, and being envious of his assistant. Also my mother was glamorous and theatrical, though a horticulturist by profession.

As a kid I was intrigued by, and made, puppets, undoubtedly because of early television shows, especially the unusually imaginative
Bil and Cora Baird marionettes. (I was in second grade in 1950 when
we got a TV, a "Phoenix," so I'm a card-carrying member of the very
first TV generation.) Spike, a stick puppet, exerted a special fascination—every afternoon at 5:30 he sat at a funky upright honky tonk
piano at the beginning of every show while playing and talking under
and over the music, almost confidentially, in simpatico camaraderie
to us kids at home—filling us in on the real scoop, the "dirt" or low-
down, about what was about to happen or what was really happening. He had a gaunt face, like a steely tough, with a cigarette dangling
nonchalantly from the corner of his mouth, slits for eyes, heavy eye-
lids, and uncanny, mimetically mysterioso movements—jerky and
quixotic like a pixilated phantom—droll, diabolical and scary (a
spoof supposedly of the renown jazz pianist Hoagie Carmichael). The
way the (almost hidden) rods, connected at the wrists, controlled his
taut, sharply angular verticality made the asymmetrical syncopation
of his hands slightly disconnected, unreal and suspect, enhancing his
spooky but captivating, endearing anonymity; there was something
about his identity that was, or had to be, concealed. (His movements
suggested something that could only be surmised, since I probably
had no real idea of mystery at that age. Who today might remember
this children's puppet show?) Spike gave me the chills, intriguingly
quickening the prescient sense of mystery and play; he inspired a secret allure, allied with the forbidden and unknown.

Later, my parents had a puppet stage built for me as a Christmas
gift, which could be used for both marionettes and hand puppets,
with a red velvet draw curtain, stage apron and little footlights. I
made my own puppets—out of almost anything—and constructed
and performed homemade shows for my friends and baby brother,
Grant, in the cellar playroom (a real underground). One was an exaggerated Tallulah puppet, with some Auntie Mame mixed in—an
imperious, unreal and archly ridiculous voice. Looking back I realize
there's another virtual ontology to the animation of puppets that suddenly transforms them from static and sometimes simple objects into
beings that seem to have a life of their own—a kinetic semblance that
is both a "virtual illusion" and *more*! The disembodied kinetics of

puppetry—being moved *from beyond* the confines of the body, and the transformation of inspired play and shifting textures of imaginary voices—impacted my early dancing. I guess I secretly wanted to be all the puppets and still be able to pull the strings!

We would go to our grandparents' large, old house for Thanksgivings (over 150 years old, with over twenty rooms, built with wooden pegs instead of nails); their third-floor attic, hermetic and remote, had drawers, closets and trunks full of vintage clothing and turn-of-the-century costumes. My cousins and I loved going through the outdated garments and gear and dressing up in outlandish costumes. After Thanksgiving dinner we would try to do impromptu shows, but the grown-ups always passed out—sounds *avant-garde*, right? It was also in their attic that I found a variety of fabrics for my puppets, and where I first sensed invisible presences.

Another early TV show that had a big impact on my imagination was *Beat the Clock*. It was sponsored by Sylvania, with a large lit-up second-hand clock to measure the allotted time for each stunt. Married couples were the contestants, and the handsome, smooth, and charming emcee (Bud Collier) had a fetching, blond assistant, Roxanne—sort of a 1950s X-rated "fantasy gal" in a snug, black, lowcut frock or cocktail dress, who sparked the proper *innuendo*. There were basically two kinds of *fraught*, unreal stunts for the contestants attempting to win tempting prizes (appliances, vacations, etc.)—the first type featured improbable and near impossible riggings with props, stands, containers with fluids and relay races. Each couple as a team was more often placed in baleful opposition to one another; the wife had to try coordinating some difficult tasks with gear like fishing poles, tilted platforms, precariously balanced cups or containers and whipped cream (their favorite) to avert an accident involving the husband getting squirted, mauled, pummeled, whipped-creamed or clobbered (not so subtle revenge). Roxanne was always there to clean up the embarrassed or humiliated husband, emerging ruefully with a withered look from his plastic, protective suit, while the audience howled. People replicated the scenarios at parties. The other task involved *language*—a curtain opening rapidly to reveal a blackboard with a famous scrambled aphorism or saying. Each word had magnetic holds so they could be quickly repositioned. The time element and the large, loud ticking clock itself (twenty seconds, usually) were anxiety and suspense provoking. This is what a writer is *always* doing to syntax—repositioning every word to gainsay the sentence . . . The show's improbable stunts, paraphernalia and bizarre accouterments were an obvious, humorous set-up, and undoubtedly the irrational, motley collection of improbable props and gear influenced my early dances. I still trace my fascination with sex perversions to this show— it was like pop Krafft-Ebing turned into not-so-sublimated *charades* (later I found an old, yellowed edition hidden in my parents closet!). TV *is* perverse.

(1993)

Rereading Hegel's *The Phenomenology of Spirit* (1807) reoccasions inquiry into the problematics of reflexivity. Hegel's seminal work is the source for a complex dialectical investigation of mind, reinvented in a new key at the turn of the twentieth century by the founder of phenomenology, Edmund Husserl (*Ideas*, 1913), and later advanced in its existential incarnation by Jean-Paul Sartre's magnum opus, *Being and Nothingness* (1943). The theoretics of reflexivity (and *theoremics*—the accumulating payload of poststructuralist theory and postmodern polemicizing) combines the prereflexive, reflexive and self-reflexive in a synthetic and synergetic enterprise that remains the protean, transformational centerpiece of a constantly evolving, ongoing movement that undoubtedly will carry its formidable momentum into yet another century.

Reflexivity is the cognitive component of the mind's movement to mirror its own complex functions and *cognitize* itself, a kind of double (re)turn, ontic radar, or metanoia—the cardinal supplement of Hegel's famous *in itself* that, in turn, revises and exceeds the homeomorphic extensions of Spinoza's *natura naturata*. (The word cogni*tize* is, in part, metaphorically analogous to magne*tize*—what the mind has to enact autonomically in order to solicit or activate insights into its own processes and operations.) Reflexivity is the philosophical capacity that mirrors the functionings of perception, apperception and cognition, whether actually, conceptually, and/or virtually, in and through experience; polemically it informs *how* we know *what* we know. And although Hegel was a prodigal nineteenth-century German thinker, the last several decades of ambitious— seemingly limitless—advanced theorizing has occurred predominantly on the French (post)structuralist writing scene (e.g., Alexandre Koyré, Alexandre Kojève, Emmanuel Lévinas, Maurice Blanchot, Georges Batail- les, Pierre Klossowski, Jean Hyppolite, Michel Foucault, Jacques Derrida, etc.). For the philosophy of science and verification theory, the analogue of the idea of reflexivity demands a technic whereby the mind tests its premises and hypotheses about any conceptual given, constellation, as- semblage or network of facts, theoretical canon or methodology (while simultaneously recognizing the physicist's dictum that measuring alters the means).

Reflexivity as a technic should clarify, eliminate or transcend meta- physics per se (i.e., metaphysical speculation). Hegel's three-step program of consciousness, self-consciousness and reason followed Kant's categori- cal indexing of the mind's operations, which induces what now may be called a kind of virtual metatripping—watching *(how* one is) watching (apprehending), looking at *(how* and at *what* one is) looking (appercep- tion), and seeing (what one is) *seeing* (cognition; the virtuality of seeing and esthetic reflexion generate still other hyperthetic modes and catego- ries). In the realm of cogitation, it also denotes how one *apprehends* ap- prehension, *discerns* discernment, and ultimately cognizes (the reflexively kinetic signs of) cognition, processing the virtually extendable ciphers of knowing. On the other hand, the concrete *metaflexions* of sense data, per- ception, apperception, apprehension and cognition actually engage sev- eral simultaneously interpenetrating logical strategies that range across, through and over the grids of transdisciplinary systematization. Merleau- Ponty's reminder that phenomenology is first about perception enjoins one to attend to objects, art works, esthetic issues, visuality and virtual experiences. One of the most challenging canons of (post)modernism is that an art work reflect itself, and/or reflex the observer's perception and understanding, or both, via a (double) synergetic reciprocity. The si(g)ns of the wor(l)d—the dialectics of exteriority and interiority and the lin- guistic exemplifications of thought—are assayed in *motion*; language and thinking have *kinetic* gradients, parameters and margins, as well as kine-

lexic indices and interactive registers that can become hyperdimension-
ally reflexive. Art accomplishes this project through its hypertrophic plays
of forms—how the assemblage of materials and (the mixing of) formal
principles deploy its elements, structural relays and/or delays, signs, symbols and strategies to render systemically transparent the virtuality of its
construction. And ultimately, on the frontier of phenomenology's *meta-
methodology*, reflexivity produces the cognition *of* cognition, a kind of
double monitoring or metaflexion, ideally an automirroring function or
paraphilosophical analogue that might be likened to a magnetic resonat-
ing imagizer of psyche and perception; a semiothesia. (Movement assures
sympathetic bonding and empathetic transferences—what you see is not
not you, or, in metagrammatical parlance, what one is being being seeing
is not *not* synonymous with subject or self . . .) Metaflexion doubles and
thus reflex(iviz)es perception, apperception and reflexion, thus also pro-
ducing the reflexion *of* reflexion, the mirroring *of* mirroring, a meta/*metanoia*. (Jean Beaudrillard and Paul Virilio have written about the para-
technological and metaontological dimensions of hypervirtualized
spacetime and the paradoxes of the digitized hypertrophizing of temporality and consciousness.)[1] Nam June Paik's famous video sculpture of
the Buddha contemplatively sitting cross-legged in the lotus position stoically facing his own reflectively virtualized image on a *television monitor*
(an impassive, hypervirtualized reflexion) is both an iconic and ironic self-
reflexive commentary on reflexivizing beingness(ence).

I will argue here that being (being) (em)bodied and the phenomenon
of corporeality create, figure prominently in and constitute their own hyperdimensional landscape of (self-)reflexive functions; the implicit as-
sumption heretofore has been that reflexivity is a purely mental affair of
consciousness and not achievable by, nor located in, corporeality. (Corporeality: the ontothetics of physicality, incarnation and the physiogenics
of sentience, feeling, sensibility and the motivity of desire.) And dance,
being (being) the art of the body in locomotion, virtualizes corporeality
and is thus a primary instrument for clarifying some of the pivotal, conceptual extensions of (its) motor reflexivity. This is afforded, in part, by
scrutinizing the work of certain (post)modern choreographers, a topic
that as yet has received little or no attention by dance writers, theorists,
philosophers or critics; obviously it's time to make amends. Movement,
motion registers and the constantly shifting kinetic gradients intercon-

necting the dialectical, kinaestholexical ideosigns of physicality, objects and bodies animate the larger transactional proportionalities of the human landscape (while also entraining another sociocultural dialectic between bodies, doxa and ambient) and generate the *geomimetric* filaments of world and temporality as well as the subliminal ontolexical substrates and subaltern gestalten of shadow, double and Other that (pre)constitute identity and selfhood and animate and sustain bicameral consciousness.

One of Husserl's systemic advances after Hegel revolves around the concept of bracketing the contents (*noema* and *noemata*) and substrates (*precepts, percepts, traces*) of perception and conception—the holistic composites and components of the signs and data of experience—by a sort of eidetic suspension of the mind's modes of representation, like freeze-framing a transparency or slide of mental reality to ascertain or analyze its spectra of essential components or compositing essences. Husserl thus supplied a technic that made it possible to bracket subject, field and agent, as well as any constitutive factor including negativity, negative space or any component of mental life—a very complex idea in Hegel's vast project, a lever or switching device for a highly active, rapidly alternating polaritizing methodology that constantly contraposes, converts, inverts and transposes the kinetics of differences, principles, paradoxes and the antinomies of reality, space, events, ideas, conception, representivity, etc. Space, too, in dance, is conceived as having a "negative" component—this creates its virtual, dialectical and magnetic relationship with the *invisible* and activates and contrasts a kinelexic dialexis (or double read) between bodies, isomorphs, signs, tensions, time, qualities, forces, presences, place, structures and dimensions—like a photographic negative that reverses the recording or resolution of gestalten by inverting the compositives and components of its images, revealing the paramechanics of appearance, sight and perception that are physicalized and defined by its trans(per)mutable (con)figurative alterities. Corporeality and movement are inextricable; placements, positionalities, axes, contexts and meanings are cocorrelational and (co)compossible. Also, our digital, technomediated world, especially since, and because of, television, movies, computer and Internet, magnifies the reflexivization of hypertrophized imagining capacities circulating through extended networks (which also, in turn, both reinforce and deeply inculcate conditioned stereotypes

and relentless, "hidden" propagrandization; celluloidal bombardment
burns image *syndromes* into the unconscious, causing collectivized con-
flicts, ructions and traumas).

Reflexivity has its primal, prescientific roots in mythology, whose pop-
ularizations usually obscure its actual (ontogenic) meanings, transliterated encipherments and mythopoetic encryptizations, e.g., Narcissus's
fateful calamity resulted from fixating his selfsame reflection on the surface of the pool as his "own," mistaking it as an other and falling in love
with the simulacrum of his virtualized double (a neurotic entrapment),
rather than being able to recognize, look through or beyond it—mistaking himself as his own (non)identity. In Jacques Lacan's collection of essays *Ecrits*, there is extensive treatment of the necessary developmental
phases of the mirror stage(s), whose ontology of reflection reflexes psychoanalytical (or psychotropistic) insights into an infant's formative ideo-
motor processes.

Art is a concrete means and tool for cognizing the symbiotic, semiotic
and symbolic processes of reflection, reflexion and self-reflexion, or the
dialectics and polemics of metaflexion. Poetry and theater may of course
perform that cognization more immediately at hand—the cadencing of
lines and the dramatic impact of vocalization and delivery, break and re-
connect (the schemata) of typographemized space and presentational
frame, engaging a collective enchantment. Hypnotic rhythmicities turn
language, character and psyche back on their transactional axes and circuitous route(s) of sender/receiver, pivoting signifiers and signifieds in
spontaneous, double-coiled weaves while permuting and concatenating
their contexts and contents. Gertrude Stein's *The Making of Americans*, a
century after it was written, remains one of the most radically innovative
exemplifications of a highly kinetic, self-reflexive syntax (and a hybrid
genre too—the first "systems novel"). Stein's animated, mantra-like
modes of rhythmicized repetition continuously accelerate and advance
while circuitously circling back to reengage and reweave their permuting,
fissionating cadencings with concatenative ontolexic branchings. Her
steady-state cascade of smooth, syntactically reiterative chains and her
prose's adept semiotropic spiral phrasings weaving back upon and
through their conceptual pivots create a complex virtual ontology that
reiterates and reignites its permutating paraliterary extensions through
dense, hypnotic accretions that uncoil with fluid digital finesse, like a re-

lentlessly unwinding spool or pneumatic motor, auto(re)producing itself. This novel of a family's history generates a vast network of cognitive modalities constantly being reconfigured by its hypertrophic grammatology— her incantatory use of double gerunds (seeing, feeling, thinking knowing, etc.) makes them into timeless disembodied agents that conflate cogent amalgams of mnemonic valences filtered through a rarified, teletemporally suspended, intergenerational continuum.

Before considering some modern and contemporary exemplifications of reflexivity in dance, it should be noted that vigorously executed, rhythmic body movement has always been a means that autogenerates ontic doubling—the similarity of accounts of shamans from many different cultures noted by Mercea Eliade in his extensive studies of the anthropology of comparative religions involves reflexivizing processes that universally mirror man's inner, pre- and paracognitive capacities. Shamans are primarily healers who use song, chanting and dance in ritualized processes of transformation.

What are the factors and elements that make reflexive an art form, work, genre, technique or experience (or, in the case of dance, its kinelexic indices of movement and motion registers)? Dance's primal level is constituted by an upsurge of motor impulses that are routed as flexions— the near instantaneous branchings of a neural and corporeally extended signaling system that propels the articulated coordinations of animation, expression, locomotion and performance while weaving manifolds of gestural and isomorphic matrices that may be casual, situational, geometric and/or loaded with psychological portent or mythic import. Its primary level is constituted by bioenergetic vectors and meridians that breathe, pulse and weave to (inter)connect movement with its ambient, and that are thus prestructural. (Not all kinetic structures and structurations are identifiable, reach a conscious threshold, become definitively readable or have specific imports.) Reflexivized movement belongs to the highly articulated ability of a dance artist who cannot only execute but teach and explain the technique and structural capacities of its execution. And, of course, performance itself can tacitly reflex audience and performer(s) to and for each and one another.

Dance offers different models and orders for the exemplification of corporeal reflexivity. What and how we know through the body, physicality, and corporeality (which involves all the phenomena of *being being* a body) is still a nascent philosophical frontier. Because dance is a non-discursive art, it is easy to overlook its complexities simply because the means to articulate them remain mute, or unavailable. The scope and range of dance writing during the twentieth century has grown immensely but still lacks sufficient philosophical and theoretical underpinnings for it to have kept pace with the comparative volumetrics of advanced writings about the other arts, e.g., literary criticism and semiotics. And coordination of both mind and body, a given in yoga, has not been a pedagogic priority for most dancers, probably indeed only for a rare few; this is more likely to occur in the choreographer's precinct, where technique and composition are prerequisites to transforming the principles of physical motivity into artistry and the capacity to structure, transmit, teach and explain. Because modern dance is constantly undergoing transformations of its vocabularies, its repertoire of styles and techniques are made trans(per)mutable; choreography reflexes their fission through its performative processes and pedagogies—the formal principles of movement structuration, style, kinesiological harmony, etc., are exemplified through the transformational strategies of composition.

Beginning in the twentieth century, the reflexivity of the dancing body became a primary esthetic project. The virtual semblances of Isadora Duncan's dance, supple ease and virtual repose, were characteristic of its lyrical flow and eideticized by its grandiloquently robust, highly stylized sculpturality, which mirrored classical music's majestic harmonies and architectonic rhythmicities and catalyzed its uncanny mimetic plastique, rendering a formal (double) reflection of movement—of natural forces, deity, heroic human strivings, spiritual proportionality—keys to its larger kinelexic reflexivity. Duncan insisted that the dance develop the dancer's intellect. Martha Graham's and Mary Wigman's expressionistic styles were more weighted and chthonic; their darker, psychologically motivated movement gestalten supplied an anguished, existential reflexion of the conflicted psyche. All three of course had read and studied Nietzsche and Schopenhauer.

In ballet, Balanchine's *Symphony in Three Movements* reflexed the ballet lexicon in a protomodernist mode well-known as neoclassicism, set to Stravinsky's brash, atonal score, with its clashing, irrupting and interrupted arhythmic weaves that disjunctively sutured textures, activated discontinuous structural decoys, distorted amplitudes and shattered timbral relays that rebounded visually and kinetically, musically and choreo-graphically, spatially and tactillicly by twisting, angling, and decentering the dancers' lines, shapes and axes, and vectoriing their disjunctivated phrasings with skewed, unexpected upsurges of fleet, fast-paced, rapidly transforming momenta. The highly asymmetricalized interfacings and in-tricately overlayered interplays of its ensemble action purposely warped the dance fabric and twisted the palpable density of the bodies' trajecto-ries while splaying the dancers' limbs in off-centered, cantilevered poise as they were swept along with spikey ballast or carried through unusually surprising, sweeping or suspended spatial deployments. In order to per-ceive the fractionating excess and knotty complexity of the dense, hyper-active stage picture, one's eyes had to move quickly through an unusual tangle of eccentric configurations to decipher its hyperactive overlays of simultaneously erupting articulations, which could be likened to navigat-ing a thick underbrush of gnarled vines and exotic, leafy obstructions or reading *by* reading laterally across several columns of text at once to dis-cern tacit lexical weaves. Here, too, one again realizes the initial excite-ment of the formal abstraction of ballet—geomimetric complexity super-sumes narrative, character, psychological underpinnings or motivation within a rich formal superscape teaming with unusual detail and unfa-miliar juxtapositions of overactive gestalten that transcend literalization.

Merce Cunningham's choreography investigates and extends innumer-able self-reflexive palettes of synergetic structures; some works, such as *Torse, Sounddance, Landrover, Points in Space, Enter* or *Ground Level Over-lay*, seem to invent a separate lexicon for each dance.[2] He utilizes balletic principles of alignment and locomotion but interrupts, supplements, ex-tends and synergetically overlays another vocabulary, one motivated by the geometricity of the spine's ability to axialtropize an extended reper-toire of (omni)vectorial plays that dialecticize verticality and directional-ity through rapid shifts of balance, focus, torque, placement and dynamic change. His works range out into space, virtualizing its deep recesses, but the individual phrases of each dancer always seem to return to their own centers, and his dense compositional weaves refract and fractilize space and the margins and parameters of their constantly permuting, (mi-cro)intervallic alignments while being propelled though fast, fleeting vis-tas and indelibly mysterious terrains—sometimes baffling but always af-fording an internal reflexion of each dance's cohesivity. The modes of

abstraction and great formal invention (created by a variety of chance
methods and, later, computer) are further catalyzed by a dynamic fission
that varies from performance to performance. Unlike almost all other
choreographers, Cunningham reflexes an open continuum and synergized contexting of organizational principles, raw kinetic "data" and visceralized immediacy of movement. True, the dense, profuse reflections of
his dances might (initially) seem like distorting kaleidoscopic gestalten, a
dymaxion house of mirrors or the quixotically scrambled mirages of
dreamscapes, but the semiotrop(h)ic collaging of ideosigns and accreting
motion ratios always relink and rerelate the dance's material to itself
while simultaneously sparking interactive ranges and registers of associations personal, transpersonal and cosmic.

Reflexivity can result from the juxtaposition of various temporal modalities and dimensions within the performance of a dance and thus initiate a (micro)mnemonics—memory and recall are counter-and supraposable, fractilized in the continual (de)constructive collaging and
recollaging of kinetic components orchestrating the totality of the work's
passage. The assemblage of materials and the transsectionizing of temporality includes fleeting images, discontinuous overlays, flashes of insight,
shards and flexions (i.e., upsurges of impulses and signals whose motoric
thrusts are emitted by an autonomous, steady-state pulse, like the heart-
beat or planetary sidereal). Thus, the semiotic components of watching a
dance and reflecting on *its* reflexionizing of materials *and* its beholders
set up double perceptual tracks—attention to the supernumerary details
of an art work (the primary, secondary and tertiary transparencies of its
virtual illusion, which Susanne K. Langer has treated in her aesthetics),
which disclose a plurality of meanings that can be (proto)symbolic, linear, literal, synchronistic, situational, discontinuous, inferential, self-
referential or coupled with the (simultaneous, copresent) discernment of
how the form arises and how or why its structural concatenations are so
deployed. (The term *art work* also has analogical references to *dream
work*—how the collaging, assemblage and internal compositional
logic(istic)s of a work (dance) resemble modes of oneiric display, envisagement, visualization and recall, as well as modes of condensation, dis-
placement, super(im)positionality, etc.) The formal array of elements,
principles, images, impulses, qualities, design factors, vectorization, composition, etc. gives one "clues" to its subliminal logic(s), organizational

dynamics and transposable registers—its construction of continuous and/ or discontinuous modalities that coalesce in the synthesis or overall impact of its structurations, the surmise of motivation, causes, reason or being—like the two halves of the brain, which relay different, intraleveraged modes of perception—linear and/or chaotic, rational and/or irrational, logical and/or atrophic, symmetrical and/or asymmetrical, analytical and/or intuitive, to create a spectrum of intermeshing, virtual dialectics between the processes of apperception and cognition.

Other choreographers who have contributed to the experimental momentum in recent decades have made other strides that have questioned the hierarchical organization of a dance, dance company and/or its institution. Yvonne Rainer, one of the leading founders of the Judson Dance Theater during the 1960s, made an early dance, *Three Satie Spoons*, to Erik Satie's *Gymnopédies*—a kinetically witty, ingeniously constructed solo that juxtaposed simple sequences of incongruous, nonsequitur gestures, poses and passages that, in spite of their discreteness, temporal delays and mimetic slippages, made a continuous, fluent continuity that seemed to *italicize* and foreground movement as *syntax* and reminded me (years later) of why Jacques Derrida's word "grammatology" could also well apply to the variety and modes of performance styles that originated with the Judson choreographers, who focused on deploying colloquial, everyday movement to make dances that reflexed structural principles and were thus systemic. Discontinuous, discrete, isolated units and unexpected, supraposable gestures and activities were linked in Rainer's dances with a clear, concise delivery, and they were made emphatic in *Three Satie Spoons* by their whimsically uncanny musicalized counterpoints, which played with the cancellation, decoy and subversion of metrical cadencing while contraposing the harmonic elements of Satie's facetiously fractious melodic structure. Her well-known *Trio A*, from *The Mind Is a Muscle* (1966), initially performed by three dancers in canonic delay, took this mode of composition to a more comprehensive formal embodiment with a more varied spatial deployment.

Sally Silvers and Wendy Perron are two choreographers who, during the 1980s, evolved unusually distinctive, eccentrically inventive vocabularies that broke the "codes" of compositing movement by reconfiguring the paramechanics of composition and thus what constituted the permutational displays of cohesion and dispersion of isomorphic units, defini-

tion of shape and readable gestalt through a continuum of moving bodies within an original lexicography; they did this in part by subverting
expectation and logical sequence. Both choreographers could seem beguiling yet guileless as they executed the unlikeliest logic, choices and
odd links as if tying and untying assorted movement knots, thereby reflecting individualized grammars that telegraphemized their signatures in
space and that, in turn, refreshingly exposed the usually tacit, conditioned assumptions and traditional preconceptions underlying most conventional choreography. Perron and Silvers uniquely broke the accepted
frameworks of movement readability that gainsaid the play of qualities by
incorporating shrugs, tics, decoys and even sloughing to alter the legibil-
ity of context, contrast, placement and phrasing, thereby releasing other
modes and indexes of articulation that amplified unusual kinelexic registers and structural possibilities within their formal deployments. Their
dances seemed to vividly reveal and thereby reflex how they assembled
themselves by appearing to reveal the meta-premises of composition, and
they consisted of highly individualized, nonordinary, quirky, deconstruc-
tivist units whose seams, like Gertrude Stein's prose, seemed to be simultaneously disassembled and rewoven before one's eyes, diversifying the
fragmentary arrays, movement palettes and possibilities of dynamic (and
dramatic) overlays. Their styles were also embellished with witty kinetic
squiggles, rhythmic subterfuges and ironic juxtapositions that recom-
pos(it)ed the logics and whimsy of fluid connectivity—Silvers's style
gamin and ungainly, purposely gauche and harder-edged, adventurously
packed in lots of zany but brainy pretzel permutability; Perron's softer,
more sensuously indelible and permeable and more structurally oblique—
she slyly slid registers and craftily decoyed nuances between the gears of
her phrases.

Since the 1970s, choreographer Marjorie Gamso has utilized quasimi-
nimalist modes of repetition to accrete and vary the kinetic microincre-
ments that subtly permute the accumulation of a dance's phrases. In *At
the Stake* (seen in preview at the Construction Company Studio in 1994
and performed by soloist Karen Strand), a woman in the purported role
of a condemned witch performed a carefully calculated, cogently alert
and meditative dance in front of a two-piece wooden stake on which
hung a red jacket. She moved forward and back, inscribing vertical tracks
that advanced toward the audience in shifting, oblique angles filled with

close, cove(r)ted nuances. Her repetitive advancings, retractions and re-tracings, inlaid with cryptic gestures, refracted the incremental notches of her path with sharp vectored changes, tilting torso and extending legs that reached out, punctuated and transected the planes of space. While maintaining a stoic containment within her advancing ambient, the dancer emphasized how dialectical shifts of verticality and axis and the accretion of precise, repetitive motor flexions etched the contours and re-flexed the nuances of a mysteriously conflicted psyche. One repeated ges-ture in particular, poignant and poetic, occurred as she premeditatively raised the back of her hand to her brow; it suggested a spectrum of mul-tiple emotions, feelings and connotations, as well as alternative ways to *read* the concatenations of their mimeticized reenactments. This single gesture inscribed an entire inner psychological landscape—of fear, woe, being overwhelmed, daunted, wrought, obsessed, distressed, preoccupied and/or persecuted, as well as states of hesitancy, thinking, doubting, grieving, pausing, considering, probing, plotting, etc.—to the threshold of it becoming an indelibly transmutable cipher for perceiving the accu-mulation of the dance's entire network.

When the dancer reached the downstage vicinity near the audience, with her halting, raised arm, her suspended gaze surveyed a vista beyond the confines of the room, so that the dynamics of her placement and its arrested virtualized semblances connoted or inferred the sense of the au-dience (as space, vista or locale) disappearing, or that she herself was on a crescent of disappearing (a double and double/double mimetic reflec-tion/reflexion). Then, again, she recursively retreated to retrace her path. These rebo(u)ndings of structural accretions reflexed their performative impact (formally, not expressionistically) and, in turn, reflexed the mythic psychophysiognomics of the (condemned) figure/character, while also reiteratively reflexing the viewer's acts of watching, looking and see-ing, and they cast virtualized ontolexical reflections with and between the implied/implicit/implicated placements and nuances of this, her selfsame (shadowed), double. Time too seemed paradoxical. The dialectical inter-play of accumulated mimetic traces and the interactive tracings of vectors interspliced with the recursive reiteration of tracks, reinforcing the trans-formation and suspension of the dance's virtual temporality and spatial dimensionalization, which simultaneously (a)bridged the sense(s) of time passing, *also* foregrounded the prescience of each present, durated mo-

ment. The intraleveraged interweavings of these vectorialized filaments,
the repetitive, transmutable eidetic contours and the (re)inscribed recursivity (re)traced by her limbs in an arc around and above her body, reflexed concatenating motoric relays that assembled a continuum both
formally concrete and dramatically replete with covertly synchronized
psychomimetic (and psychoanalytic) innuendo. Curious too was how the
dance(r)'s viscerality foregrounded the kinetic cryptopoetic double reflec-
tions/reflexions while a subtle feminist polemic neutralized the historical
(and tropophorically, hysterical) stereotypes of the outsider "subject"—
the witch.

Vectors are lines, but more than lines too—their virtual, bioenergetic
extensivity produces elasticized reflexions that flex the audience's sightlines and shift the dimensionalities and registers of stage and world. They
also reflex the vibrating eidetics of sight and (re)constitute the meridians
of body and planet—the biophysiogenics of any ambient/field—while
their virtuality generates the geomimetric filaments and interdimensional
transparencies of perception and apperception. Those trajectories deliver
and insure knowledge. Analogously for the written word, concepts connect the vectors between ideas and their syntactical components; their
agents connect words and images and cause hosts of vectorized transferences to catalyze virtual linkages that coordinate the elements and matrices of signs and semblances that move and interact with, through and
across the schematic grids of different discourses, vocabularies and areas
of knowledge—and also across the electronically digitated topologies
ranging between grammatology and hypertext. In his posthumously published *The Visible and the Invisible*, Maurice Merleau-Ponty traces the
proliferating interfusions and often simultaneous interfacings that constitute the dimensional intertwinings of interiority and exteriority connecting the complex mental vectors of perception and cognition.

Choreography and language analogically share different kinds of spacial and typotopological organization, pattern coordination, code transfers, rhythmic overlays and intradimensional configurations. Many experimental choreographers have also worked with language and included a
variety of texts that reconfigure simultaneous contexts and counterpoints
within, and as lexical supra(im)positions of, their dances. In my own
dances, I have explored a performative intensity that challenges linear se-
quentiality by raising the frequency of the body, which enables the tran-

sectioning of limbs to pack in more microrhythmic details with simultaneously erupting impulses, omnivectorizations and virtual transcriptions of the limbs with mimetic delays that probe, energize or extend directional and dimensional changes. I call it "synapsulating" movement, i.e., interrupting the movement flow by driving and overriding the generation of (im)pulses to gun the ante of rapid gestic play that motorizes the animation of the body's pulsions through space, incorporating Merce Cunningham's axialized, decentering, rotorizing isomorphs and pulsing spinal contractions. Though I use musical accompaniment for certain dances, I also use texts (some recorded, some spoken live) that have included dense, philosophical essays (like this) to create several simultaneously interactive semiolexical counterpoints and conceptual exchanges to reflex the brain's interactive bicamerality.

Intermedia transpositionally bridges the discursive and nondiscursive to create virtual anlagen akin to Hegel's original dyadic transformer of thesis/antithesis, so that a new synthesis—or *scursis*—of combined modes of articulation occurs both continuously and discontinuously as well as visually, verbally, audially, kinetically, conceptually and neutropically while listening to *and* watching the simultaneous kinetic leverages that occur between these intramediated alteric polaritizings. This endeavor might be a response to the fact that our culture's vast visual and auditory thresholds, ratios and density perception capacities have become increasingly more specialized, spacialized and acute in tandem with the digitated development of electronic media and our increasing cyberphilic involvement. These contrapuntally intermediated capacities also amplify the exchanges between imagery and languaging, whose subliminal paralexical ratios supply the raw data and circuitry that mirror the transfer(ence)s between envisagement and conception, (con)figuration and schem(at)atizing that play, in turn, with perception and apperception. The relational threshold complexities between ideas and images are often trans(al)l(iter)-ated into pictures (cf. Einstein's quick shorthand sketches for physics problems, models or solutions, or Wittgenstein's metareflexive parallels between propositions and pictures). An excess of images/imageries are virtually telescoped in a dance and are subliminally and kinelexically processed, digested and (inter)digitated by thinking (while also reflecting) about them—converting converging signals and signs, codes and ciphers into thoughts, conjectures, multiple concrete readings and permeably

transposable, eidetically controvertible scapes. The transpositions between
art forms, ideas, logical languages, systems and their inferences and implicit transferences also become motional reflections of reflexivity.

Because theater is not only an adjacent art but can be as viscerally and
kinetically engaging as dance, a few examples are also worth citing. Richard Foreman's Ontological-Hysterical Theater comes immediately to
mind—his sustained achievement and uncanny transpositions of poststructuralist philosophy have inspired a long career of plays that consistently explores the spectrum of reflexive modalities and the ironic
displacements of subject and identity and reflects as well his indirect in-
debtedness to the kinetic inventiveness of the Judson Dance and Poets'
Theaters (that grew in part out of Happenings). His plays often include
wittily staged dances incorporating elements of mime, heavily stylized
and spiked with an excess of parodictic and hyperbolic irony. His trademark string, which virtualizes visuality's vectors, sometimes dotted with
black and white demarcations, (a)bridges distances and connects strategic
sightlines to underscore semiospatial perspective plays and thereby concretizes how the mimetic actions of vectors animate interactive processes
and reflex the ratios of perception and apperception. They're also an
ironic foil for what is obviously not *not* obvious!

Elsewhere, too, I have written about Athol Fugard and the late Reza
Abdoh. Fugard's poignantly courageous, passionate ethical commitment
leads to artwork that consistently confronts the oppressive trials, tribula-
tions and predicaments caused by South African Apartheid and the political transition of its presciently uncertain aftermath. His plays always
transcend their subject matter, characters and circumstances while reflexing a complex transvaluation of values politically, artistically and psychologically. (Fugard writes, often directs and sometimes acts in his own
works, brilliantly, of course.) His plays always arouse pathos, which is an
essential, distilled reflexion of ethicality. The maniacal hyperkinetic reflexivity of the late Reza Abdoh's theater was engineered by the density of
interactive multimedia—in his last work, *Quotations for a Ruined City*,
the actors double-flexed one another by their rapid, intricate mimetic exchanges, which mirrored, amplified and subverted their erratic, manic
and complex behavior and actions: texts and languaging were counter-
(com)mande(re)d by simultaneous presentations on two overhead, foregrounded video monitors against which the performers lipsynched their

own prerecorded voices which cogently dialecticized several counter-contrapuntal, supraposable overlays. A double mimesis also was tele-scoped by films of trains racing through fleeting stations and landscapes involving rapid transformations of perspectivity that were simultaneously projected on two rear, overhead upstage screens that further accelerated, and offset, the frenetic, if not hysterical, overlapping mis-en-scenes—devices within devices, spaces within spaces, (virtual) mirrors within (virtualized) mirrors, but in the conceptualized service of reflexing a still larger cognitive (and political) circuit. The Wooster Group also manipulates multimedia to deconstruct, reconstruct and thereby reflex the un-suspected, secret underpinnings of famous historical plays such as Chekhov's *Three Sisters* or O'Neill's *The Hairy Ape*, often with highly inventive, unpredictably thrilling, ludicrously subverting stagings that surprisingly reappropriate, revitalize and recapture their protohistorical essences.

Whether and why art should be reflexively cognitive—or the many ways directly and indirectly, explicitly and implicitly, overtly and covertly it can so function—and its relationships with a polemicized pre- and *re*presentation are intriguing (postmodern) esthetic concerns that also galvanize larger issues at hand. In a world of unprecedented, incessantly accelerating complexity, including the simultaneous orders of information retrieval and transmission and alongside the attendant problems of overload and psychic pollution, reflexivity becomes a spiritual necessity, too. After two centuries of building an indelibly formidable momentum, the long-distance reflexivity race has finally gotten off to its marathon start, with multiple frontiers but no finish line in sight, only a wide track facing an open-ended, indefinitely expanding horizon.

(*1997*)

Metagexis (Joseph's Song)[1]

(Excerpts)

Intimations of a *trialectic* •

Mappings for a motion, •

or *meta-grammar*

The *double negative* as denouement •

For four voices:

ANYONE

SOMEONE

NO ONE

and a Proxy

"How can the word 'not' negate?"—"The sign 'not' indicates that you are to take what follows negatively." We should like to say: the sign of negation is our occasion for doing something—possibly something very complicated. It is as if the negation-sign occasioned our doing something. But what? That is not said. It is as if it only needed to be hinted at; as if we already knew. As if no explanation were needed, for we are in any case already acquainted with the matter . . .

Ludwig Wittgenstein,
Philosophical Investigations[2]

Western philosophy and the art of logoic reflexion have grown out of dialectics. When there is an occasion for unimpeded action, the specifiable distances between subject and object, doer and deed, seer and seen, knower and known, dancer and dance disappear. A trialectic would thus test, proxy and monitor all metareflexive (and/or preconceptual) choices of moves, available options, alternatives, structures, perspectives and positionalities. NOTE: *The reader should not be deterred by the tricky play of conundrums and twisty syntax but move through this text rhythmically, which will deliver up its modalities and meanings as much as would trying to puzzle them out literally and conceptually.*

For Joseph Devadesa (His name should be on the cover!)

I. TRIALOG

The aesthetic*s* of the double negative cannot (not) posit that which is *not* unless it is absence. (Whether it is or can be absent [to itself] is what selects its mode of inquiry.) It is not *not* useless, neither useful. The aesthetics of the double negative is about the possibilities of pinioning positionality in the face of total absence. -That is, the double negative as an ontological *decoy*, or (meta)esthetic *d e p l o y*. A meditation on negation.

No minds do different things. Different things *do* do minds; or, minds do *do* different things. Remember Hegel: philosophy begins with negation. (The concept of exemption by absence.) "Those who *would* would know."

No notes cannot *not* be made. Anything that cannot, cannot *not* be. -It is important to accept starting anywhere, except when happenstance is benign, and thus *working* with what is offered.

Either is not nor nor not not or. *Neither* is not or nor not not nor. If there *is* Nothing then there is (even) no finality. What is not *not* a possibility cannot be left unsaid.

Nothing may or may not be. There are no ideas, only bodies. (There are no bodies, only ideas!) A *body* of ideas is a contradiction in terms, no? The only o u t may be an *AUTOBIOPATHY*![3] I'm carrying a metaphor. It's loaded. I'm carrying an umbrella.

I'm carrying *the* umbrella. It is a concealed, "sawed-off" umbrella, i.e., half-size; portable. Modern equipment. The ethicality of intrigue, remember, begins with . . . *ESSENCESPIONAGE*! (-We report therefore only what cannot *not* be found and duly spy on ourselves.) Pronouns are our only salvation: they proxy purposely by their incipient misappropriation! NO ONE has to be convinced. SOMEONE m u s t be convicted! ANYONE escapes. *Everyone* is sentenced! Pronouns are anti-bodies. I am an antibody. I am a dancer.

The tongue in my left shoe is also a metaphor because it keeps falling out. I am *falling out*! See! -I can take *this* tongue out of my shoe. (Only by having one metaphor stand *proxy* for the other [one] does disclosing do one one's *cree*dentials.) "Falling out"—a popular colloquialism for losing awareness, passing out, or over; or having a rift. "But it's not as if one is not *not* certain nor cannot be."

(Grammar, *doing* grammar, is like quicksand; the more effort we exert to extricate ourselves from the turgid turmoil of our sacred dilemma of sounding out *its* limits only brings us undeniably closer to the brink of our denouement. Magic word: *denouement*—it makes the tip of the tongue tingle.)

No notes cannot *not* be made. Nothing may or may not be. Nothing may or not be unknown. -If it is unknown it may be a mystery. (If it's a *myth*stery it's the mastery of misery . . .) If it's a mystery it is not unknown, but *unknowing* is a mystery. Nothing neither is an isn't nor is it limited. It *is* a paradox to begin.

The courtyard looks out on a window. Noise is a k-n-o-t. Knowing *k-n-o-t-s* notes nearness Nous *not* news. By untying its substance the untidy conditions of its appearances uncoil. Noise is knotted notes. Noise uncurls but notes uncoil. The nose never knows but without it knowing could not be *un*stated! That which is truly mysterious is not unknown. Not everything that is unknown is a mystery.

-The double negative *is* an ontogrammatical "k-n-o-t." Its action works like a concealed switch because it forces one to move forward in thought logically while also *simultimelessly* moving irrationally backwords.

That which cannot be *can* see. That which is not *not* being *is* seeing. Non-being is not not-being. Looking into what is not not known is *being* being shown. Looking into what cannot not be *un*known is being *being* sown . . .

What we cannot be we cannot *not* see. (What cannot be cannot be being seen without being being *seemed*.) "But it's not as if one cannot *not* be certain." (One can be sure, but never certain.) "But it's not as if he is not not certain nor cannot (not) be."

The double negative does not affirm opposites but promises positing the path and possibilities (or possible positionalities) of and for p r o x y. Proxy monitors, then reflexivizes, all possible premises, precepts, positionality options and perspectivity selection-modulations. Proxy is a virtual monitor for the parameters and conditions constituting the reflexions of the Other, and/or shadow, and/or the d o u b l e (or any combinations thereof), and the attending, and attenuating, aesthetic, psychological, ont(olog)ical and theotropic coefficients that accrue. Proxy happens only when the "shadow" is made transportional or translucent to itself; i.e., when all psychological moves are apprehended, exposed, apperceived. Motives are concealed; intentions—revealed. There is Nothing to teach and everything to learn.

-No conditions cannot *not* be m e t. This is maybe why and also not *not* an explanation as to *why* aesthetics and theology do not see eye to eye. One is busy *a p p e a r i n g* while, or so that, the "other" can be *being being* busy *disappearing*. Only on the orders of there not-being being (the primal contradiction?) can cancellation be effected. Whoever is not holy has not *not* be ordered!

Being spoken is not not being being heard, so being said need not be without *lessening* to listen, lusting to lesson. Throats thrust thresholds to try trusting thrushes thrashing in twilight twittering their thirsty thankless thoughts. Two are only tunes, not *not* for thinking only when they are *not* held in abeyance. ANYONE who is *is* lazy! -There, we've find*ally* got *that* said, which is as good as being being dead. (-That which is being being dead could never not *not* be said!) SOMEONE who is not *not* trying cannot help *but* understand. ANYONE who understands and tries to help cannot *not* be attentive. No notes cannot not be being being made! NO ONE who cannot cannot agree!

II.

Like a coin, this two-sided motion (or meta) grammar consists of what is not not separate and involves reciprocally activated double plays: on one side, *not not*, and on the other, *being being*; investigating the double action and ontological correlatives of metasemantic reflexion. (BEING BEING read, which is not *not* said, initiates a sign circuit that notates the actions of the eternal recurrence.)

-Cannot the usage of the double negative imply a specially sanctified *mode* and *code* of action and reflexion? -Or a special kind of "acting"—intentionally? -Doubtlessly we've all accepted the dictum learned in school—that the double negative is always equivocally redundant, and, as such, grammatically forbidden. What is not *not* news is necessary; what is not *not* necessary: n e c e s s i t y!

The double negative does not *not* n e c e s s a r i l y cancel itself, denying only what cannot *not* be doubted. Thus its option (action) is to make exempt what cannot *not* be specified. It is thus a device (deed-vice, too) for recircuiting our complacency in the wake of watching that which can-

not be seen and yet not *not* observed! ("-What is o b s e r v e d *is* what is
not *not* seen? Wait a minute! -Is *this* the hidden implication by metaphorical extension of the contradictory concept of negation?") In the
sense that before we can account for, and then cancel, the imposed (and
inherent) dualistic grounding of language and symbolic presentation, we
have to come *to* knowing as *as* is in an intrigue, bartering and bantering
the interpenetrating sets of "dual-correlatives" to e x p o s e what is not
not immanent (and expouse what is not *not* transcendent!).

    -Dual correlatives: the necessarily contradictory modes of getting *any-
thing* said: "I'm moral, *not* ethical; honest, *not* truthful; religious, *not*
spiritual; I have emotions, *not* feelings; motives, not intentions; so I'm
modern, not contemporary; democratic, not egalitarian; I have taste, not
style . . ." -The extension of reflexive metaphoricality cancels the contradictions of existence and reveals the immanent paradoxes of being . . .

    The *aesthetics* of the double negative as a kind of psychological *decoy*,
or philosophical deploy—it reveals only what cannot *not* be (m)asked (or
symbolized); so it extends the *concept* of the metaphor as a kind of ontological trigger, and acts as a surreptitious psychic switching mechanism—
not unakin either to a double tracking device. In a treatise on meta-
esthetics the 'subject' *never* makes an appearance but only (s)peaks out
cautiously from behind tightly drawn curtains. We reveal ourselves only
by not *not* telling our secrets. (What cannot not *not* be heard *is* what is
known.) "To know it you must not *not* show it." Emotional inference is
implied by what is not said; while its divinely devious inflection *can* connote what cannot *not* be left unsaid! So there! -What is not not limited is
implied, while what is cancelled, complies. (An existential demise: *salvation as* C A N C E L L A T I O N .) And that sublime, always unsavory metaphor about having to t r i c k ourselves into *unknowing*. (-Why can't we
go about *that* process—unknowing—directly?) What we *can* not not
wade into *is* the Unknown, and finding ourselves looking (for It) is already (being) *being* over our heads . . .

III.

    T E L E T E C H N O T I C   A N E C D O T E : holography necessitates a
metagrammar; the *teletechno(s)tic* transfers by means of complicated mirror monitoring mechanisms and supertransistorized laser beaming apparatus are t e l e m i t t e d over long distances—"piping" and duplicating a

whole event from one coast to an other. This augurs the necessity of these two metagrammatical structures, as paraontic deedvices: *being not not here*, and *being being there*. An unusual, unprecedented d o u b l i n g effect—phantomic transferences of people-processes as light bodies—not *not* as substitutes, replicas, *or* proxies . . . (Note, too, the implicitly concealed connotation and ontical ambiguity of "the other coast." *What* other coast?) What is invisible is not not real. What is not not invisible is virtual. What cannot be named cannot *not* be thought. What is being (being) seen cannot not be left undisclosed . . .

IV.

Every holy thing wishing to remain holy surrounds itself with mystery.
—*Stephan Mallarmé*[4]

What could be said to be the signs employed for g e n e r a t i n g a *meta*grammar? -A grammar that maps out its *own* constitutive conditions, without necessitating or i m p l y i n g a "subject." A grammar that clears a space for b e i n g but does not have to become, fill or inhabit it. -Or, speaking metaphorically, a grammar that empties (a) space for being being absent . . .

-Constructing a kind of virtual bridge for metamethodologically s u r - v e y i n g a territory (and not *not* a terrain?) on which to situate a floating schema—a kind of *motion grammar* . . .

SENTENCES FOR RANSOM. BEWARE: BARKING DOGS! No one will not *not* understand. If it can be n a m e d it is not *not* something. -If it can be sung it is not *not* Nothing! ("You're making me *un*become what I cannot not [even] be!" Being cannot not be being being seen.) Being is being being naught when awe is not not sought. Being is being being caught when awe is not (not) without ought. That which is sought is not not caught but by being *being* naught. Being being without and without ought is no nuisance for any body! -Anyone who would not be would not NOT see! SOMEONE who could not not be *would* see. ANYONE who would not would not not be being (being) seeing. ANYONE who could not be sought would not not be caught. -But, SOMEONE who could not not be being caught would be being being sought. ANYONE who could w o u l d be caught and so would not want not to be unsought! SOMEONE who could would be being being caught and so not be b(r)ought. ANY-

ONE who could would be being caught and would not be wanting not not to be being bought, etc. (But, someone who *is* consenting *could* be forsaken!) *ANYONE* finding feeling fondles folly. Being caught is naught when not *not* having an ought. (BEING BEING CAUGHT IS NOT *NOT* HAVING O U G H T!)

He ought to be being being caught so as not not to be naught. NO! He ought to be being being s o u g h t so as not not to be caught! NO! He ought to be being being naught so as not not to be caught!

BEING AND BEING BEING WITHOUT AND WITHOUT OUGHT *OUGHT* NOT *NOT* TO BE UNREDEEMING! BEING AND BEING BEING WITHOUT AND WITHOUT OUGHT OUGHT NOT *NOT* TO BE UNREDEEMING! (Yes! This bespeaks the ethical demise of an aesthetic *d i s g u i s e* not *not* worth the catching!) What is out of time or not without it is not *not* without catching!

THE WORK OF BEING BEING WITHOUT AND SEEING THE SAME *AS* THE SAME IS SEIZING FOR THE SAKE OF SAYING *THAT* WHICH COULD NEVER NOT BE STATED. THE WORK OF BEING BEING WITHOUT AND SEEING THE SAME *IS* THE SUM OF SEIZING FOR THE SAKE OF SAVING THAT WHICH COULD NEVER NOT *NOT* BE STATED. THE WORK OF BEING BEING WITHOUT AND SEEKING THE SAME AS THE SAME IS THE SUM OF SEEKING FOR THE SAKE OF SAVING *THAT* WHICH COULD NEVER NOT BE S(T)ATED. THE WORK OF BEING BEING WITHOUT AND SEEING THE SAME AS THE SUM IS THE SAME AS SEIZING THE SAKE OF SAYING THAT WHICH COULD NEVER NOT NOT BE *BEING* STATED. THE WORK OF BEING BEING WITHOUT AND SEEING THE SAME AS THE SUM IS THE SAME AS SEIZING THE SAKE OF SAYING THAT WHICH COULD NEVER NOT NOT BE BEING (BEING) STATED. THE WORK OF BEING BEING WITHOUT WITHOUT AND SEIZING THE SUM AS THE SAME IS THE SAME AS SEEKING FOR THE SAKE OF SAYING THAT WHICH COULD NEVER NOT BE BEING BEING *UN*STATED. THE WORK OF BEING BEING WITHOUT AND SEEDING THE SAME AS THE SAME IS THE SUM OF SEEKING FOR THE SAKE OF SAYING THAT WHICH COULD NEVER NOT NOT BE *UN*STATED. (Isn't *this* the r e a l task?)

BEING BEING CAUGHT *WITH* N A U G H T should be *the* exemption! STEP IN WHATEVER YOU CANNOT PUT YOURSELF INTO! Step into w(h)om(b)- ever you cannot not show yourself to be! Coping or carping that being caught is *being being* without ought *ought* not to be an impossibility! (Isn't *this* the definition of necessity?) Carping that being being n a u g h t is being without ought *ought* not to be an impossibility! (Is this n o t the definition of contingency?) Being being without ought is not not without being sought. NO! Being without ought is not not without being *being* caught. (Thus there *is* a safety device after all in what cannot *not* be [left] unsaid! -There *is* a paradox on e i t h e r side of the fence that cannot and not NOT be.) -It's close to how we cannot *not* figure out how what we cannot be WE are!

-All situations a p p e a r and APPEARANCES seem contradictory until they cancel themselves in the sense that they are not *not* being what they cannot be being being. (Cancellation as salvation. "What is not not said can be being being dead. So there!") The conditions of any state become contagious when they go without saying; saving.

-*A wick and a whisper and a wish for each whisker. Watching a wick washes watching. Watching whispering washes w i s h i n g. A wick that is not not a whip is wishing watching were w o n d e r i n g! -Paradox is built into the cosmos but ambiguity must be being being sewn into the universe! -An oasis is no time for prudence; for practice a panther for pathos. There's a wick in our wishing that watching a whisper washing is not not an indecent way of wondering why W O N D E R I N G must always be being being without and not not worrying. -A pity that piety is not not a pieta!*

IRONY WITH SARCASM MAKES MALICE. SARCASM WITH I R O N Y MAKES MALICE MELT. THE GHOST WHO HAS HO(S)TS SPIES THE OTHER('S) COA(S)T. RELIGOSA: the d r a m a t r a u m atizing of mystery (misery). -The transfiguration of the shadow into, or through, the Other (but not otherness?) is the differinference between practice and praxisma: art and science, ontology and theology. -IT'S ANYONE'S GUEST; GUESS!

"If there *is* Nothing then there is (even) no finality." . . . What we cannot *not* put into words we leave dangling on the edge of silence (science) . . .

V.

AGONY IN THE GARDEN

Passion often makes fools of the wisest men and gives the silliest wisdom.
    —*Francois, Duke de La Rochefoucauld*[5]

One has to be true to Mystery before It can be Truth to itself. One has to be true to oneself, before Mystery can be being being itself. -One has to be two to be being being true before the Mystery of the Other is Our Mother. "I

do not doubt you My Father now that I can not not doubt myself!" Truth is
not not Mystery; Mystery is being being Truth.

So let us enter now into what cannot *not* exist and sow be being being
seeing. An invitation is not not an invocation and so either way the
plight of lending light is being being not without fright. Being being light
is lending and *is* is not not a blight. There cannot not be authority nor
not (its) ascension. IN THE GARDEN APPEARING *IS* A G O N Y AND THE CUP
IS NOT *NOT* EMPTY. The enemy is not *not* myself. "My soul is sad even
unto death, wait here and watch with me."

DOING c o u l d be being being; being could be doing. SEEING could
not not be doing. BEING could not not be seeing. -These are the meta-
premises for all sˢoᵒrᵃtʳsˢ of pos*sibyl*abilities no one would not want *not* to
be thinking!

Being being h e a r d cannot not be (but) absurd! By listening to what
is not *not* stated and hearing what cannot be said, Mystery discloses itself:
I AM Truth's Dancing Partner. "Then, coming to his disciples he found
them sleeping. And He said, 'Could you not, then, watch one hour with
me?' "

We have to push grammar to its limits and then further. (Further is
what is not not beyond? Double one is not not a sum; double two is being being true, a clue for *you* who are Th(r)ee!)

Double negation appears magical (since it is without logical precedence) because it can expedite the automatic cancellation of contingency
and causality—but only by "excess exemption" (*i.e.*, by standing, or a p -
p e a r i n g to stand, by being (being) standing outside of all circumstances, conditions and positionalities). *It* speaks only through metaphors
and not *not* in parables. "I AM neither Thee nor not *not* He who *is* being
being Three!"

If it's one thing it cannot *not* be an other. If it's two things it can be
being being *the* Other. Double one is not not a sum. Double two is being
being true. To see (through) Three is not *not* to be! The double negative
is a slippery catch for u n d o i n g a non-existent l a t c h: ANYONE, SOME-
ONE and NO ONE are also virtual metaphors for the enactment of triadic
reflexions (the Trinity transfigured?) whose combined action = a theo-
thetic or telethe(le)tic technic over impossible distances. The reflexivizing
of past participles and gerunds in *double* relief cauterizes contingency.
("*Being* being caught without ought ought to cauterize contingency . . .")

The ethical task of the phantom writer *ex nihilo* is to be being being ex-posing the concealed, ambivalent presuppositions of linguistic reflection.) "Seeing is deployed when being being a decoy. Being a decoy is *being* be-ing d e p l o y e d. To be one one must not *not* be a sum. To be two is being being due. To see(k) three is not *not* to be . . ." -Too easy would it be to claim the demise of the double negative as a hybrid aesthetic ac-complice, as an "ally" or alibi of sorts—since only riddles can ax-complish but by what cannot be specified . . . -It's not the point of having to become selfless nor not not selfish, only reminding ourselves, or being *being* reminded, of nothing: "*Echos etch the Void.*"

When "Nothing" is used to signify "not anything" it cannot *not* be stated. -The purposeful ambiguity of using the word no one to mean not and not *not* anyone—and then expecting relief—or exemption! (no one as a telethetic metaphor or theotropic phantom. Maybe anything that is not is not not Nothing!) Turning synaptic/synoptic logic (and the body) inside out, like pockets. Joseph: "Isn't there a way of saying (sav-ing) it, without stating (staking) it (id)?" Anything that is known is not not revealed. Something that is not *not* known is being being shown! -That which is not not known is not necessarily *un*known. Being not-known *is* not not *un*known. Anything that is *is* concealed. Anything that is revealed is also reviled. (Nietzsche: "He that taught to bless also taught to curse."[6]) Ontic demise is its own disguise (or its owner disguised!). -The intricately intriguing "subject" of ethical ambiguity and the ontical paradoxes of anything a p p e a r i n g . . . "To be one one must not *not* be a sum . . ."

-The ambiguity of using the word n o t h i n g to mean "not anything" and then expecting a discount! here it is! (Ontology is not not without cash d^{d}e^{i}v^{v}a^{i}dends, either!) Theology is transcendental metaphysics, by the books, *boys*! Theosophy, transcendental theology, under the counter, *girls*! -The awareness and cathexis of non-recordable realities: coming to terse with terms—this is a "*trialectomy*":' working out the *theoptics code.* (The shadow transformed becomes Other; the Other t r a n s f i g u r e d : p r o x y . . .)

-It is because there *is* Nothing that there is contradiction. -It's not plain, the plan of having to become selfless nor not not selfish but simply of giving heed to the fact that by removing greed *being-being* is the creed. Anyone can not not be somebody! Heed the need of being being the creed so someone's credentials *can* be *un*believed! (News is what is not not new.) In a flash his flesh was flush with flee(c)ing. A pity that p i e t y is not not a pieta! (Pathos that is not NOT pity *is* p i e t y!) -The *final* statement about UFOs, Little Green Men, and Saucer Flying People in tandem: "THEY'RE THE U L T I M A T E MYTHOLOGY OF pure THOUGHT!" -That which cannot *not* see can be being being seen. Salt *is* the soul! Incidents that cannot not happen are accidents. Accidents that cannot NOT happen are coincidences. Anyone who is not not NO ONE is SOMEONE. SOMEONE who is not not anyone *is* NO ONE. NO ONE cannot NOT be holy. (Holy is *being* b e i n g held, and higher is in esteem!)

What is invisible is not not real. What is not not visible is what is unreal. What is not not existent is virtual. What is not not virtual is invisible. What cannot be named cannot *not* be thought! What can be known and what can be said are NOT two different things! Perhaps all this is a perfect search (a la Gertrude Stein) for an explanation that is being *being* description, or better still, a description that could not *not* be an explanation.

What is not not an instant is a moment. An instant is not not a second but a moment has the most weight. (A moment does not not have duration.) That which is not not here is everywhere. Surely these sentences are exercises that are spontaneous but not not random, for SOMEONE who *could* not not exist. -So this *IS* a Holy Mission, after all! Being being everywhere is not not here and is *is* the same as the sum so the sun cannot not be being being heard, herded, hoarded. It is simply a chance occurrence that is not not a coincidence. (A metaphor *is* without retribution!) A feeling is not not an emotion. (Emotion is *being being* feeling.) What I cannot *not* doubt I conceive. And what I cannot not conceive is being being believed! What can I say? Only what I cannot NOT *do*! What can I not n o t do? Only what is being being done. It's permissible but not allowed. (What is not *not* allowed is what everyone does!) -It is simply a chance occurrence that what is not not a coincidence is being being decided . . .

Today I met a friend completely unexpectedly in the park not near where either of us live, and it turned out to be his birthday! It was simply a chance occurrence that could not not be but being being coincidence. It was spontaneous but not not random. -The difference between destiny and fate is what cannot not correspond. Fate is what cannot *not* happen and destiny *is* best left to decide. (Destiny is best left to be being being deciding . . .) -Not that *I* could have known it nor not NOT noted it! What is not n o t known is indeed descri*babble*! That which is random is not not spontaneous; it is simply a chance happenstance that *that* which is being being random is not not spontaneous and *this* is NOT a coincidence! -THIS IS AN EXPLANATION AFTER ALL!

After all! -What is the point that what cannot *not* exist maps out a metagrammar?! The point is exactly what cannot *not* be stated, so precision is staked by being not being being indisposed to ma(s)king itself. Black holes cannot be (in) my imagination. My imagination cannot not be *in* my head. My head is not not my brain! My brain is not not my mind! THERE! This surely settles everything once and for all! Why has no one NOT thought of this before? NO ONE HAS NOT *NOT* THOUGHT OF THIS BEFORE! By existing ANYONE can not not be listening. (An explanation is of no consequence only if it is not NOT a description?) -An artist employs his imagination so *everything* he says cannot not be unbelievable, either. (The ambiguity of an aesthetic is guaranteed by an ethical paradox?) -It's a special clause for what cannot not be being being consigned. RESIGNED ARE THOSE WHO *ARE* THEIR EXPLANATIONS!

Whitehead may have said *the ultimate morality is style*, but then the Ultimate Ethic is ontology. (Ontology is the science of Being.) Ethics is a system of juridical principles arranged in a purposely operative order. Anything with purposive order *must* be ambiguous, but ambiguity is being *being* ordered. (Prudence is *anyone* with purposive intent.) -Morality is the way *someone* misbehaves; style, the way they pose. Losing composure is *not* without its own equilibrium! Everything in its own proportion is not in its entirety. DON'T ENCOUNTER ME; CONFRONT THE ISSUE! Everything that is not not in its own proportion *is* entirety? (Losing composure is not *not* without its own equilibrium.) In a flash my flesh was flush with fleeing . . .

(*I'm now thinking of ontology as "the psychology of the beyond . . ."* -*What do we mean by saying someone comes to the understanding of the concept of metaphoricality?*) Isn't one, or NO ONE, a metaphor? Joseph: "Isn't the Self itself the shadow and not not beyond a doubt? -Or, isn't the Self itself the shadow and not not beyond being being doubt?" -We can escape only what we cannot not doubt. (And what we believe leaves

us no room for rummaging.) Thank goodness there's a paradox on either
side of inquiring into what can and cannot *not* exist! The day saves itself.

Becoming a "pool"—disappearing. (This points to an *other* meaning
of the Narcissus myth: looking *at looking* at (and of) oneself, adjusting
one's position so as to go or "see" through the mirror, surface of the
pool, and image, reflecting the *reflexion,* so one v a n i s h e s . . .) "We
who are not and who are without are not not without Love." Only when
I look out at you through time (or—only when there's being [being]
looking t h r o u g h you *out* of time—another *imposture*ability?)—is *it*
(ID) looking out of itself . . . (Or, only when I see you looking out of
yourself does time disappear . . .) -Disappearing and unbecoming (or de-
creation) as correlative analogies metaphorically e n a c t e d .. ("What is
not not known *is* being being s[h]own . . . and, what is not not *un*known
is on loan . . .) "What I cannot not see *is* me . . . What is not *not* me can
be . . . What is not not me can be being being seen . . . What cannot not
be seen is being being seemed . . . The virtual is not *not* opposed to the
actual, or the actual to the "real"—the relative remodulation of "opposites" . . . i.e., whatever is registered or received is also resisted and deceived (i.e., becomes conditional). "I cannot *not* be what I *do* see!"
"There can be no reason that we do not not have bodies. Excess exemption is remandatory. Holy Contagion *is* Nothing: Unknown!

The d o u b l e is not not the Other, so the shadow *can* be twice the
sum! That which is sun is s u n g and thank goodness inquiry cannot not
exist! Being being (w)rung is being won. Being one is being being sung.
(Being being sung is not *not* having a sum.) "Only when I am not *not*
myself can a feeling be a facsimile. A likeness to what is not not a fact *is*
a simile, and a f a c s i m i l e bears no resemblance to it (id)! -is what is
not not suspect, the *subject*? (The basic idea of these preliminary mappings for a motion grammar is to keep being being moving so that the
subject is not not the body. This definitely explains the mystery of dancing and being in *one* sentence!)

The aesthetic(s) of the double negative only asks (not) what I cannot
mean, o n l y what cannot *not* be said. Be afraid only of what cannot be
being being (t)read, not what is dead. Be afraid of only what cannot
pierce the heart and the pieces with which *you* cannot part. The double is
not not the Other, so the shadow *can* be being being twice the sum. The

opposite of oneself is not *not* the "Other." The Other is oneself only when the opposite is not not being (being) itself. (The double is not not the Other.) When the Other is not not itself, p r o x y is being *being* possible. THERE! I've find*ally* got that said, which is as good as being being dead. That which is not not dead IS being being *said*. -Duality and contradiction are the trigger mechanisms of holy universe: they enforce the (illusory) contingency of the separated self. (They—contradictions—turn on our "motors," but if we do not know, or note, it, the motor cannot be kept running. THAT THE WORLD IS A CONTRADICTION ACCOUNTS FOR THE FACT OF APPEARANCES. THAT THE WORLD IS A CONTRADICTION AC- COUNTS FOR THERE *BEING BEING* A P P E A R A N C E S . . .) No notes cannot be made.

No notes cannot *not* be made. What is not not derived is being being describing. The day saves itself. It *is* Paradise, after all! I can now explain e v e r y t h i n g but by not not describing anything! There is no reason that we do not NOT have bodies. "What I cannot see is not *not* me!" "I cannot not be what I *do* see!" Everyone believes everything. NO ONE conceives Nothing. Anyone *will* tell anything. ANYONE cannot *not* believe nothing! No one cannot not exist! What is not not said can be being being (t)read. OR: what is not said cannot not be left unsaid. What is not seen cannot not be left undisclosed. What is seen can not *not* be observed. What is not *not* seen cannot *not* be being being observed! Everyone who always shows up cannot (not) be my imagination. EVERYONE WHO ALWAYS SHOWS UP CANNOT NOT BE *IN* MY IMAGINATION! It *is* a party, after all!

NO ONE can not not exist. This is being being (un)believing. What is not *not* believed is relieved and what is not not cancelled, concealed. My imagination cannot not be in my head. My head is not not my brain. My brain is not not my mind. My mind is not not unsettled. Listen to lessen that which could not *NOT* be *un*stated! What is not not *you* CAN be being being true. Only the core of my awe ought not not to be being being caught. The core of his awe is caught by his ought: so ought he not not to be without it? PLEASE!

DOING c o u l d be *being being;* being could be doing. SEEING could not be doing. BEING could not *not* be seeing. Now it's perfectly clear. Why hasn't ANYONE not thought of this before? NO ONE has not *not* thought of this before!

(Why hasn't SOMEONE not not thought of this before? Possibly because NO ONE could not not be seeing being being thinking! What is not
not here is everywhere.) This of course *is* to explain Nothing and not *not*
something. The core of my ore is awe and we ought not not to be being
talking (about) it. These *are* the metapremises for all sorts of pos*sibyl*abilities, including mappings for a motion grammar NO ONE would not want
not to be thinking! What is not not sought is taught. What is *un*stated is
what is not not said. What is unstated is what is not not being *being* said.
What is not not forbidden entices us. What is not not taboo solicits our
attention. We give thanks after all. What I cannot not pretend to be I AM!
Pathos that is not *not* pity *is* p i e t y. What is not not a k n a c k *is* worth
knowing. What is *not* worth knowing is worthy showing. When the
d o u b l e is not not the Other the triple *can* be being being twice the
sum. Anyone who is not not someone is being *being* NO ONE. So SEE, this
is being being a description and not not an explanation, after *all*!

(*1972–1973*)

One has to be true to
Mystery before It can
be Truth to itself.

—Unknown Voice

One comes to dramatization in necessarily summoning the power of the Unconscious, the Great Reservoir, the Ocean; the Mother Sea. -One must see t h r o u g h, penetrate the husk ("projection") of the dramatization process to see the seeds, source of transcendental personification, however possible, the numinous, seductive mysteries of divinity.

But knowing itself (piety) must, in some capacity, be dissolved not only into, but so that, understanding can be. The "Gate" opening opening is a stateless state: radiation. It is unbounded. It bonds. Knowing beckons us to dissolve its forms; its own forms of owning. The albatross soaring and swooping in cyclocircular rings sings signs following the wave and wake of The Ship, and one must not attempt to seize or kill him.

I've been concerning to resolve myself, and absolve myself too, as far as possible, by degrees and decrees, of the i n t i m i t a t i o n s, or *intimidinundations*, of identity as it conditions dramatraumatizing one's center (or one's sense of center), then this projection onto and as personification—theurgy; of power(s), of divinity . . .

A picture: a disembodied hand twirling and spinning a rope issuing from a cloud conditioning different kinds or se(c)ts of appearances might be metaphor or analogy enough of how illusions perpetuate the multifoliate wiles of divine sanction. -The "rope" in its marvelously intricate, intimately embellished tricks of cosmic projection assumes different appearances and guises, the finesse of the hand . . .

-How far can one see into and through the soar sore sauce source of this perpetual perpetuating p a r a d o x has been the inspiring motive and motif. This was written on the eve of my birthday, the metaphor of a gift, mappings for a metatheology. Krishnamurti: "Being as nothing is not negation."

BLACK is to Nothing, of Nothing, for Nothing: The Great Abyss, The Eternal Void, the Exemptiness of knowing, the cancellation of necessity that perpetuates crisis; contingency.

BLACK is for Nothing: for The Supreme Silence! Hearing having and showing Black is for there being Nothing, a kind of a kind of b e i n g l e s s n e s s e n c e whose qualities quaver; measured by decrees of absence its meticulousness is beguiling; measured by degrees of intentional removal is this its rapport in this is this is Silence.

There is no stillness. Stillness occurs when there is an illusion of the appearance of Silence. Stillness is sacred, Silence omnipotent. Black is Silence. It is the absence of color, of form, of shading, of inference, of difference, of deliverance, of absence. Devoid of definition (i.e., divinity) its shapeless manners of being being bothersome are its intentional conditions of transparency.

And so, devoid of all appearances It is deemed devout. -And, so devoid of all illusions It is deemed divine! And so devoid of all Mystery is It truly devoided. -Only on that condition are there none! Only on that ground is there cause for Holiness. Or, only on that account are there never none. Names. Names (k)need numbness.

It is because there is Nothing that there is contradiction! We can only infer the absence of All in the tangled testimony of contradictions. We can only infer the absence of All in a testament of where there is a Where there is being no contradictions. ((Ascertaining is not (not) ascension.)) Until there is Nothing is there separation.

NOTHING: the radiation of emptiness of, almost the heat of, of hovering a heart vaporous after the coiled creation of Creation's appearance, the manifested sanctuary of beatified illusions dissolving into fragile unformerness: flames fanning fires fire feeding fires frees not not without flames nor not without radiation is The Great Unknown.

Because It does not have properties nor cannot nor poles so in assisting us is there not being the unaccustomedness to noting Nothing's negative: Nowhere. Nowhere is NOW HERE! (Never was there never was there going without saying. Never was there never was there going was without saying!)

Disquietude disclaims and disdaining detains! There is no opposite to be in the position of disclaiming. There is no opposite to be in in the position of disclaiming. Where there is no opposite to be in in the position of discoursing Nothing obtains!

NOTHING is beyond, below, before and above personification, for there "is" no It, which is the appearance of appearance(s) shifting its invisible gale and guise under The Great Guide Void. Less us deserve not disdain. Let us desist not detain. Let us discard not disclaim.

Because it is without gravity there is no fear of striking its center. Only on the cancellation of one's own conditions (contingency) can It be met, penetrated possessed, but then, confusion surely becomes those who would profess its intentions.

Personification is a whirlpool of forces for farces for for faces freezing faces likened to being likened to being (being) likened to a liquid lightness loophole: a variegated vortex. (He can be seen!) A vortex(t) is vacant not void. The Void is not even not not invisible! (The invisible is not *not* invincible!) Being vacuous is not even being being vacant. -Unknowing is marked marred masked martyred but by its own n o n - e x i s t e n c e!

By looking It cannot be seen. By being said It cannot be stated! By being found It is never disclosed! By being revealed It is not obtained. And by being being revealed It is only further concealed! -The ambiguity of there being (being) appearances and anything at all forestalls all sanctification! It cannot even be sought, save thought! Or, it can be caught but never taught. But then, it can be received, deceivingly achieved! -Thus one finds fends owning anything friends by its smile redundant!

Nothing is a guarantee of anything. Anyone enforces something. Anyone fortifies somebody. Some body parries. Something is sure to produce nobody. Somebody might be making sure to produce nothing. Someone might be masking sure to allow Nothing. Anyone will go on. He does not try. Truth tries tricks. (Tricks to trust.) -To thrust: tried trying trusts truths.

Nothing is a guaranty of anything! Nobody knows Nothing. Everybody knows something. Anything owns somebody. Someone complains. A brisk briefing is brusquely beguiling. Anyone works as hard as they can. Some body works harder than they can. Someone, becoming nobody, works harder (yet) than they are able! Yes, pronouns are precious, even pious proxies. -Let anything stand proxy for there being (being) conditions of ambiguity, something for the wager of contradictions concomitantly co(ur)gent. Nothing could be It: The Supreme Paradox!

Succinctly is its smile sown and shown and so devotedly devoid dutifully disclosing Nothing. Nothing appears to be understood; but noted It is never known.
-Being known is or implies a contradiction. Being known implies there being a contradiction. Nothing is forever and forever Nothing so we rejoice in It. Anything is opposed to Nothing.

NOTHING is not opposed to anything. Nothing is not not opposed to Nothing, that is, Nothing is not opposed to itself, which is to say that anything being anything is (thus) its being opposed to itself because anything becoming something still is not stillness.

Nothing does not, dares not, darts not, devours nothing. Nothing does not do anything. Nothing does not do nothing. Nothing does not not do Nothing! Something suffers. Someone hears. It cannot exist! Since It subsumes atoning there is no expedient exile, much less expectant ecstasy in the whim, wave, wake of ceaseless ties (tides tidy themselves). Treasures. Treasures unto treasures cease. Cease speaking and sow seeping. Cease seeking!

-It befits benefitting us little to ladle to litter to tell talk taut teach tire tend trust touch tout about the bout that what we are we cannot be cannot tire of that which is Nothing, of Nothing, for Nothing except to exempt to feel full falling foolishly like a flimsy feather amidst the fearlessessence of our own feeble foibles and follies praising It and magnifying The Great Unbounded Void for its sublime Nothingnessence.

-For an image Friends will Friends will an image will it (not) bind blind us to wishing worshiping something which of itself must muster master mustier become unreal, creating illusion? Illusions' puns pounce down dunce dutifully dunces dare dancing dumb dances doing deeds. Illusions rebounding resound deedliverance. Deedliverance breeds d e p t h c e p t i o n. (This is the sublime reflection of folly: to be knighted by nonsense!) Since there is no need nor necessity but only night whining wide for that why which is forgiveness's needs there also not be no mighty seeds for forgetfulness's self as swell as The Well wails The Void, The Great Nothing Supreme stows without stirring.

Still bounds stillness.   Stillness bounds itself.   Still bonds bound stillnesses.   Nothing bonds stillness. Stillnesses bound stillness. Nothing cannot surround Nothing. Nothing bonds nothing. Nothing bonding Nothing bears beauty. Breathlessly a bounty bends and boundaries bind blessings blind its would-be seekers for where there is the mistaken proXspect of identity then there is posing pausing there causes, crises too for catching, which is not to save the future isn't itself without whispers.

Since there is Nowhere to go we cannot linger nor not not be going so we might as well be well on our way merrily! Forward! (Our guesses surmise themselves and surprise ourselves.) Devoid of all contradictions Being would be (for It) another illusion! There is no rest in certainty or repose revealing divinity's disguises in the device of mobility's momentum.

Rather than! Rather then. Holders containing Emptiness. Emptiness obtaining Holiness. Emptiness overflowing its portals is a paradox (unto itself); pray please play not pay but ply the contradiction its heed. -Praising folly reminds us of Nothing so we can call voiding devotion. Praising foolishness reminds us to note Nothing so renouncing renaming we surprise ourselves surmised!

(We worship in stillness not Silence. We can worship in stillness not Silence. Silence is won not One! WE CANNOT WORSHIP IT; THIS IS THE SUPREME HOLY HOSTED HOAX AND GRIEVOUSLY PIOUS PARADOX, THE ABSOLUTE UN-ISNESSES OF ITSELF!)

Nothing radiates The Unknown. For all the e m p t i n e s s words can connote is The Unknown The Unmanifest. (The same is Its not being like likened or similar or unto anything.) Because it is devoid of all appearances its Mystery is its intentional reminder of Holy Absence. TO NOTHING AND FOR IT: Eternal

Black. Because It is devoid of all illusions its Mystery is in the d e p b t h s of barteraurgering with its own non-existence! Illusion and personification are the instrumental adapters of The Unknown uncharting itself, unleashing and unlicensing Its Holiness with which It is beyond the practiced beyond the beyond then behind the art-if-acts of imagination, benediction, diplomacy and reason!

Let us desist not resist! Let us refrain not reclaim! Its holiness that is is The Void is is not emptiness is is not beyond emptiness beyond is is not not the practiced acts of acts of comprehension, of facts, of formulation, of fantasy, of folly. We who are not are not without Love appreciating the mighty entanglement of divinity unwinding The Great Coil in which echos etch in which e c h o s form The Form of the sacred serpent Void.

But is not It and is not.

If IT purports naming or measuring whether even divinity IS or is in motion is still is stillness but not being not Nothing lands us in the p r o p h f u s i o n s of aptsurdity, which is still sorely sacred! When we began we believed. When we believed we deceived. When we believed loving lost loving until knowing brought wrought us to unreconciled rejoicing in atoning for the everlasting contradiction of pondering (much less worshiping) anything! -Let us not be unnerved who are we are too unwholesomelessly s(h)own? The Void is Supreme.

WE WHO ARE NOT WITHOUT LOVE ARE SOLITARY IN OUR APPREHENSION OF DIVINITY, WHICH IS IN ITSELF OUR OWN REFLECTION OF EXPECTATION. APPREHENSION APPROACHING ITS OWN REFLECTION IS FOLLY. WE WHO ARE NOT AND ARE WITHOUT LOVE LOVE.

SINCE THERE "IS" NOTHING, THERE IS (EVEN) NO FINALITY. T H U S THERE IS CONSOLATION IN FINALLY FINDING N O T H I N G IS OF CONCERN!!

-WOULDN'T THE SUPREME ABSURDITY OF THE CANCELLATION OF ALL CONTRADICTIONS (AND ALL APPEARANCES?) BE *ITS* NON-EXISTENCE? HOW HELPLESS WE ARE! HOW COULD NON-EXISTENCE "BE"? HOW COULD IT EXIST OR NOT EXIST! (WE PLAY TRICKS ON OURSELVES AND ON OUR TRICKS TRULY BUT HARDLY CAN WE FIND OURSELVES FOOLED INTO ENOUGH KNOWING!) THE VOID IS SUPREME. WE REJOICE IN NOTHING.

-WE CAN RESOLVE EVERYTHING BUT R E C O N C I L E NOTHING! LET US REJOICE! NO SUCH THING AS NOTHING!—BUT, BECAUSE NOTHING IS OR NOTHING'S I S N E S S E S ARE NOT AND BECAUSE NOTHING IS NOT NOT SOMEWHERE IT IS H E R E! WE REJOICE IN IT!

WE GIVE THANKS TO THE HOLY ABYSS, THE VOID, ABSOLUTE NOTHING, ABSENT BLACK ETERNAL SUPREME EMPTINESS! NO, NOT WITHOUT HAVING RADIATION IT IS NOT ETHER AND EITHER NOT OR OF NOR OF ITSELF EITHER NOT NOR (NOT) TO BE FOUND, FEARED, FOOLED, FRIENDED, AND, BECAUSE IT CANNOT PURPORT TO BE ANYTHING OTHER THAN WHAT IS IS NOT, IT IS NOT OF MOTIVE, OF MISSION, OF MAGIC, OF PREDILECTION, OF REASON, OF MISERY . . .

LET US REJOIN REJOICING IN NOTHING, FOR NOTHING AND UNTO NOTHING THAT IT ISN'T! -THAT THERE IS NO SEPARATION AND THAT BLACK, THE ABSENCE OF ITSELF AND OF DIVISION, BECOMES THE S Q I N T E S S E N T I A L ASCENSION OF THERE BEING THE HOLY ABSENCE OF THE SYMBOL (SYMPTOM) AND OF HAVING, AND OF HALVING, AND OF OF, AND OF CONDITIONS AND OF NEEDING THE NEEDLING CANCELLATION OF RATIONS, REASONS AND RAISONS, WHICH IS OF THE FESTERING APPEARANCES FOOLISHNESS REVELING IN REVEALING THE REPRESENTED NECESSITIES OF NO-WHERE: NOW HERE, WHERE THE CRISES OF ITSELF BECOMING HOWEVER MUCH UN-SO MUFFLES ONLY THE IN*DEED*IENCY OF EXPOSING THAT WHICH IS NOT *NOT* BEING OF, AND IS NOT OF REJOICING, AND NOT OF ONESELF AND NOT C A L L E D NOTHING!

AUMen! O M e n !!

(1972)

Transmedia (pp. 3–14)

1. Originally published in *Further Steps: Fifteen Choreographers on Modern Dance*, edited by Constance Kreemer, New York: Harper & Row, 1987.

Digital Body/Millennial World (pp. 15–20)

1. Published in *Movement Research Performance Journal* 20 (winter-spring 2000), whose theme was the impact of ever-advancing technology on the moving body.

Through Me Many Voices (pp. 21–26)

1. *The Principles of Psychology*, New York: Dover Publications, 1890, chapter 24, "Instinct," pp. 407–408.

2. Why this holds such a particular, perennial fascination led me, too, in part through play and patter, to develop a dance theater program of real and imaginary characters, *Dancing Wor(l)ds* (1990–1992), that featured a parrot, Sam (screeching, manic and ironic), and his slick partner, Wilmer Wilmerdingdong, a talk show shyster announcer conning a gullible public; a daffy, authoritative Mr. Snail—languorous, ponderously slow and goofy in a philosophical adult children's fable; Mr. Pontease Tyak, a former vaudeville actor turned vagabond philosophy professor dissembling in a hybrid guttural mix of Slavic, German and Yiddish; Patrick Duncan, Isadora's lost son, whose voice is his dancing body; Tallulah

Bankhead, deep androgynous basso caught up in a telephone monologue from paradise; Herbert McGillicuddy, a clownish clod and jester secretary to Tallulah, yammering out a satirical riff from the *National Enquirer* on how to tell if your coworker is a space alien; and a gruff, nameless, mock mysterioso spy concealed by a black raincoat, hat and shades lurking surreptitiously in an absurdist *danse noir* to a disembodied recording mauling a bastardized amalgam of French, Italian and Spanish—reminiscent of the disjunctively coordinated soundtrack of a foreign flick; and a series of impossible tongue twisters delivered in several foreign accents.

3. Maurice Merleau-Ponty, *The Prose of the World*, Evanston: Northwestern University Press, 1973, p. 5.

4. Jacques Derrida, "Form and Meaning: A Note on the Phenomenology of Language" in *Speech and Phenomena and Other Essays on Husserl's Theory of Signs*, Evanston: Northwestern University Press, 1973, p. 119.

5. Ibid., p. 87.

WORD RAID (Impossible Tongue Twisters for E. E. Cummings) (pp. 27–31)

1. *WORD RAID* was previewed at a Poetry Project Benefit in the fall of 1978 at St. Mark's Church, New York City, performed by Robyn Brentano and myself while I danced; it premiered at the Kitchen, New York City, in February 1979. In 1984 it was performed with Pamela Tait in French and English at the American Center, Paris, and in German and English at the New Dance Festival in Munich. It was originally published in *The Soho Weekly News* (February 1979), reprinted in *The Paris Review* (fall 1979, Vol. 21, No. 76) as well as in the anthology *TEXT-SOUND TEXTS*, edited by Richard Kostelanetz, New York: William Morrow & Company, 1980. Many of the tongue twisters were rendered in foreign accents or disguised character voices that are noted in parentheses.

2. A type of missile.

From Out of the Field of Vision (Or Finally: The Internet) (pp. 33–50)

1. New York: Simon and Schuster, 1983 p. 295 (Hodges's emphasis).

2. Lady Ada Lovelace was the first historical programmer for Babbage's Analytical Engine.

3. New York Anchor Books/Doubleday, 1999 (originally published in the United Kingdom in 1997).

4. Hodges, p. 292 (Hodges's emphasis).

5. Kant, *Critique of Pure Reason*, translated by Max Müller, New York: Doubleday & Co., 1966, p. 100.

6. Ibid., p. 112.

7. Ibid., p. 313.

8. See especially chapters 5 and 6, "The Artist's Idea" and "A Chapter on Abstraction," respectively, Baltimore: Johns Hopkins Press, 1968.

9. *SuperLecture* was published in *The Young American Writers*, edited by Richard Kostelanetz, New York: Funk & Wagnalls, 1967, pp. 221–237.

10. *Pardon My Leak (Scandals in the Presence Tense)*, eddy 7 (winter 1975–76), pp. 34–47, and *DON'T BLOW MY C-O-V-E-R*, eddy 9 winter 1977), pp. 52–64; both articles were published pseudonymously under the alias Zora A. Zash. The dance event was performed at Washington Square Methodist Church in New York on May 14, 1971, and simultaneously broadcast on WBAI radio.

The Telaxic Synapsulator (The Future of Machine) (pp. 51–71)

1. The original text was recorded and first presented in May 1974 as the last part of *Praxiomatics*, performed by Kenneth King and Dancers at 597 Broadway, New York City; it was performed as a duet with Wendy Perron. A mock-up Synapsulator with a silver slatted reflective revolving cylinder drum was constructed for the occasion. The text was originally published in a special issue of *Shantih* ("The Literature of Soho"), vol 4., nos. 3–4 (winter–spring 1982), edited by Richard Kostelanetz. The litanized mantra repetitive text in the right column was written for performances of *DANCE SPELL/THE TELAXIC SYNAPSULATOR* at the Brooklyn Academy of Music, premiered March 13, 1978, with choreography for my company's ten dancers with music by William-John Tudor, projections by Kerry Schuss and a streamlined hi-tech Synapsulator designed and built by Steven Crawford. The second text was published in *File*, a Canadian magazine, in its fall 1980 issue (vol. 4, no. 4), guest edited by Sylvere Lotringer. The texts have been combined and updated.

2. New York: Oxord University Press, 1973, p. 8.

Stravinsky's *Oedipus Rex*: Julie Taymor—Seiji Ozawa—Jessye Norman (pp. 75–87)

1. Actually, according to Julie Taymor's Director's Note (1992), the inspiration was the similarities between the early Haniwa sculpture of Japan and the pre-Greek sculpture from the isles of the Cyclades (3200–2200 B.C.). Anyway, highly stylized, primordial masks of the human form with no eyes or mouth.

2. Sophocles, *Oedipus the King*, translated by Stephen Berg and Diskin Clay, New York: Oxford University Press, 1978, p. 45.

3. Ibid., p. 72.

4. Ibid., p. 86.

5. Ibid., p. 66.

6. Ibid., p. 90.

7. Ibid., p. 59.

Writing Over History and Time: Maurice Blanchot and Jackie O. (pp. 89–96)

1. Sections from this text were read at The Poetry Project at St. Mark's Church, New York, on November 20, 1995.
2. See esp. "The Work and Death's Space," translated by Ann Smock, Lincoln: University of Nebraska Press, 1982, pp. 19–34; orig. Editions Gallimard, 1955.
3. Ibid., p. 33.
4. *Baudrillard Live—Selected Interviews*, edited by Mike Gane, New York: Routledge, 1993, p. 85 (interview 9, "Games With Vestiges").
5. "The Work and Death's Space" in *The Space of Literature*, p. 91.

Dreams and College (pp. 97–110)

1. *Hyperspace: A Scientific Odyssey through Parallel Universes, Time Warps and the Tenth Dimension*, New York: Oxford University Press, 1994. For the better part of two decades I have been an avid listener of Dr. Kaku's weekly science program *Exploration* on WBAI radio, during which he has often discussed string theory, hyperdimensionality and the paradoxes of space and time.
2. *The Coming of Age*, translated by Patrick O'Brian, New York W.W. Norton, 1996, p. 524.
3. New York: Collier Books/Macmillan, 1966.
4. Jean-Marie Chauvet, Eliette Brunel Deschamps and Christian Hillaire, *Dawn of Art: The Chauvet Cave—The Oldest Known Paintings in the World*, translated by Paul G. Bahn, New York: Harry N. Abrams, 1996. See also Paul G. Bahn and Jean Vertut, *Journey Through the Ice Age*, Berkeley: University of California Press, 1997.
5. See chapter 17, "Symbols and the Evolution of Mind, in volume 2 of *Mind: An Essay on Human Feeling*, Baltimore: Johns Hopkins Press, 1972. I am indebted to Susanne Langer's work for many insights contained herein.
6. Maurice Merleau-Ponty, "The Indirect Language" in *The Prose of the World*, translated by John O'Neill, Evanston: Northwestern University Press, 1973.
7. Chapter 18, "Symbols and the Human World," in *Mind*, p. 337.
8. "*De somnis (On Dreams)*" in *The Basic Works of Aristotle*, translated by J. I. Beare, New York: Random House, 1966, p. 618.
9. See *The Poetics of Space, The Right to Dream* and *The Poetics of Reverie*.

Sight and Cipher (pp. 111–115)

1. This text was recorded and accompanied a solo of mine, *UPPER ATMOSPHERIC DISTURBANCES*, performed at PS 122, 150 First Avenue, New York, April 13–16, 1995, on a shared program with choreographers Tina Croll, Douglas Dunn and Wendy Perron.

1. Joseph Cornell show at the Pace Gallery, 32-34 E. 57th Street, New York. (This captioned quote by Cornell was prominently displayed at the entrance to the show [1/31/87].) Ideally, readers should have one of the innumerable books that display Cornell's work beside them while reading this text.

2. Gaston Bachelard, *The Poetics of Space*, translated by Maria Jolas, Boston: Beacon Press, 1969, p. 58.

3. *The Philosophy of Aristotle, Psychology*, book 4, New York: New American Library, 1963, p. 274.

4. *Zettel*, translated by G. E. M. Anscombe, Berkeley: University of California Press, 1970, Entry #94, p. 17 (emphasis mine).

5. *The Psychology of Imagination*, Secaucus, NJ.: Citadel Press, p. 245.

6. Translated by Carelton Dallery, Evanston: Northwestern University Press, 1964.

7. Ibid., p. 171.

8. Ibid., p. 268 (emphasis mine).

9. Ibid., p. 272 (emphasis mine).

10. Ibid., p. 214.

11. *Stroll with William James*, Chicago: University of Chicago Press, 1984, p. 211.

12. Ibid., p. 59.

13. Ludwig Wittgenstein, *Tractatus Logico-Philosophicus*, translated by D. F. Pears and B. F. McGuinness, London: Routledge and Kegan Paul, New York: The Humanities Press, 1963, p. 117 (orig. German ed. 1921; emphasis Wittgenstein's).

14. *Thus Spoke Zarathustra* in Walter Kaufmann, *The Portable Nietzsche*, New York: Viking Press, 1973, p. 435.

15. *The Principles of Psychology*, volume 2, chapter 24, "Instinct," New York: Dover Publications, 1950, (orig. ed. 1890), p. 409.

16. Ibid., volume 1, p. 140 (emphasis mine).

Autobiopathy (pp. 135–151)

1. Originally published in *Footnotes: Six Choreographers Inscribe the Page*, text and commentary by Elena Alexander, Amsterdam: G&B Arts Int'l (Overseas Publishers Association)/The Gordon and Breach Publishing Group, 1998.

2. Cf. Susanne K. Langer, esp. the introduction and first part of *Mind: An Essay on Human Feeling*, volume 1, Baltimore: Johns Hopkins Press, 1968.

3. Georges Bataille, *Inner Experience*, translated by Leslie Anne Boldt, Albany: State University of New York Press, 1988, p. 60 (emphasis Bataille's).

The Body Reflexive (pp. 153–168)

1. See esp. Paul Virilio, *The Lost Dimension*, New York: Semiotext(e)/Autonomedia, 1991.

2. I have written about Merce Cunningham at length in "Space Dance and the Galactic Matrix," in *Merce Cunningham: Dancing in Space and Time*, edited by Richard Kostelanetz, Pennington., N.J.: A Capella Books, 1992.

Metagexis (Joseph's Song) (pp. 169–183)

1. *Metagexis* was previewed on October 22, 1972, as part of the Soho Arts Festival to Elect George McGovern, at Super Nova, 451 West Broadway, New York, and read by Elaine Luthy, Duskin Shears and myself. Excerpts were taped by Elaine Luthy and myself for a dance event that accompanied it on November 3 and 4, 1972, at Exchange for the Arts, 151 Bank Street, New York, as part of their opening celebration. The dance was premiered on April 2, 3 and 4, 1973, at Exchange for the Arts, with Linn Varney as Anyone, Carolyn Lord as Someone, Jim Neu as No One, Eva Pietkiewicz as the Proxy, myself as Channel/Proxy who doubled as a dancer, with dancers Maher Benham and Kyra Lober. A videotape was made by Exchange for the Arts and is in the Dance Collection of the New York Public Library for the Performing Arts at at Lincoln Center, New York. The writing of *Metagexis* was made possible by a fellowship from the Creative Artists Public Service Program (CAPS), 1972. An excerpt was published in *eddy*, a dance periodical, in the spring-summer 1976 issue. This is an abridged version.

2. Translated by G. E. M. Anscombe, New York: Macmillan, 1953, p. 147 (entry #549).

3. The idea of an *Autobiopathy* was germinated herein in 1972 but wasn't written until 1992.

4. See *Mallarmé*, Baltimore: Penguin Books, 1965, p. xi.

5. See *La Rochefoucauld: Maxims*, translated by L. W. Tancock, Baltimore: Penguin Books, 1959, p. 35.

6. *Thus Spoke Zarathustra*, in *The Portable Nietzsche*, edited and translated by Walter Kaufmann, New York: Viking Press, p. 299.

Appeal to the Unknown Prayer to the Great Void (Mappings for a Metatheology) (pp. 185–191)

1. Presented as part of *Simultimeless Action*, a collaborative performance event and installation with Pierre Ruiz, musician-composer, and William Steward, painter, at the Greene Street Gallery, 110 Greene Street, New York, June 1972; published in *Art & Cinema*, summer 1986 (vol. I, no. 1).

About the Author

Kenneth King © Johan Elbers; costume by Heather Samuels

KENNETH KING is a dancer/choreographer and writer, and former Artistic Director of Kenneth King & Dancers/Company. Since 1964 he has presented a wide variety of dance, dance theatre, dancetext and performance art at many venues, MOMA and the Brooklyn Academy of Music. King earned his B.A. from Antioch College. He has taught, lectured and mounted dances at numerous colleges and universities.